Hitting the Target

(Focusing your discipleship)

Don Loomer

Hitting the Target
(Focusing your discipleship)
by Don Loomer

Printed in the United States of America

ISBN 9781609572471

www.xulonpress.com

Table of Contents

Preface

As a young man growing up in rural America, one of the things I learned from my dad was how to hunt and fish. My dad was part of a group of men who enjoyed hunting and fishing together and when I was old enough, he took me along and taught me the elementals of both sports. He took the time to teach me how to properly handle a gun as well. But I was never a very good hunter. For whatever reason, I had a hard time keeping both eyes open, following the bird and squeezing the trigger all at the same time. But I really enjoyed the fellow-ship and camaraderie so much that it didn't bother me that I rarely hit the target.

Western Christianity seems to have the same attitude toward church as I did toward hunting: We enjoy the fellowship, the camaraderie, the pro-grams we run and the meetings we attend so much that it doesn't bother us that when it comes to making disciples, we don't seem to hit the target very often. So we go from year to year, program to program investing time and energy in this "thing" we call the church, enjoying the process but not seeing much progress in "making disciples." Could it be that we have never taken the time to define what a "disciple" ought to look like?

As a young man, fresh out of college I started work as a research engineer. In the early months of that time, through the suicide of a roommate,

God got hold of my attention and I gave my life to Jesus Christ. I continued to work but about two years later sensed God's call to pastoral ministry and left engineering to go to seminary. Two years into my training, I started pastoring a small church on the weekends and have followed in pastoral ministry for the last 45 years.

Part of the thing I struggled with was even though people talked about "making disciples" as the heart of the Great Commission no one ever gave me a definition of what a "mature disciple" should look like. One day I heard a speaker say, "Anyone can hit the bull's eye if you draw the target after you take your shot." That statement brought into focus for me what I had been struggling with. I had learned how to translate Greek, how to oversee a Christian Education program, and had gained an understanding of the Old and New Testaments as well as church history but no one had helped me understand both what a disciple was and then how you "make" one.

Since seminary I have attended numerous "church growth" seminars run by people who have been "successful" at some facet of church ministry, who have seen their churches grow from small to large as everyone was to learn from reading the advertising material. But no one helped me understand what the "target" was and how you "hit" it.

Jesus said, "Go and make disciples…."[1] Those who heard him had watched him do what he was telling them to do. They had been the recipients of his training and teaching so for them it was obvious what a disciple was to look like. But for us who live two millennia later, who have inherited the cumulative results of change, relevancy, and contemporary methodologies, the picture is not that obvious. The result is that people can be an integral part of a "normal" church for years and not be much closer to being conformed to the image of Jesus than they were to start with. They assume that if they attend church on Sunday, serve in some capacity in the life of the church, read their Bibles and pray and perhaps become part of some smaller group structure in the church that maybe by osmosis they will grow into maturity. Only it doesn't happen.

With all of this in mind, it has caused me to spend a great deal of time and prayer trying to give definition to the word "disciple." What follows is my definition of a "mature disciple."

I am certain this book is not the final word. It is a working definition that I have developed which has been helpful in evaluating my personal life and the content and direction of the ministry I have been involved in. I commend it to you as a place to start. Use it as a target to put up on your wall. Shoot at it, redraw it, rethink it for yourself. But for God's sake (and yours) — find a target and shoot at it.

The apostle Paul said, "Him we proclaim, warning every man and teaching every man in all wisdom, that we may present every man mature in Christ. For this I toil with all the energy which He mightily inspires within me." [2] What does it mean to "present every man mature in Christ?" Toward that end I set forth the following definition and working manual.

Introduction

How do we define a "disciple?" Do we define it in terms of church attendance, or belief system, or habit patterns, or serving on various boards and committees, or number of people they have led to Christ, or ability to "walk by faith," or how they respond to trial? Do we define it by one's ability to sing praise songs, or repeat the books of the Bible, or repeat certain clichés, or quote a certain number of Bible verses from memory or the regularity of the "quiet times?" What standard does one use as the measuring stick?

I attended a management seminar when I was younger in the ministry in which the presenter suggested that in interviewing people for various positions within an organization, the interviewer should look in three specific areas. He called it the "A-S-K Paradigm."

A - stands for attitudes.
S - stands for skills.
K - stands for knowledge.

I have never found a better viewfinder through which to look when doing a personnel appraisal than this simple an acronym.

This book will be broken into three sections corresponding to each of those letters. In each section I will present an introduction in which I will define what is meant by the word or concept. Then I will define six specific, different characteristics that I have found are the most crucial in this area and will devote a short chapter to each. I will then close out each section by giving some very practical ways that those characteristics can be developed in the life of a believer. These will be things you can do that I have found helpful from my experience and that of others. *Thus the book is intended not just to define what a disciple looks like but will enable us to have some practical, hands-on methods for developing these qualities in the lives of other believers.*

These methods need to be varied for each individual because God does not use cookie cutters in our development of disciples. Each person is created uniquely different, like a snow flake and thus must be treated individually but these are some general, suggested ways that you can start. As we pray for those we are working with, God will bring to mind some different ways of helping them that will reflect their uniqueness.

There have been times throughout my ministry that I have wished I could become a carpenter. The reason is that when a carpenter finishes his day, he can look back across the day and say, "I started here and finished there." He can see his progress and go home internally rewarded because of the obvious progress. But working with people is different. You cannot stand back at the end of the day and see much significant personal transformation. This kind of change usually happens over a long period of time. This book is an attempt to give us some kind of plumb line against which we can measure our activities so that from time to time we can look at individuals and measure growth in some specific areas. Then you will be able to say with the apostle Paul, "For what is our hope or joy or crown of boasting before our Lord Jesus at his coming? Is it not you? For you are our glory and joy."[3]

May God help you to become a "maker of disciples."

Section 1

Attitude

Chapter 1

Attitude

B ack in the 1950's Earl Nightengale, one of the early founders of the "power of positive thinking, personal motivation" movement produced a twelve record series of motivational talks entitled "Lead the Field." They are still available in other formats. The first "talk" was entitled, "The Most Important Word." As he presented it he said that the most important thing about a person was their attitude. He said that we can't control our circumstances but we can control our attitude toward whatever it is that happens to us. He said it is this ability to control and change our attitude that determines whether or not we will be successful in life.

But just what is "attitude?" Webster's defines it as "a position, disposition, or manner with regard to a person or thing." Wikipedia defines it as "… a hypothetical construct that represents an individual's like or dislike for an item. Attitudes are positive, negative or neutral views of an "attitude object": i.e. a <u>person</u>, behavior or event."

When we think about a person's "attitude" we generally refer to the way a person responds to certain things or events in their lives. For example we say, "They certainly have a bad attitude." By that we mean that the way they are responding to some situation is certainly not positive or healthy. If we say "They have a good attitude" we usually mean that their response to a certain event or person was what we consider positive.

When we think of specific attitudes we would include such things as happy, grateful, consistent, hard-working, positive, enthusiastic, faithful, trustworthy, optimistic, alert, fair-minded, etc. on the positive side or stingy, critical, negative, complaining, sour, picky, reckless, egotistical, standoffish, etc. on the negative side. Attitudes describe our internal way of responding to life, the way we just naturally, spontaneously respond to life and circumstances.

Why are attitudes important?

Attitudes are important because they determine the way we interpret and respond to life. A person with a negative attitude tends to always read the worst into any given situation. If something happens to them, they take it personally and react with, "Why doesn't he like me?" or "Why does God always allow these kind of terrible things to happen to me?" or "I knew it would be this way." They interpret life through the lens of something or someone being against them personally. They read this negativity into almost everything and everyone with whom they interact and thus it becomes a self-fulfilling prophecy. The same can be said when something happens to a person who lives life with a positive attitude. They interpret the same facts from a totally different perspective and see the good that can come from whatever has happened to them.

In his book, "Man's Search for Meaning" Victor Frankl describes this very effect. Dr. Frankl was a Jewish doctor from Austria prior to World War II when Adolph Hitler rounded up Jewish people and put them into concentration camps. Many of them eventually died. Being a psychiatrist he worked with the other prisoners to help them stay mentally and physically healthy. It gave him time to study the responses of people to severe adversity. In his book "Man's Search for Meaning" he wrote, "If a prisoner felt that he could no longer endure the realities of camp life, he found a way out in his mental life - an invaluable opportunity to dwell in the spiritual domain, the one that the SS were unable to destroy. Spiritual life strengthened the prisoner, helped him adapt, and thereby improved his chances of survival."[4] What he discovered was that those who had an attitude of optimism and a desire to help others actually survived longer and were healthier than those who did not have that attitude. He discovered that attitudes are extremely important in the way a person handles life.

So attitudes are crucial to becoming a truly mature disciple or follower of Jesus Christ. When Paul wrote to the Philippians he would say, "Your attitude should be the same as that of Christ Jesus……" (Phil 2:5 - NIV) He was writing to them about the way we are look at one another and work together. He said if we are to work successfully in the environment of the body of Christ, we need to have the same attitude toward our relationships that Jesus had when He gave away His life for other people. Then he goes on to write about adopting the attitude of a servant and being willing to go even so far as death for the benefit of others. But he sees the main issue as that of having the right attitude.

So we begin our description of a "disciple" with the matter of a person's attitudes. These form the motivation out of which a person operates and with which he responds to all of life. A person can have been trained in all the skills necessary to live

19

the Christian life but if there is not within them a desire to be obedient the skills will seldom if ever be used and then only out of a sense of obligation or duty. They can have all the necessary information and knowledge they need but if there is not a heart to follow Jesus with all of one's life and glorify Him in everything they do, they may be able to win some intellectual and abstract arguments, but there will not be the "abundance of life" that Jesus said would come from following Him.

There are six attitudes that I have found are crucial to a person's spiritual maturity:

1. A desire to know God
2. A desire to glorify God
3. A desire to become like Jesus
4. A desire to love people
5. A desire to serve people
6. A desire to be involved in the Great Commission.

Chapter # 2

A Desire to Know God

Being a Christian involves far more than simply praying some kind of prayer, making some kind of decision, joining a church or being baptized. The essence of Christianity is knowing God. This does not simply refer to an accumulation of information or data about Him as important as that might be. Rather, it refers to a knowledge that comes out of a personal relationship, out of walking with Him and sharing heart to heart with Him in a two way dialogue and commitment.

The tragedy of much of modern Christianity is that it knows very little about this kind of desire. A. W. Tozer stated it very well when he wrote, "How tragic that we in this dark day have had our seeking done for us by our teachers. Everything is made to center upon the initial act of "accepting" Christ (a term, incidentally, which is not found in the Bible.) and we are not expected thereafter to crave any further revelation of God to our souls. We have been snared in the spurious logic, which insists that if we have found Him we need no more seek Him. This is set before us as the last word in orthodoxy, and it is taken for granted that no Bible-taught Christian ever believed otherwise."[5]

How different this sounds from the writing of Paul, the apostle when he wrote, "I want to know

Christ and the power of his resurrection…."[6] He was a man who had walked with Jesus for many years and had lived his life is sharing the gospel with the people of the Mediterranean Sea basin. He wrote these words from prison toward the close of his life and still the cry of his heart is that he wants to know Christ in an ever deepening way. It is this heart-cry that permeates the entire Bible from the pens of men who had encountered the living God and were not satisfied with that initial encounter. It is the testimony of godly men down through the ages who have tasted the goodness of God and this has whetted their appetite for something deeper. Listen to what they say: "This is what the Lord says, 'Let not the wise man boast in his wisdom or the strong man boast of his strength or the rich man boast of his riches, but let him who boasts boast about this: that he understands and knows me…"[7] "Let us know, let us press on to know the LORD; His going forth is sure as the dawn; he will come to us as the showers, as the spring rains that water the earth."[8] "Then Moses said, 'Now show me your glory."[9] "Be still and know that I am God."[10] "I want to know Christ and the power of his resurrection and the fellowship of sharing in his sufferings, becoming like him in his death…"[11] I keep asking the God of our Lord Jesus Christ, the glorious Father, may give you the Spirit of wisdom and revelation so that you may know him better."[12] "His divine power has given us everything we need for life and godliness through our knowledge of him who called us by his own glory and goodness."[13] A prominent pastor who has gone on to be with the Lord once wrote, "When I was thirty I wanted to be a great preacher; when I was forty I wanted to build a great church; but when I turned fifty, I only wanted to know God in an ever deepening way."

This kind of knowledge of God as a living Person forms the foundation of our spiritual lives and becomes the basis out of which everything else in our Christian life grows. That is why it is the most crucial attitude a person needs to have to build the rest of their lives upon.

WHAT IS MEANT BY KNOWING GOD?

Knowing God means primarily two things:

1. Having an understanding of the truth about God. This ventures into the area of theology. Years ago, I determined that as I read through the Bible that year, I would write down everything it had to say about God. I tried to systematize it as best I could and at the end of the year I started to work through putting what I had discovered into some semblance of order. It was an amazing study and one that gave me an entirely new appreciation for Him. The study contained many areas that were helpful in my walk with Him as well as many areas in which I simply stood in awe, not being able to completely comprehend what I had written down. But since it was God I was trying to understand, that is to be expected. Paul wrote, "Oh, the depth of the riches of the wisdom and knowledge of God! How unsearchable his judgments and his paths beyond tracing out! Who has known the mind of the Lord? Or who has been his counselor? Who has ever given to God that God should repay him? For from him and through him and to him are all things. To him be glory forever! Amen."[14]

If we are grow in our relationship with Him, this is essential in the same way that an increasing knowledge about one's wife or husband is essential to the ongoing of the marital relationship. Having been married 44+ years and looking back, I thought I "knew" my wife when we were first married. How foolish that was. Over the years I have come to know her and understand her character and temperament in ways that I did not know at the outset. I could sit down now and write a much fuller description on what my wife is like now than I ever could have attempted years ago.

The same is true in our walk with God. If I do not know that He has made me promises, I will never come to Him and inquire about them. If I do not know that one day I will stand accountable before Him, I will live my life very differently. If I do not know what the "fear of the Lord" is, I may live my life out of the wrong kind of fear. If I do not know that my ways are not His ways, I may try unsuccessfully to "pull it off" by my own ingenuity and effort and then stand and wonder why things didn't work out the way I had hoped. So a factual knowledge about God is essential if we are to grow in our walk with Him.

2. <u>To be involved in a personal relationship with Him.</u> This is what Jesus was referring to when he prayed, "Now this is eternal life; that they may know you, the only true God, and Jesus Christ who you have sent."[15] He was not referring to an intellectual knowledge based upon a research of factual information, he was speaking about a relationship that one person can have with another person. Again Tozer writes, "God is a Person and can be known in increasing degrees of intimate acquaintance as we prepare our hearts for the wonder. It may be necessary for us to alter our former beliefs about God as the glory that gilds the Sacred Scriptures dawn over our interior lives. We may also need to break quietly and graciously away with the lifeless textualism that prevails among the gospel churches, and to protest the frivolous character of much that passes for Christianity among us. By this we may for the time lose friends and gain a passing reputation for being holier-than-thou; but no man who permits the expectation of unpleasant consequences to influence him in a manner like this is fit for the kingdom of God."[16]

This kind of knowledge can be cultivated just as any other human relationship can be cultivated. Since God is a Person, He can be known in the same way any other person may be known. The word to "know" can refer to intellectual information but it can also refer to a deep, intimate relationship. It says of Adam that he "knew his wife; and she conceived, and bare Cain, and said, I have gotten a man from the LORD."[17] In this context it is a reference to the intimacy of the sexual relationship, so "knowing" another person refers to more than an understanding of certain factual information. When Jesus said to the Jewish leaders who questioned Him, "Though you do not know him, I know him"[18] He was not saying that they did not have a certain theology about God or that their theology was wrong. He was saying that they did not have a relationship with Him.

This is not an instantaneous thing, it is a life-long process of ever-deepening involvement. It is something that can be compared to the court-ship-to-marriage process. It beings with an aware-ness of one's existence. Then there comes a time of cultivating the relationship. If marriage is to come, it means there is a time of commitment in the engagement and finally a coming together in an open, public commitment of lives to one another. But that is not the end of the process. The knowl-edge then grows and deepens as the couple continue to live out their lives in a new kind of intimacy and familiarity. Knowing creates a desire to know and one of the joys of marriage is the privilege of watching the relationship blossom into an ever-deepening intimacy. The same is true with our relationship with God. It is with this in mind that Moses, after having encountered God in the burning bush and walked with Him during the coming out of Egypt had the audacity alone with Him on the mountain to ask, "Lord, show me your glory."[19] He had been enabled to see what an amazing Person this God is who had called him to lead the people. Because of this, Moses wanted to have God open Himself up in a way that he had never experienced before. This is desiring to know God.

WHY IS THIS IMPORTANT?

   1. It is important because all of our activity must proceed out of this relationship. G. Campbell Morgan writes, "The proportion in which I know the Lord is the proportion in which I am prepared to serve Him. Is it not certain that when I know as I am known I shall be more perfectly prepared to serve?"[20] Unless we live our lives out of this relationship, we will live out of inadequate resources and for the wrong reasons. It will cause us to be motivated by guilt or feelings of duty and obligation or out of a desire to please or impress someone else. All of these are wrong reasons to serve God. It is the depth of the relationship that causes me to trust Him when He asks obedience of me that I have never been challenged to before. It is the depth of the relationship that causes me to take stands in public in which I often have to stand alone. It is the depth of the relationship that enables me to know that He is walking with me into circumstances that are beyond my ability to handle. It is the depth of the relationship that enables me to say, "Even though I walk through the valley of the shadow of death, I will fear no evil, for you are with me...."[21]
   2. It is important because of the things that people who know God are able to accomplish. The following is a listing of some of the things the Bible says that people who know God are empowered to do:

*   They will take action against the forces of godlessness present in their culture. (Dan 11:32)

* They will defend the cause of the poor and needy. (Jer 22:15)
* They will show love to others who know God. (1 John 4:7-8)
* They will be enabled to maintain unity within the body of Christ. (Eph 4:11-13)
* They will be able to obey the Bible, (1 John 2:3-4; Tit 1:16)
* They will have the right attitude toward sin. (1 John 3:6)
* They will have an ever-increasing ability to trust God. (Psa 9:10)
* They will be able to listen to others who know God. (1 John 4:6)
* They will be enabled to grow in grace. (2 Pet 3:18)

All of this comes about simply as the result of knowing God. Accomplishment comes out of relationship and those who have known God the deepest are those who have been enabled to accomplish the greatest things for Him. They have been men and women who hungered after God in such a way that they were not satisfied until they, like Jacob would not let go their search until they had realized the goal of their pursuit.[22]

HOW DOES ONE PURSUE THIS KNOWLEDGE?

1. It begins by coming to know Jesus Christ. This is what Jesus meant when he prayed, "Now this is eternal life: that they may know you, the only true God, and Jesus Christ whom you have sent."[23] Jesus came that we might have life (John 10:10) and that life begins when we invite Jesus Christ to become the King of our lives and begin to build our new lives around Him. When we do that, He by His Spirit, pardons us of all our sins through His sacrificial death and simultaneously comes to dwell in our physical bodies in the person of the Holy

Spirit. It is such a new life that Jesus referred to it as being "born again." (John 3:1-21) This is like saying "I do" in a wedding ceremony. It inaugurates a new relationship into which a person enters. There are many different ways the Bible describes that transaction but they all refer in essence to the receiving of a new life and entering into a new relationship. This is the beginning but by no means is it the final step of knowing God in the same way that saying "I do" is not the end of what takes place in this new marriage.

In the movie "Mary Poppins" there is a scene where Bert the chimney sweep is cleaning out a chimney. One of the children looks up the chimney and exclaims, "Oooh — it's dark up there." Bert looks up and says, "Oh no, that a doorway to a land of enchantment." This initial decision of inviting Jesus Christ to become the Lord of one's life may look foreboding from this side but when made, it becomes a doorway to a land of the Spirit in which the greatest privilege is that of being able to grow in our relationship with the God of the universe.

2. Asking God to reveal Himself to you. One of the greatest privileges of pastoral ministry is the confidence people place in you that gives them the freedom to open themselves up to you about many of the deepest issues of their lives. It is not a privilege one takes lightly because when someone has shared with you some of the deepest personal things about themselves, they are vulnerable and at your mercy. Often, to have them do that, I have had to ask deep, probing questions in an effort to get them to reveal themselves to me. Relationships are deepened as we lose the fear of revealing things about ourselves to another because the only way we can get to know someone is if they choose to reveal themselves to us.

In the same way, the only way we can grow in our knowledge of God is if we choose to reveal

ourselves to Him and He chooses to reveal Himself
to us. He has already revealed Himself through His
creation and His word (Psalm 19:1-11). His final
and fullest revelation came to us in the person of
Jesus. God has invited us to probe the depths of
His personhood. He has offered to reveal Himself
to anyone who has a seeking heart. When God came
to Samuel to speak to him concerning his future,
it says, "The word of the Lord had not yet been
revealed to him."[24] When Samuel invited God to
speak, God shared Himself and His future plans with
him. All he had to do was ask. Moses came boldly
and asked God to reveal Himself to him.[25] When Paul
prayed for the Ephesians he prayed, "I keep asking
that the God of our Lord Jesus Christ…may give you
a Spirit of wisdom and revelation so that you may
know him better."[26]

Since the final revelation of God has come to
us in Jesus Christ, we can not expect that there
is some part of His person that He has kept just
for us alone but we can expect that He will enable
us to catch glimpses of Him that will enable us
to deepen the relationship in new and meaningful
ways. Paul prayed that the Colossians would grow
"…in the knowledge of God…"[27] Thus one of the ways
we grow in our knowledge of Him is by asking Him
to reveal Himself more deeply than He has in the
past.

3. Spending time in God's word, the Bible. Since
God has spoken to us clearly in the Bible and has
chosen to record certain revelations concerning
Himself, His nature and ways in the Bible, it only
makes sense that we would spend time reading it to
discover those things. Not only will it give us
informational things but we will get a chance to
understand His ways of dealing with people and situations. Since God always acts consistently with
His nature, He will like deal with us in similar
ways in similar circumstances. He said to Moses,
"I am the Lord. I appeared to Abraham, to Isaac

and to Jacob as God Almighty, but by my name the Lord I did not make myself known to them."[28] God had enabled Moses to see something about Himself that those who had preceded him had not seen. Now we have that revelation written for us in the Bible and by reading it and meditating on it we can come to the same kind of understanding that they had. Granted this is factual information, but that material can become the source of our meditation and out of that will come new and deeper appreciations of the quality of our relationship. How can one meditate on Abraham's discovery that in the moment of deepest obedience he found that God would provide everything he needed to complete his commitment and not come away with a profound change in our relationship with the same God? (Gen 22:1-19) Knowing that He will supply our need in moments like that will change forever the kind of relationship we will develop with Him. Reading about how the people in Hebrews 11 lived by faith and how their faith was honored in ways they never anticipated, how can we not also live by faith because the God who fulfilled His promise to them will also fulfill His promises to us?

   4. Cultivating a hunger to know God. Certain things are obtained only because we purposely choose to have them with a longing that becomes almost insatiable. Such was the situation with the psalmist when he wrote, "As the deer pants for streams of water, so my soul pants for you, O God. My soul thirsts for God, for the living God. When can I come and meet with God?"[29] As one reads this you can hear the longing in the heart of the writer for the kind of intimacy with God that we have been thinking about. Certainly God would not put such a longing within the heart of a person unless there was the anticipation that the longing could somehow be satisfied. It was C. S. Lewis who said, "If I find in myself a desire which no experience in this world can satisfy, the most prob-

able explanation is that I was made for another world."[30] David writes from the desert of Judah, probably being chased down by Saul, "O God, you are my God, earnestly I seek you; my soul thirsts for you, my body longs for you in a dry and weary land where there is no water."[31]

These are the cries of those who have tasted the delight of knowing God and have become so thirsty for more that they have found the longing nearly all-consuming. This is a thirst that when partially satisfied only creates a greater thirst. Jesus said, "Blessed are those who hunger and thirst for righteousness for they will be filled."[32] Those who have hungered have found that in the filling there is created an even greater hungering and thirsting. This desire to know God is a spark that can be fanned into flame when focused on. It is a conscious choice we make that determines the focus of our hearts. As David said, "On my bed I remember you; I think of you through the watches of the night."[33]

5. Learning how to be still. In Psalm 46:10 the writer said in the voice of God, "Be still, and know that I am God; I will be exalted among the nations, I will be exalted in the earth." The word translated "still" means "to sink, relax, sink down, let drop, be disheartened." He is addressing a problem we in our modern world understand only too well: the problem of hurry and busyness. If we are always running too and fro, occupying our minds and lives with things too numerous to elaborate, we find it becomes impossible to slow down long enough to focus well on any one thing. We are bombarded with responsibility, with noise, with activities of our own making or of the decisions of others that impinge upon our lives. We carry our cell phones on our belts and hang some hearing device from our ears and then wonder why we don't hear God speak to us.

The psalmist had discovered what Jesus knew to be true, if you want to listen to God, you must take time to slow down, be still and make yourself able to hear. Good relationships take time to be together and to cultivate. They grow in no other way. It took a "gentle whisper" for Elijah to finally be able to hear what God was saying. (1 Kings 19:10-13) It took being alone on the mountain top for forty days for Moses to finally come to the place where he could ask God to show Himself. (Exodus 33:18) It took being alone on the far side of the Jabbok River for Jacob to come to grips with the call of God on his life. It took all night in prayer for Jesus to finally be able to make the selection of the twelve to follow him and be trained. (Luke 6:12-16)

Learning to be still is an art that must be cultivated if a person is ever to come to know the living God in the manner that He intended.

Shortly after Harvard College was founded in 1636, the Trustees of the school wrote, "Let every student be plainly instructed, and earnestly pressed to consider well that the maine end of his life and studies is to know God and Jesus Christ…. and therefore to lay Christ in the bottome, as the only foundation of all sound knowledge and learning." This was true then and is still true today. In his book, Knowing God" J. I. Packer writes of a friend. "I walked in the sunshine with a scholar who had effectively forfeited his prospects for academic advancement by clashing with church dignitaries over the gospel of grace. 'But it doesn't matter,' he said at length, 'for I've known God and they haven't."[34]

The first characteristic of a mature disciple is that they have a desire to know God and that desire burns deep within their heart.

Chapter # 3

A desire to Glorify God

People are inherently self-centered. We tend to think about ourselves before we think about anyone else. We will take credit for things we have not done if it is to our advantage. We dress so we will be noticed and commented on. We spend the vast majority of our wealth on ourselves and think nothing of it.

Thus, one of the greatest evidences of a genuine work of the Spirit is that God takes a person's focus off themselves and doing what they do for personal gain or recognition and transfers the credit and focus to God Himself. This is called "glorifying God." As the first question, the Westminster Catechism asks *What is the chief and highest end of man?* The answer comes back, *"Man's chief and highest end is to glorify God, and fully to enjoy him forever."* Therefore a mature believer is a person who has a deep desire to see God glorified in any and all circumstances.

A friend asked Mrs. Thomas A. Edison, "Have you ever asked your husband where he gets all the ideas that make him so famous?" Thoughtfully, Mrs. Edison replied, "Yes, I did ask him once. He didn't say anything. He just pointed upward and smiled!" This is the heart of "glorifying God.

What does it mean to glorify God?

1. The first definition of glorifying God means to praise Him or thank Him for either who He is or what He has done. The words which are translated "to glorify" are also translated, "to honor, to magnify" and some of the newer translations use the words "praise and thank." This aspect of glorifying God is seen especially throughout the ministry of Jesus. When he healed a paralytic it says, "when the multitudes saw it, they marveled, and glorified God, which had given such power unto men."[35] When He had healed a number of people with various physical ailments we read, "...when they saw the dumb to speak, the maimed to be whole, the lame to walk, and the blind to see: and they glorified the God of Israel."[36] After Jesus had raised a widow's son from the dead, we read, "And there came a fear on all: and they glorified God, saying, "That a great prophet is risen up among us; and, That God hath visited his people."[37] This kind of response could be demonstrated from many other incidents in his life.

From this we see that one of the evidences of a mature person is that their lives are filled with gratitude and praise to God for both who He is and what He has done. Knowing this, the mature person has within them a deep desire to see that God gets the credit for the things that have happened and it is this giving credit to God that is one way in which we glorify Him. Three hundred years after Paul lived John Chrysostom, a good and brave man who preached very plainly against iniquity of all kinds. The empress was not a good woman, so she schemed to have him falsely accused and banished. He died an exile from his home. Thirty years later, his body was bought back to Constantinople for burial in the imperial tomb. Chrysostom's motto was inscribed on the tomb: "Praise God for everything!" As his friends testified, "When he was

driven from home, when he was a stranger in the
strange land, his letters would often end with
that doxology, 'Praise God for all things!' This
is the heart of a person who wants to see God glorified in all things.

2. The second definition of glorifying God means
that we give Him the credit for what He enables us
to do.

We see this in the incident out of Daniel's life
when Nebuchadnezzar said to him, "Are you able to
tell me what I saw in my dream and interpret it?"
Daniel's response was, "No wise man, enchanter,
magician or diviner can explain to the king the
mystery he has asked about, but there is a God
in heaven who reveals mysteries."[38] We see it in
Joseph's life when Pharaoh came to him and said,
"I have heard it said of you that when you hear a
dream you can interpret it." Joseph responded by
saying, "I can not do it but God will give Pharaoh
the answer he desires."[39] Joseph knew that God had
given him the ability in times past to interpret
dreams that had been shared with him but he did
not want to be presumptuous and think that because
he had been enabled to do it in the past he could
automatically do it now. He wanted Pharaoh to know
that it was God who had given him the ability to
understand and interpret those dreams and that if
He wanted to, He could do it again. This is giving
God the credit for what He enables us to do. It is
not a sense of false modesty that causes us to say,
when we are complimented for the completion of a
task that was beyond our ability to do, "God gave
me the strength or wisdom to do the task." This
is the spirit of the athlete who, upon scoring
a touchdown or completing a great task, bows in
the end zone or points heavenward as their way of
saying that it was not them who accomplished the
feat but it was God who enabled them to do it and
they want to make certain He gets the credit He
is due.

Thus having a desire to glorify God means that a person genuinely wants to see God get the credit for what they have done. A number of years ago there was a young woman who was a part of our congregation who was a relatively new Christian. She had been asked to do a poster for an upcoming woman's function and had done the very best she knew how to do. When she gave the poster to the woman who had asked her, the response she got were the words, "Is this the best you can do? We can't use a poster like that!" Then she proceeded to throw the poster away. The young woman was devastated and came to me, wanting to quit. I asked her, "Who did you do the poster for?" She thought for a minute and then she said, "For Jesus." I said, "Was he pleased with your work?" She thought and responded, "Yes." Then I said, "Did you do it so you would get the credit or did you do it to please Him?" She thought about it and started to cry. She said, "I did it for Him and He was pleased." "Then," I said, "it doesn't make any difference what this other woman thought." She had done what she did to please God and to glorify Him. When one does their work in that way, God gets the credit (glory) and we can walk away content in the knowledge that He was glorified whether anyone else appreciates it or not. When this is the attitude out of which we live our lives then we can take rejection and abuse. This is what Peter means when he wrote, "Yet if any man suffer as a Christian, let him not be ashamed; but let him glorify God on this behalf."[40]

Why is this an important attitude to desire?

Having a desire to glorify God is important for four reasons:

1. God deserves it. In Revelation chapter four the twenty-four elders are described as laying their crowns before the throne of God and saying,

"You are worthy, our Lord and God to receive glory and honor and power."[41] The reason He is worthy to receive glory is because He created all things. Everything was created by God and they have their existence as a result of His power. There is really only One who deserves the glory and the credit for the creation of the world as well as for all that occurs within the creation and that person is God. If an artist deserves praise for the quality of what she paints and a carpenter deserves praise for what he builds and an athlete for what he or she achieves then truly God deserves our praise or glory for all that He has done. Not to give Him glory is to snub the greatness of His work and the wonder of His being. Not to glorify God is to refuse to acknowledge Him and the majesty that He possesses and is a statement of pride and independence of His sustaining power over His entire creation. It is to exalt oneself over what has been made as if we somehow had a hand in bringing it into existence or maintaining its stability.

When David brought the ark to Jerusalem and put it inside a tent he had erected, he committed to Asaph, the chief of the singers, a song to be sung which included the words, "Ascribe to the Lord, O families of nations, ascribe to the Lord glory and strength, ascribe to the Lord the glory due his name."[42] David recognized that God deserves to be glorified for who He is and for what He has done.

2. God demands it. It may sound egotistical of God to demand that He be glorified but it is not. If He was not worthy of being glorified that would be another matter, but He is worthy of such glorification and therefore He is not reluctant to demand it from His people. He knows that we were created for such a purpose and when He demands that we glorify Him He is only demanding what is rightly His due and what will ultimately be in our best interests. When Moses was first setting up the tabernacle and consecrating the utensils and

the people to be involved in this kind of sacrificial system, two of his nephews, the sons of Aaron came to offer to the Lord unauthorized fire. John Calvin says of this fire, "The 'strange fire' is distinguished from the sacred fire which was always burning upon the altar: not miraculously, as some pretend, but by the constant watchfulness of the priests. Now, God had forbidden any other fire to be used in the ordinances, in order to exclude all extraneous rites, and to shew His detestation of whatever might be derived from elsewhere." It was not fire that had been taken from the altar as God had prescribed for them to do. As a result fire came from out of the presence of the Lord and consumed them and they died. God said to Moses and Aaron, "I will be sanctified in them that come nigh me, and before all the people I will be glorified."[43] God was saying to them, "I demand to be glorified and I will deal harshly with anyone who does otherwise." At first glance it seems to be a small thing for such a dire consequence but God wanted to establish forever the principle that His people are not to take coming into His presence or doing their duty lightly or offhandedly. God said, "I am the LORD: that is my name: and my glory will I not give to another, neither my praise to graven images."[44] And He also said, "I will not give my glory unto another."[45] God demands that we glorify Him because He will not share His place of honor with anyone else. This is not because He is like a spoiled child who thinks that he ought to have everything go his way but because He knows that there is no one else who is worthy of receiving the glory that ought to go to Him. It is simply a fact that is true. When a parent demands obedience from a child they do it because they simply know what is best for the child. In the same way when God demands that we glorify Him, He does it simply because He knows that He deserves it and that it is in our best interests to do it.

3. It is the antidote for pride. Pride is unquestionably the most dangerous sin in the vast array of sins. Pride causes a person to believe that they somehow deserve to be the recipient of not only their own praise but that of others as well. As Solomon so aptly stated it, "Pride goes before destruction, and a haughty spirit before a fall."[46]

Pride is the internal motivation in the human heart that wants to take the credit for who we have become and what we have accomplished. Jonathan Edwards said, "Pride is much more difficult to discern because its nature consists in a person's having too high a thought of himself. No wonder he who has too high thoughts of himself does not know it; for he necessarily thinks that the opinion he has of himself has just grounds, and therefore it is not too high; if he thought such an opinion of himself was without grounds, he would therein cease to have it."[47] It is the spirit of Henry Kissinger when he said as he was speaking to a roomful of notable people, "I haven't seen so much talent in one room since I was in the Hall of Mirrors."

But what is the antidote for pride? It is the act of giving the credit to another. This is exactly what glorifying God is; it is giving God the credit and praise for what we are and what we have accomplished. It is desiring that God gets the glory for those things that we have done.

Ramon Piaguaje, a Secoya Indian born and raised in the rain forest of Ecuador, won the Winsor & Newton Millennium Art Competition, the largest painting competition in the world. His painting "Eternal Amazon" was selected from over 22,000 entries by professionals and amateur artists from 51 countries and was on display at the United Nations. Ramon, who started drawing as a teenager over 30 years ago, was not introduced to oil painting until 1993 in Quito. The young man who has captured the attention of the art world was first encouraged in his efforts by Orville and Mary Johnson, Wycliffe Bible Translators working in his village.

The Johnsons recognized a God-given ability and had encouraged him to keep drawing. When they left his village in the early seventies, having completed their translation of the New Testament, the belongings they took with them included 30 drawings by Ramon. Since then, Ramon has met the Prince of Wales and the secretary general of the United Nations, and "Eternal Amazon" has been viewed by ambassadors, artists, dignitaries, and members of the press and public from around the world. Ramon is quick to give the Lord credit for the acclaim he has received. "I can't take pride of the gift that I have as an artist, for it is God that has given me this talent, and I want to use it for his glory."

When the elderly missionary couple heard about the exhibit at the United Nations, they decided to surprise the South American artist. They entered the exhibition hall and found Ramon surrounded by many people. As he looked beyond his admiring fans, he saw the Johnsons and began to cry. They hugged and wept for several moments. In Secoya, Ramon repeated over and over to Orville and Mary, "You are the ones that should be honored, not me . . . for you came to give us the gospel, and I believe that is why I now can be here."

This is the antidote for pride in the life of a believer.

4. It keeps us from wrong thinking. When people stop glorifying God, there is a subtle change that begins to creep into their thinking that causes them to lose a proper perspective on life and reality. When Paul was writing to the Romans to explain why God's wrath was being poured out on the civilization of which he was a part, he wrote, "For although they knew God, they neither glorified him as God nor gave thanks to him, but their

thinking became futile and their foolish hearts were darkened. Although they claimed to be wise, they became fools and exchanged the glory of the immortal God for images made to look like mortal man and birds and animals and reptiles."[48] Then he describes what an entire culture looks like that has stopped glorifying God. But the downward spiral comes out of the futile thinking that comes from not giving God the credit that He is due in all the areas of life.

So we see that it is crucially important that we continually glorify God as God. This is why one of the key attitudes that a mature disciple ought to have is the desire to glorify God in everything. But how do we do that? To that we now turn our attention.

How a person glorifies God:

1. By verbally acknowledging that it is God who has enabled us to accomplish whatever we have done. This verbal identification is crucial if people are to understand why you do what you do. Jesus said, "Let your light so shine before men, that they may see your good works, and glorify your Father which is in heaven."[49] How can they know to glorify God unless there is some verbal communication from us as to why we have done the good works they have seen. Samuel Shoemaker said it well when he said, "No man can tell that Jesus died on the cross for their sins by watching the way you live."

This was the way Daniel handled it when he was brought before Nebuchadnezzar. Nebuchadnezzar had dreamed a dream but could find no one to help him understand what it meant. Even the wise men and the astrologers could not interpret it because Nebuchadnezzar refused to share the dream itself with them. Anyone can take a stab at some interpretation if they know the dream but apparently he was finished with their appearance of wisdom. When

Daniel found out about his dilemma, he went to the king and asked for time so that he would be able to interpret his dream. Daniel went back and shared the situation with his friends and asked them to pray about it with him. In the middle of the night God revealed both the dream and its interpretation to Daniel who then went to the king with its interpretation. When the king asked if he was able to give him the interpretation, Daniel replied, "No wise man, enchanter, magician or diviner can explain to the king the mystery he has asked about, but there is a God in heaven who reveals mysteries. He has shown King Nebuchadnezzar what will happen in the days to come."[50] He had to verbally communicate that it was God who had revealed this to him or else the king would have never known that and given glory to God. Rather he would have praised Daniel and probably raised him up to some high position in his kingdom. But because Daniel verbally communicated that it was God who had enabled him to do what he did, Nebuchadnezzar ended the time by saying, "Surely your God is the God of gods and the Lord of kings and a revealer of mysteries, for you were able to reveal this mystery."[51]

<u>2. By becoming a continuously thankful person.</u> David wrote, "Whoever offers praise glorifies Me"[52] to a people who were in danger of forgetting God. The giving of thanks is indicative of a person who desires to honor or glorify the person to whom they are thankful. It is a method of praise and glorification. To stop giving thanks to God is to start down the road to unbelief. Thankfulness is a characteristic of a person who realizes that God is the source of all we have in life and, who, because of knowing that fact is continually coming to God to thank Him for all He is and all He has done. At one point in his life, David was asking God to teach him His way so that he could walk in God's truth. He asked God to give him an undivided heart, a heart that is not ambivalent about

following the ways of God. Then he said, "I will praise you, O Lord my God, with all my heart; I will glorify your name forever."[53] This is a statement of thanksgiving to God for what David knew was coming.

Thanksgiving is one of the most obvious evidences of a genuinely mature believer we have. When we are thankful toward God, we are acknowledging that God is the giver of all things, and as such deserves our praise and glory. When Paul writes to the Roman church he encourages them to accept one another. Then he writes about how Christ became a servant to the Jews to confirm the promises he made to the Old Testament patriarchs (presumably Abraham in Genesis 12:3) so that the Gentiles would glorify God for the mercy that had been extended to them.[54] He then goes on to quote 2 Samuel 22:50 which says, "Therefore I will praise you among the Gentiles; I will sing hymns to your name." Praise and hymns of praise are vehicles of thanksgiving which are offered up to God in gratitude for what He has done for His people. We glorify God when we thank Him for all He is and has done.

3. By asking the Father for things in Jesus' name. In his last conversation with his disciples Jesus said to them, "And I will do whatever you ask in my name, so that the Son may bring glory to the Father. You may ask me for anything in my name and I will do it."[55] We don't normally think of praying as a means of glorifying God but here Jesus explains to his followers why this is so. Jesus had a deep desire to glorify the Father. When he prayed in John 17, Jesus spoke of glorifying the Father repeatedly. It is a prayer that is full of His concern both to glorify the Father and of receiving back the glory that had been His from before the world began. One of the ways in which Jesus can glorify the Father is if we come to the Father with our requests and ask in Jesus' name. He was the One who made it possible for us to

be able to have any relationship with the Father. So when we come to the Father, the only way we can do that is to come through Jesus. Hence we come in Jesus' name. We have no right to access through any other means. So, when we come to the Father in Jesus' name with our requests and He hears and responds to them, it gives Jesus the opportunity to once more glorify God by hearing and answering our prayer. It is an unfathomable thing that God somehow limits what He does in our world to those things for which we come to Him in prayer. Being omnipotent He can do whatever He chooses to do but one of the things He chooses to do is to wait until we pray before proceeding with what He is doing. This is why Jesus told his disciples that whatever they asked the Father in His name He would do and in the doing, the Father would be glorified.

4. By using the abilities God has given us through the strength which He gives. Peter writes, "Each one should use whatever gift he has received to serve others, faithfully administering God's grace in its various forms. If anyone speaks he should do it as one speaking the very words of God. If anyone serves, he should do it with the strength God provides, so that in all things God may be praised (doxazw — glorified) through Jesus Christ. To him be the glory and the power for ever and ever. Amen."[56] Here Peter is exhorting his readers to use the abilities (spiritual gifts) that God has given them to serve other people. This includes, but is not limited to the special abilities that each one of us has as a unique creation of God. We each have different physical, mental, emotional, temperamental and spiritual abilities whose combination is unique to us. These are not simply given to help us make a living or have a better life. They are given so that we, like Jesus, might give our lives away for the benefit of other people. We cannot duplicate the work Jesus did for us on the Cross but we can live with the same kind of self-

sacrifice which He did and give our lives away with equal unselfishness. But we can only do this with the "strength that God provides."

As Jesus used the unique abilities the Father had bestowed upon Him both through the unique genetic makeup of his mother and the divinity bestowed upon Him by His Father, so, too, we can use the unique genetic abilities we have been given and the supernatural power that comes through the new birth and the habitation of the Holy Spirit to live our lives in such a way that we give our lives away in the service of others. This is true whether the abilities are for some special "religious" ministry to which a person is called or whether it is for the humble service as a gardener, a research scientist, a scholar or an auto mechanic. These God-given abilities are to be used appropriately and in that use, we will glorify God. It may not be in some big display of public recognition and in fact it may never be recognized in this life — but if done with the right attitude, it will result in glorifying God.

This is what Paul had in mind when he wrote, "Do you not know that your body is a temple of the Holy Spirit within you, which you have from God? You are not your own; you were bought with a price. So glorify God in your body."[57] He sees the human body as more than a flesh and blood mechanism. This is how many in our generation tend to look at it. He sees the human body as on a parallel, with the magnificent temple in the Old Testament which became the dwelling place of the holy God of Israel. In the same way, our physical, flesh and blood bodies have become that kind of temple which is the dwelling place of the Spirit of God. As such they have become a place where we can glorify God, if we use it properly. One of the ways that we use it properly is to use the abilities which we possess to serve other people. When we do that, we glorify God who has called us and gifted us with our uniqueness.

5. By completing the work that God has given us to do. When Jesus was praying with his disciples in the Upper Room, He prayed, "I have brought you glory on earth by completing the work you gave me to do."[58] He prayed this on the eve of His death and thus He was looking back across what He had done. He saw that what He had been assigned to do by the Father was completed. The only remaining thing was the Cross which was the culmination of His work. What He was saying to the Father was that He had understood the task the Father had given Him, the task of healing the sick, proclaiming the good news of the kingdom, and selecting and training those who would remain after Him to begin to carry out the final injunction He had given them in Matthew 28:18-20. The sum total of all of this was "the work" he referred to. He had yet to face the cross.

But God not only gave Jesus a work to do with His life, He has given each believer a work to do with their lives. Ours may be quite different in outward manifestation but it is a significant work nonetheless. God has a purpose in Creation and He calls each of us according to that purpose.[59] Thus He has in mind a specific life for each of us to live. Jesus could understand exactly what His part was in the total purpose of God and each believer ought to be able to discern with the same clarity what God's purpose is for their lives. As we discern that purpose and then focus our lives to accomplish that calling, we will be enabled to glorify God in the same way that Jesus did. Each believer ought to be able to say at the conclusion of their lives, "I have brought you glory on earth by completing the work you gave me to do."

We will look at this more completely in Chapter 13 when we think about understanding our unique temperament and abilities. But if a person does not have the desire to glorify God in everything they do, they will not use their temperament and abilities properly no matter how well they understand them.

Conclusion

We have seen the necessity of having a desire to glorify God if one is to become a mature person in Christ. It is crucial because of what it does with the person's view of both God and themselves and who is going to get the credit for how they invest and live out their lives. To come back to the Westminster Catechism's question, "What is the chief and highest end of man?" The answer remains, *"Man's chief and highest end is to glorify God, and fully to enjoy him forever."*

Chapter # 4

A Desire for Christlikeness

As a young man, I recall seeing portraits of Jesus that were of a white European male, feminine and soft with a well-kept beard, flowing white garments and well washed, shining hair. He was the image of gentleness and likeableness personified without a touch of the healthy hardiness that comes from being a laborer in the carpenter's shop. It was no wonder that as a young Christian, when I was exhorted to "be like Jesus" it created a revulsion in me that I did not understand. Yet as I grew in my walk with God, I realized that God was in the process of conforming me into the likeness of His Son[60] and as I began to rethink that it brought me to a place where I realized that a desire to become like Jesus was an attitude that ought to be an obsession of every believer. This becomes my rationale for including this as one of the attitudes a mature believer ought to have.

WHAT DO WE MEAN BY "CHRISTLIKENESS?"

To understand this we must retrace our history as a human race and go back to the dawn of humanity. In Genesis 1 we find God creating first the physical world, then the plant world and then the animal world in simple succession. Each was created and pronounced good, with no further comment. But when God created man, He said, "Let us make man in our own image, in our likeness and let them rule over the fish of the sea and the birds of the air, over the livestock, over the earth, and over all the creatures that move along the ground. So God created man in his own image, in the image of God he created him; male and female he created them."[61] Man was created in the image of God. This makes him different from all the rest of the created things. This was not a physical image but rather a likeness of another kind. The words translated "image" in the Bible both refer to a moral likeness, not only a physical one. Man was created with a mind so he could think like God thinks; with emotions so he could feel like God feels; with a will so he could make moral choices in the same way God can make moral choices; with creativity so he could experience the joy of creating new things, not from nothing but out of all that God had created. This is how we were intended to be from the outset of creation, made in the image of God.

But when the man was given a choice, he chose to try and become like God in a way that he was never created to be. When he did that, it not only altered his relationship with God but it changed forever the image of God that he had been created to be. He could still think, but his mind would never function the way it had been created to function. He could still feel emotions deeply only now there would be the continual temptation to follow through with the emotions in ways that would be destructive. He could still make some moral choices but his will would forever be so enslaved to his selfishness that his tendency would always be toward self-expression and self-fulfillment and not toward those things for which he had been created. He was separated from the very thing he had been created to be — a creation made in the image of God. Jackson Lake lies at the base of the

Tetons in Wyoming. Sometimes early in the morning when the lake is perfectly calm, the reflection of the Tetons is magnificently reflected and mirrored on the lake's surface. The interesting this is that if you were to take one little flat stone and skip it across the surface of the lake, the image of the Tetons would be distorted and marred. In the same way, when Adam committed that first sin, God's image in man was distorted and marred.

When Jesus came, he came as the image of God.[62] He came as what we were created to be, His divinity excepted. He came with the full abilities that we had all been created to possess. He came in order to do something for the human race that would make it possible for every human being to find a way back to that image for which we had been created. He came to make full restoration possible.

This is the essence of what the Bible calls salvation. When a person receives Jesus Christ as Lord and Savior[63], a supernatural work is begun in their inner being that beings the process of restoring them back into the full image of God that they were created to be. This is what Paul is writing about when he says, "For those whom he foreknew he also predestined to be conformed to the image of his Son, in order that he might be the first-born among many brethren."[64] Jesus is the image of the invisible God[65] and when God began a work in our lives He began in us the work of conforming us to the image of Jesus Christ. The word translated "conform" means "having the same form as another, similar." It has the same root as the word "transform" which appears in Romans 12:2 and speaks of us being transformed by the renewing of our minds.

But transformed into what? We know what we were, but what are we being transformed (metamorphous — metamorphosis) into? We are being transformed into the image of Jesus Christ. We are being made into people who are like Jesus Christ, not in outward appearance but in our inner being.

WHY IS IT IMPORTANT FOR US TO UNDERSTAND THIS?

1. It is important for us to know that God has begun a process is us. When we gave our lives to God, He began a process of gradually and inevitably changing us into that image for which we were originally created. This is the work of the Holy Spirit and is called sanctification. It is a work that will not be complete until we stand in His presence. John wrote, "See what love the Father has given us, that we should be called children of God; and so we are. The reason why the world does not know us is that it did not know him. Beloved, we are God's children now; it does not yet appear what we shall be, but we know that when he appears we shall be like him, for we shall see him as he is."[66] John realized that this process of becoming Christlike would not be completed until either we die or Jesus appears in His second coming. Then the process will be complete and we will be fully restored back to that original. This is the only hope for mankind. It is the ultimate hope for the believer.

Paul had this process in mind when he wrote to the Philippians. He said, "Indeed I count everything as loss because of the surpassing worth of knowing Christ Jesus my Lord. For his sake I have suffered the loss of all things, and count them as refuse, in order that I may gain Christ and be found in him, not having a righteousness of my own, based on law, but that which is through faith in Christ, the righteousness from God that depends on faith; that I may know him and the power of his resurrection, and may share his sufferings, becoming like him in his death, that if possible I may attain the resurrection from the dead. Not that I have already obtained this or am already perfect; but I press on to make it my own, because Christ Jesus has made me his own. Brethren, I do not consider that I have made it my own; but one thing I do, forgetting what lies behind and straining forward to what lies ahead, I press on toward the goal for the prize of the upward call of God in Christ Jesus. Let those of us who are mature be thus minded; and if in anything you are otherwise minded, God will reveal that also to you."[67] He knew that he had not yet attained total Christlikeness but it was the heart-cry of his life. He desired it so greatly that he even wanted to die the same way that Jesus had died, laying down his life for the church. Then he too, like Christ would be raised from the dead. It is rather like the story of Jack Katz. The scene was the campus of the University of Florida in the early 1960s. The football team was in practice session. They were running wind sprints for conditioning. One of the large linemen, Jack Katz, who played tackle, had proven himself to be the fastest lineman on the team. Katz walked up to coach Ray Graves and asked if he might run sprints with the faster backs. Permission was granted.

For the next several days Katz managed to finish last in every race with the backfield runners. Nobody was surprised. The coach asked if he wouldn't rather be a winner with the linemen than a loser in the competition with the backs.

Katz responded, "I'm not out here to outrun the linemen. I already know I can do that. I'm here to learn how to run faster; and if you've noticed, I'm losing by a little less every day." This ought to characterize our lives as believers, we may not be as complete as some who have walked with Him longer, but we are becoming a little more like Him every day.

It is important that we see that we are involved in the process of growth so that when we look back across the time since we first gave our lives to Christ, we can see measurable progress toward becoming like Jesus. We will not get discouraged when we don't experience instant maturity or when we may not be growing at the rate we would desire. But we will be content that we can see the progress and that will assure us that God is at work in us to do His good will.[68]

2. It is important because it gives us the model for maturity. A few years ago I listened to a Christian psychologist say that at the time there were over 360 distinctly different schools of psychology. This means that there are over 360 different models of what maturity is. There is the Freudian model, the Rogerian model, the Skinnerian model, etc. Each different school sets before their students a model of maturity toward which they believe they need to motivate their clients in order for them to become whole and healthy. In this variety of definitions, how do we know which one is right? How do we know which one to steer people toward who come to us for counsel and help? Each of the different models have their goals and methods of getting there. I am certain that each one of them holds some aspect of truth and help or else they would never be set forth as able to help people come to maturity.

For the Christian, Jesus is the model of maturity toward which we are moving. When Jesus was speaking to the crowd, he said, "A student is not above his teacher, but everyone who is fully trained will be like his teacher."[69] This is the process of apprenticeship. When someone comes to be apprenticed, you place them alongside of another who already has mastered the necessary skills and attitudes for the job. By working alongside the craftsman and watching what he does, the apprentice gradually comes to develop the attitudes and skills necessary for the task. Each day he becomes more and more like his teacher. This is why Jesus called his disciples to "Follow me." As we follow someone we inevitably become like the one whom we follow as he or she sets before us the example of what they want us to become.

Because Jesus is to be our model, many of the writers of the New Testament used some aspect of Jesus' way of handling life as an example of how we should respond. When Paul was writing to the Philippians about what they needed to do to be able to get along with one another, he said, "Have this mind in you which was also in Christ Jesus."[70] Then he went on to describe how Jesus became a servant. When Peter was writing to his readers about how they should respond when they do good and are mistreated because of it. He wrote, "But if you suffer for doing good and you endure it, this is commendable before God. To this you were called, because Christ suffered for you, leaving you an example that you should follow in his steps."[71] Then he goes on to describe how Jesus responded under similar circumstances. When the writer of Hebrews writes to his readers about how we are to run the race set before us, he urges us to "Let us fix our eyes on Jesus, the author and finisher of our faith, who for the joy set before him endured the cross, scorning its shame, and sat down at the right hand of God. Consider him who endured such opposition from sinful men, so that you will not lose heart."[72] The examples could be repeated numerous times.

When Paul wanted to encourage the Corinthian believers to do everything for the glory of God, he used himself as an example and wrote, "Be imitators of me as I am of Christ."[73] He was not afraid to ask people to live life exactly as he did because he was focused on living his life exactly as Jesus had done. It was not that he thought he had his life completely together as you read in Philippians 3:10-18 but he was focusing on "…becoming like him in his death…" The model for maturity as Paul understood it was the person of Jesus Christ. This was true he said because "...it is no longer I who live but Christ who lives in me."[74] For this reason he was not ashamed to ask people to imitate him.[75] It is to be the same with every believer. Our desire to be Christlike is to be so evident and consuming that we will be unafraid to ask other people to imitate the way we live because we are endeavoring with all the strength that God provides to live like Jesus.

HOW DO WE BECOME CHRISTLIKE?

1. We must build a correct mental image of who Jesus was and how he lived. For many of us this will take some major rethinking. Philip Yancey in his book, "The Jesus I Never Knew" shares with the reader his personal struggle in this area. He writes, "The more I studied Jesus, the more difficult it became to pigeon-hole him. He said little about the Roman occupation, the main topic of conversation among his countrymen, and yet he took up a whip to drive petty profiteers from the Jewish temple. He urged obedience to the Mosaic law while acquiring the reputation as a lawbreaker. He could be stabbed by sympathy for a stranger, yet turn on his best friend with the flinty rebuke, "Get behind me, Satan!" He had uncompromising views on rich men and loose women, yet both types enjoyed his company.

One day miracles seemed to flow out of Jesus; the next day his power was blocked by people's lack of faith. One day he talked in detail of the Second Coming; another, he knew not the day or hour. He fled from arrest at one point and marched inexorably toward it at another. He spoke eloquently about peacemaking, then told his disciples to procure swords. His extravagant claims about himself kept him the center of controversy, but when he did something truly miraculous he tended to hush it up. As Walter Wink has said, if Jesus had never lived, we would not have been able to invent him"[76]

What he works through in the book is more than worth the time a reader would spend reading it and digesting what he says. Very few of us have ever taken the time to seriously grapple with the portrayal set forth in the gospel of Jesus Christ. We have so tamed him down that we think he is not much more than a polite, soft-spoken, gentle, effeminate person who tried his best to be "nice." This has seriously affected how we define biblical manhood. John Eldredge writes this in his book, "Wild at Heart," "I think most men in the church believe that God put them on earth to be a good boy. The problem with men we are told, is that they don't know how to keep their promises, be spiritual leaders, talk to their wives, or raise their children. But, if they try real hard they can reach the lofty summit of becoming……a nice guy. That's what we hold up as models of Christian maturity. Really Nice Guys. We don't smoke, drink or swear; that's what makes us *men.* Now let me ask you my male readers: In all your boyhood dreams growing up did you ever dream of becoming a Nice Guy? (Ladies, was the Prince of your dreams dashing…. or merely nice?)[77]

The wrong image or understanding of who Jesus was and how he responded to all of life's situations has left us with a model that we are not certain is desirable or worth emulating. Therefore we need to take the time to work our way through the gospel stories with a view in mind to try and understand the real Jesus. As we do that we can begin to correct our thinking about Him and rebuild a better understanding of the model of maturity that we are desiring to become.

To do this simply take the next four months and re-read the gospels, mentally put yourself in the situations you read about and ask yourself the questions:

* How did Jesus react in this situation?
* What was the tone of voice he used to speak to these people?
* How did he say we were to respond to certain incidents?
* What was the main thing he was driving at in this parable?
* If I had been listening to this, what would I have heard him say?
* What is surprising about what he said or how he responded?
* If I were to respond in that way in my everyday world, what kind of a response could I expect?

There are many other questions as well but these will get us started rethinking who Jesus was so that we can build ourselves a more correct understanding of what Jesus was like and how he handled life. It wills a surprising adventure for the person who does this and will open the door to an entirely new way of living life.

2. By focusing our thinking on Jesus. When the writer of Hebrews is starting into the applicational section in the book, after he has set before us the long list of men and women through the Old Testament who lived their lives by faith, he begins by telling us, "Let us fix our eyes upon Jesus, the author and finisher of our faith, who for the joy that was set before him endured the cross, scorning its shame and sat down at the right hand of the throne of God. Consider him…."[78] Under the inspiration of the Holy Spirit he wrote that the place to begin is to focus your attention on the person of Jesus. This is more than simply coming to a more correct understanding of who He is and how He responded to life. It is a conscious focusing

on Him during the give and take of everyday living with the thought in mind, "How would Jesus have responded in this circumstance? Or "What did Jesus say about how to handle this situation?" A. W. Tozer put it this way, "We tend by a secret law of the soul to move toward our mental image of God. This is true not only of the individual Christian, but of the company of Christians that composes the Church. Always the most revealing thing about the Church is her idea of God, just as her most significant message is always what she says about Him or leaves unsaid, for her silence is often more eloquent that her speech."[79]

Motivational people will tell you that if you want to become "successful" you need to write down your goals on a piece of paper and then read through them every morning after rising and every evening before you go to bed. In this way you will so implant them in your mind that you will unconsciously move toward them and will them accomplish what you set out to do. I don't necessarily agree with the motivation behind what they recommend but they have touched upon a biblical principle and used it for personal gain. In the Old testament, David admonishes us that the man who will be blessed is the man who meditates on God's law day and night.[80] When God came to Joshua to instruct him as he was about to give leadership to the nation of Israel, he said, "This book of the law shall not depart out of your mouth, but you shall meditate on it day and night, that you may be careful to do according to all that is written in it; for then you shall make your way prosperous, and then you shall have good success."[81]

When Paul wrote to the Corinthians he said, "And we all, with unveiled face, beholding the glory of the Lord, are being changed into his likeness from one degree of glory to another; for this comes from the Lord who is the Spirit."[82] What he was saying is that now that the veil has been removed from our eyes, we can gaze unhindered at the person of God. As we do that, we will be transformed into his likeness. Steve Brown, in the "Preaching Today" sermon tapes # 107 said, "Someone pointed out to me not too long ago how people who have been married for a long time get so they look alike. They start having the same kinds of expressions on their faces. They start actually having the same kinds of physical characteristics. I didn't think that was true. Then I started to look, and it really is true. Have you ever considered why that happens? Well, that's because people have abided with one another, and they begin to be like one another. It's the same way abiding with Christ. We become more Christlike. We begin to take on the characteristics of Christ as we abide in him."

There is something about focusing on someone or something that causes us to be irresistibly drawn to them and to increasingly resemble them and their style of living. This is Christlikeness in process.

3. By being obedient to the commands of scripture. Perhaps our attitude toward the commands of scripture is like those of the students of Virginia Stem Owens when she asked a composition class to write a short essay on the Sermon on the Mount. She thought they would at least respect the text since she taught at Texas A & M University situated in the Bible Belt. But their response was not expected. They said,

"The stuff the churches preach is extremely strict and allows almost no fun without thinking it is a sin or not."

"I did not like the essay, "The Sermon on the Mount." It was hard to read and made me feel like I had to be perfect and no one is."

"The things asked in this sermon are absurd. To look at a woman is adultery. That is the most extreme, stupid, unhuman statement I have ever heard."[83]

These are not uncommon attitudes toward the commandments found in the Bible. Yet upon careful consideration, every one of them is designed to make us more like Jesus. They were not given to deprive us of joy or to squelch genuine life out of us but to keep us from doing ourselves irreparable damage and discovering what the Bible means when it says, "The way of the transgressor is hard."[84] It is hard, not because the acts of transgression might be temporarily enjoyable but because the ultimate consequences are often very difficult to live with.

Jesus experienced life as it was designed to be lived. He experienced joy, laughter, satisfaction, friendships and deep interpersonal relationships, love, peace, wisdom, hope, optimism, contentment and lack of anxiety and the realization of fulfillment. To be like Jesus is to be able to experience all of those same things in one's life. This is what it means to have life "abundantly."[85] As we become increasingly like Jesus we will more completely experience these same things. Thus the commands are not given to keep us from experiencing these qualities; they are given to enable us to find them to their fullest degree. Yes there will be suffering, and sadness, pain and disappointment, self-sacrifice and rejection but no one can escape these things because that is what comes when you love and live deeply. But becoming like Jesus through obeying the things he commands leads us into a sense of satisfaction that nothing else can bring. Oswald Chambers wrote, "If for one whole day, quietly and determinedly, we were to give ourselves up to the ownership of Jesus and to obeying his orders, we should be amazed at its close to realize all he had packed into that one day."

4. By practicing the spiritual disciplines. The spiritual disciplines are exercises or practices that a person does train themselves into becoming more Christlike in their responses to the everyday world. Dallas Willard defines them as "A discipline for the spiritual life is, when the dust of history is blown away, nothing but an activity undertaken to bring us into more effective cooperation with Christ and His Kingdom."[86] In his excellent book, "The Spirit of the Disciplines" he explains the background for such disciplines and then explains the necessity for them if we are to form ourselves in the image of Christ. He likens it to a young man who wants to emulate a professional baseball player. They want to be able to perform in the same way the star does during a game. So they try and behave exactly as their hero when they play. But the thing they don't realize is that the professional can do what he does because between games, he practices the moves repeatedly so that when game time comes, they have become automatic. Willard argues that we will never become like Jesus was as he carried out his public ministry unless we master the disciplines he practiced when he was out of the public eye. It is the practice of these private disciplines that develops the character of Christ in a person's life when they are in public.[87]

To understand this more fully it is recommended that you purchase the book, "The Spirit of the Disciplines" and begin to discover these practices which if done, will bring us into cooperation with Christ and His kingdom. There is too little space in this book to elaborate adequately.

5. Make certain you are filled with the Spirit. Character transformation is not a work that a person can perform by themselves. It is a work of the Spirit. When Paul wrote to the Corinthians he

said that "we who with unveiled faces all reflect the Lord's glory, are being transformed into his likeness with ever-increasing glory, *which comes from the Lord who is the Spirit.*" (Italics mine)[88] It is the Spirit who does the inward transforming when we have our mental picture right, our focus right and our obedience to God's word. The fruit of the Spirit that Paul writes about in Galatians 5:22-23 are the character traits of Jesus that the Spirit is developing in those who are walking in the Spirit. Thus if we are to grow into Christlikeness, it will be as we allow the Spirit the freedom to the work in us that only He can do. This is, in a sense, like the working of the physical body if it is properly fed and cared for. If a child eats well, sleeps properly and exercises properly the nature of the body is such that the right cells will trigger at a time within the body without any effort on the part of the individual that will cause physical growth in the person. In the same manner, if we walk in the Spirit, have in our focus a clear understanding of who Jesus is and what He is like and we obey the commands of God, we will grow into Christlikeness by the unseen working of the Spirit internally in ways that we can't control.

But for this to happen, there must be a heart to be like Jesus. There must be in the life of the individual believer a desire to become increasingly Christlike that motivates them to do from the volitional side those things that we can do to facilitate this Christlikeness.

Conclusion

Years ago, Nathanael Hawthorne wrote a novel entitled "The Great Stone Face." It is the story of a boy, Ernest who is born in a large valley in which a legend has arisen. There is a rock formation that when looked at properly resembles a human face. The legend that has been handed down from generation to generation is that one day a child will be born in the valley who will grow to resemble the great stone face that is seen in the rock formation. As Ernest grows into manhood he often stares at the Great Stone Face and longs to see this man who will one day come. The story tells of three various individuals who come into the valley that the people think is the one they have been looking for. But Ernest, after examining each of them carefully determines they are not the one to come.

In the process, Ernest becomes a preacher in the area and a person to whom the others in the valley increasingly look to for counsel and wisdom. After determining that the past candidate, a poet was not the one they went to address the people of the valley. Hawthorne writes, "Ernest began to speak, giving to the people of what was in his heart and mind. His words had power, because they accorded with his thoughts; and his thoughts had reality and depth, because they harmonized with the life which he had always lived. It was not mere breath that this preacher uttered; they were the words of life, because a life of good deeds and holy love was melted into them. Pearls, pure and rich, had been dissolved into this precious draught. The poet, as he listened, felt that the being and character of Ernest were a nobler strain of poetry than he had ever written. His eyes glistening with tears, he gazed reverentially at the venerable man, and said within himself that never was there an aspect so worthy of a prophet and a sage as that mild, sweet, thoughtful countenance, with the glory of white hair diffused about it. At a distance, but distinctly to be seen, high up in the golden light of the setting sun, appeared the Great Stone Face, with hoary mists around it, like the white hairs around .the brow' of Ernest. Its look of grand beneficence seemed to embrace the world. At that moment, in sympathy with a thought which he was about to utter, the face of Ernest assumed grandeur of expression, so imbued with benevolence, that the poet, by an irresistible impulse, threw his arms aloft and shouted - 'Behold! Behold! Ernest is himself the likeness of the Great Stone Face."

In the process of longing and focusing and waiting, Ernest had been unknowingly transformed into the likeness of the Great Stone Face. In the same way, as we long to be Christlike, and turn our focus in that direction and walk filled with the Spirit in obedience to the commands of God, we are being inwardly transformed into the likeness of Jesus. For as John says, "… and what we will be has not yet been made known. But we know that when he appears we shall be like him, for we shall see him as he is."[89]

Attitude # 4

A desire to love people

Afew years ago there was man wearing a red wig who began showing up at sporting events across America. Somehow he had discovered which games were being televised and was able to position himself so that when the cameras panned the crowd they caught him on the screen. He did it to attract attention to himself while he held up a large poster with "John 3:16" written on it. It was his way of publicly bearing testimony to the grace of God.

God's love is probably His most publicly acknowledged attribute. Even unbelievers will refer to it in justifying their unbelief with the words, "How can a God of love allow that to happen?" Intuitionally people understand that God is a loving God even if they have never experienced it. They know, as John writes, "God is love."[90]

If, as the New Testament strongly affirms being a Christian is having the true God live in you[91] then this God, who is love will, as a result of His indwelling, love other people through the use of our bodies. He will use our hands to reach out, our ears to listen, our eyes to see need, our voice to speak words of counsel and comfort. He will enable us to become loving people. So one of the obvious attitudes that will be present in the life of a mature believer is that they will have a desire to love people. It is as John wrote, "If anyone has material possessions and sees his brother in need but has no pity on him, how can the love of God be in him?"[92]

This is why attitude number four is "A desire to love people."

WHAT DO WE MEAN BY LOVING PEOPLE?

The writers of the New Testament took a common Greek word, agape and changed the meaning of it to come to mean for the early Christian community something that the word never quite included before. W. E. Vine writes, Agape became "the characteristic word of Christianity, and since the Spirit of revelation has used it to express ideas previously unknown, inquiry into its use, whether in Greek literature or in the Septuagint, throws but little light upon its distinctive meaning in the NT."[93] It is the only word translated by the English word "love" that is used to refer to God's love. So the word itself came to mean a purely unselfish, sacrificial love for others. It is a love that thinks of others before it thinks of self. It is a conscious decision to put the concerns and affairs of others ahead of your own.[94] It is described by Paul by saying, "Love is patient, love is kind. It does not envy, it does not boast, it is not proud. It is not rude, it is not self-seeking, it is not easily angered, it keeps no record of wrongs. Love does not delight in evil but rejoices with the truth."[95]

Jesus put it this way: "Greater love has no one than this, that he lay down his life for his friends."[96] Loving other people means giving away your life to them. When Jesus commanded his disciples to love one another in John 13:34 He said "As I have loved you, so you must love one another." When he used the word "As" he was using it in a comparative sense. He was using his love for them as an example of how they were to love one another. How? By laying down their lives for others. This can be done in dramatic ways such as the man who jumps in to save a drowning person and in the process loses his own life, or the woman who during a time of war will gladly sacrifice her own life so that her children may live. It can also be given away in a much less dramatic, yet equally unselfish way as the person who takes time everyday to visit the lonely in care facilities or gives up an afternoon of their time to help someone less fortunate than themselves for no other reason than to walk with them during a particular time.

Dr. Robertson McQuilkin was president of Columbia Bible College and Seminary in Columbia, SC. His wife, Muriel was not only a wonderful wife and mother but also a painter, speaker, hostess for the college, fine cook and host of her own radio program. Then she was diagnosed with Alzheimer's. Initially the college board arranged for a companion for her so that her husband could go to the office each day. As her condition deteriorated, he was faced with a choice between taking early retirement to care for his wife or putting her in an institution for the rest of her life, In his own words, "When the time came, the decision was firm and it didn't take any heavy-duty calculation… The decision was made, in a way, 42 years ago when I promised to care for Muriel "in sickness and in health…till death do us part." So, as I told the students and faculty, as a man of my word, integrity has something to do with it. But so does fairness. She has cared for me fully and sacrificially all these years; if I cared for her for the next 40 years I would not be out of her debt…She is a delight to me…I don't *have* to care for her….I *get* to! It is a high honor to care for so wonderful a person.

It is more than keeping promises and being fair, however. As I watch her brave descent into oblivion, Muriel is the joy of my life. Daily I discern new manifestations of the kind of person she is, the wife I always loved….I also see fresh manifestations of God's love — the God I long to love more fully."[97]

This kind of love comes out of a person who has come to understand and experience the love of God that is demonstrated in the Cross. "God so loved the world that He gave His only begotten Son…."[98] "God demonstrates His own love for us in this: While we were still sinners, Christ died for us."[99]

At this point there are two things that need to be added: 1. A person can do outward things that are even very self-sacrificing and still not have a desire to love people.[100] Love can be expressed as an object of duty or obligation or simply because one is caught in a place where there is no way out but to do some act of kindness. Going through the motions of love without having a desire to love people outwardly appears to be love but in reality is may be self-exalting.

2. We need to differentiate between feeling loving and being loving. Many people were raised in environments where they never experienced what it means to be loved so they do not understand what it feels like to be loved. They have a difficult time separating doing from feeling and sometimes come away feeling like a hypocrite because even though they expressed some outward demonstration of love they did not have any feelings of love. The solution to this dilemma is to acknowledge to God that we do not "feel" love and then tell Him we are going to obediently love another anyway. If God wants "feelings" of love to arise, the responsibility for that is His. We have done the loving thing. C. S. Lewis expressed this very well when he wrote, "The rule for all of us is perfectly

simple. Do not waste time bothering whether you "love" your neighbor; act as if you did. As soon as we do this we find one of the great secrets. When you are behaving as if you loved someone, you will presently come to love him. If you injure someone you dislike, you will find yourself disliking him more. If you do him a good turn, you will find yourself disliking him less."[101]

If we ask God to give us a desire to love people He will eagerly respond to that and will present situations to us in which we can get an opportunity to "lay down our lives" in some small or great way for someone else. Mother Theresa said

"People are unreasonable, illogical, and self-centered; Love them anyway

If you do good, people will accuse you of selfish, ulterior motives; Do good anyway.

If you are successful, you win false friends and true enemies; Succeed anyway.

The good you do will be forgotten tomorrow; Do good anyway.

Honesty and frankness make you vulnerable; Be honest and frank anyway.

What you spend years building may be destroyed overnight; Build anyway.

People really need help but may attack you if you help them; Help people anyway.

Give the world the best you have and you'll get kicked in the teeth; Give the world the best you've got anyway.

You see, in the final analysis, it's between you and God; It was never between you and them anyway."

WHY ARE WE TO DEVELOP THIS DESIRE TO LOVE PEOPLE?

There are many implied reasons for doing this but there are three that stand out initially.

1. Because we are commanded to. This is probably the least intellectually stimulating reason but it is a primary reason nonetheless. He told his disciples, "A new command I give you: Love one another."[102] He told a young man who came and asked him what he had to do to inherit eternal life that he was to "...love your neighbor as yourself."[103] When debating one of the teachers of the law he said that the second most important commandment was to "Love your neighbor as yourself."[104] When Paul wrote to the Corinthians he told them to "Follow the way of love..."[105] When John wrote in 1 John he said, "And he (God) has given us this command: Whoever loves God must also love his brother."[106] This love was not just for those who love us (Matthew 5:46) but for our friends, our neighbors and even our enemies.

In our relationship with God, our obedience is the outward expression of our love for Him. Speaking to his disciples Jesus said, "Whoever has my commands and obeys them, he is the one who loves me."[107] As uninspiring as this might sound in this generation where we spend so much time singing praise music and trying to create atmospheres where people can "experience" God, from God's perspective simple obedience is the greatest thing He looks for from us. Thus to say that we love people because God commands us to is an extremely valid reason for loving them. It is in the act of obedience that we discover the joy of loving and in that joy, we find the satisfaction that we never thought would come. Teilhard de Chardin said, "Someday, after mastering the winds, the waves, the tides and gravity, we shall harness for God the energies of love, and then, for the second time in the history of the world, man will discover fire."

2. Because God is love and He has loved us. One of the main themes of 1 John is the relationship between knowing God and loving people. For John the two are synonymous. It is said that the old

apostle John insisted on being with his congregation in Ephesus for every meeting. When he was too old to walk, the people would carry him and he always insisted on addressing the assembly before dispersing. The assembly loved his sermons more than bread. What was his message? It was quite simple: "Little children, love one another."

The first time, the weakened old man could say no more and the audience was powerfully moved. And his one-sentenced messages remained the same. Later, the congregation began to consider his words insipid. Finally, someone asked him, "But Master, why do you always say the same thing?" John replied: "Because it is the Lord's command; because this alone, if it is followed, is sufficient and adequate."

John wrote, "This is the message you have heard from the beginning: We should love one another."[108] ""We know that we have passed from death to life, because we love our brothers. Anyone who does not love remains in death."[109] "Dear friends, let us love one another, for love comes from God. Everyone who loves has been born of God and knows God. Whoever does not love does not know God because God is love."[110] "Dear friends, since God so loved us, we also ought to love one another."[111] "If anyone says, 'I love God,' yet hates his brother, he is a liar. For anyone who does not love his brother whom he has seen, cannot love God, whom he has not seen."[112] "Everyone who believes that Jesus is the Christ is born of God, and everyone who loves the father loves the child as well."[113]

John is very clear, anyone who claims to have a relationship with the living God, the Father of our Lord Jesus Christ, will become a lover of other people. To have been loved is to create a life in which reaching out to others with that same kind of love is an automatic response. Not to so respond is to demonstrate that we have never experienced the truth and reality of God's unimaginable love.

3. Because it demonstrates the truth of our being followers of Jesus Christ. In the Upper Room Jesus said to the disciples, "A new command I give you: Love one another. As I have loved you, so you must love one another. By this all men will know that you are my disciples, if you love one another."[114] What Jesus was doing in this statement was giving anyone who wanted to test the validity of our love for God a concrete way to determine the correctness of our profession. If a person who professes to know God demonstrates that profession by a love for other people then the examiner has the right to say, "There is a true disciple." If, on the other hand, the person professing faith in Christ is harsh, judgmental and does not like people or want to be around them, the examiner has the right to say, "That person is not a disciple of Jesus Christ." Since it is true that "….everyone who is fully trained will be like his teacher" anyone who does not love in the way that Jesus did forfeits the right to be called a disciple of Jesus Christ. Donald Bloesch writes, "The cardinal evidence of true religion is works of self-giving love which are visible to the world (Matt 7:20; John 13:35; Rom 14:18; Jam 1:27). Such works will not be visible, however, to those who do them, for the focus of faithful doers is never on their good deeds (to which they are oblivious) but on Christ and his great work of atonement."

HOW CAN ONE DEVELOP A DESIRE TO LOVE PEOPLE

1. Realize that this is a work of God. Man is born naturally self-centered. From the first cries of demand in the birthing room to the need to be ministered to on one's death bed, our natural inclination is to focus on our own needs and desires. If a person is to develop a genuine love

for people, it is going to take a work within them to turn that focus outward. This is why Paul, when he delineates the fruit of the Spirit, begins with love.[115] He knows from personal experience that it was the working of the Holy Spirit in his life that enabled him to love people rather than persecute them to the point of death. When he wrote to the Romans he said that "…God has poured out his love into our hearts by the Holy Spirit, whom he has given us."[116] We are not called to try and generate some kind of obligatory love by an act of the will from within. This is not the self-centered drive of a disciplined person that goes against every fiber of one's being that we are commanded to demonstrate. It is rather God's love with which He has loved us being poured out through our bodies as we interact with and serve other people. We become the conduit through which another kind of love can be poured into the lives of people. The difference may seem inconsequential to a non-thinking person but it is in actuality a profound opportunity to anyone who has had their life transformed by the grace of this loving God.

There are many people who are involved in giving of themselves to help other people. When Hurricane Katrina hit New Orleans in August of 2005 it wrought devastation. It was the sixth-strongest Atlantic hurricane ever recorded and the third-strongest hurricane on record that made landfall in the United States. Katrina formed on August 23 during the 2005 Atlantic hurricane season and caused devastation along much of the north-central Gulf Coast. Following the Hurricane there was an outpouring of love and concern by many people from all over the world. The largest group that came together was Christians from a wide variety of denominations and backgrounds. And why? Because they felt a responsibility to step up and demonstrate God's love to those who had suffered through that tragedy. The stories of people who came through that and of those who became Christians as a result of the outpouring of God's love in that time is an amazing story. But those who cooperated shared publicly that it was God's love that motivated and strengthened them as they laid down their lives for those who were victims of that disaster.

2. <u>Expose ourselves to human need.</u> On one occasion a teacher of the law came to Jesus and asked what he needed to do to inherit eternal life. As part of his answer, Jesus told the story of the Good Samaritan. In the story a man going from Jerusalem to Jericho is attacked by robbers and left by the side of the road. Two religious leaders passed him right by without wanting to get themselves involved. That story hits too close to home to many of us. We are so busy with work, family, church and other time commitments that we drive past hurting people on our way around our communities and are sometimes not even aware of the needs that are there. We have insulated ourselves from the hurting and needy people that God has placed in our pathways and we often do it with "religious" reasons. I remember reading a story of some people who were visiting in India. As they walked down the street they saw a young boy with his head leaning against the window of a bakery and he was sound asleep. Seeing this, one of the parties wanted to get a picture of this and so he walked carefully into the store and took his picture from the inside. When he got back home he showed the slide to a group of friends to point out to them the poverty that existed in India. When he was finished someone in the group asked the speaker, "What did you do?" The man responded back, "What do you mean what did I do?" The person then pointed out the boy asleep against the window and said, "What did you do for that boy?" The speaker, embarrassed by the question, said, "Nothing."

The story struck a chord in my thinking because it set me to wondering how many times I have been taken aback by people in desperate need that I see or drive by and yet do nothing. The issue is not that there is no genuine human need all around us, the issue is that we are so busily involved in living our lifestyles that we drive right past without even noticing.

Stories abound about the impact that Christians are making in various communities as they begin to take seriously the people around them who are needy. Go talk with your children's teachers and ask them if they know anyone who is in need. Talk with a policeman, or a fireman, or a local social worker or your pastor or other person you know who is involved in your community. They will be able to give you multiple situations where you could begin to become involved. All the while keep asking God to open your heart and your eyes to see what is around you. We will never develop a desire to love people until we begin to meet people who are going through times of need. As we begin to touch their lives God will open our hearts to ways that we can become the conduit for His love to reach out and touch a hurting world. Richard Foster said, "One of the greatest expressions of love is simply to notice people and to pay attention to them."[117]

3. Become involved in the right kind of Christian fellowship. For many modern, American Christians church is basically a spectator experience. But Jesus never intended it to become that. For Him, the corporate body of believers in a given area had been assembled together by God to enable one another to benefit from the multiplicity of gifts and abilities that the corporate group possesses. The early church understood that and it was the intimate, supportive fellowship that enabled them to withstand the persecution that came upon them and emerge larger and stronger because of it. The writer of Hebrews admonishes his readers, "And let

us consider how we may spur one another on toward love and good deeds. Let us not give up meeting together, as some are in the habit of doing, but let us encourage one another — and all the more as we see the Day approaching."[118] Here he is writing about the importance of inciting one another to love and good deeds. He has learned from experience that we need to be constantly reminding each other of the importance of loving people and being involved in the lives of others.

This is not the kind of environment where one person is doing the speaking but where everyone in the group is sharing and encouraging each other to certain courses of action.

If we are to develop the desire to grow in our ability to love people more easily, we need the encouragement and motivation that comes from others reminding us of the importance of doing it. Mary Martin, who starred in a number of Broadway musicals was hurrying toward the stage door for a rehearsal of "The Sound of Music." Lyricist Oscar Hammerstein II was standing there looking pale and haggard. He started away, then turned back and handed her a slip of paper. "I don't know whether we'll ever use it in the show," he said, "but I want you to have it." Then he hurried away. Inside Mary met Dick Rodgers who told her that Oscar was to undergo a serious operation the next day. She unfolded the crumpled piece of paper he had given her. On it were these four lines:

A bell is no bell till you ring it,
A song is no song till you sing it,
And love in your heart wasn't put there to
    stay,
Love isn't love till you give it away.

"That was Oscar's farewell," Mary said. "I never saw him again."

<u>4. Find ways to serve people.</u> A number of years ago, our youngest daughter decided to spend three months in Africa as she had become fascinated with that continent. She initially went with a group to undertake a service project but after a few weeks they left to come back, leaving her almost alone in a country she did not know and staying with people she knew only slightly. She began to get home sick and through e-mail we corresponded with her. Finally I wrote to her and said, "Just look around for someone to serve." She did and began to come out of her home-sickness and spent the rest of the three months having a productive time. Serving others not only gets our eyes off of ourselves but it changes the focus of our interests. When we start finding ways to serve other people it opens up for a whole new world that we were unaware was there and we find a sense of meaning and purpose we have not known before.

In 1908, Irish explorer Ernest Shackleton headed an Antarctic expedition attempting to reach the South Pole. They came closer than any before but, 97 miles short of the pole, had to turn back. In his diary Shackleton told of the time when their food supplies were exhausted save for one last ration of hardtack, a dried sort of biscuit, that was distributed to each man. Some of the men took snow, melted it, and made tea while consuming their biscuit. Others, however, stowed the hardtack in their food sacks, saving it for a last moment of hungry desperation. The fire was built up, and weary, exhausted men climbed into their sleeping bags to face a restless sleep, tossing and turning. Shackleton said that he was almost asleep when out of the corner of his eye, he noticed one of his most trusted men sitting up in his bag and looking about to see if anyone was watching. Shackleton's heart sank within him as this man began to reach toward the food sack of the man next to him. But Shackleton watched as the man opened the food sack and took his own hardtack and put it in the other man's sack.

It is when we get our eyes off ourselves and onto others that we discover that in the giving away we have really gained what we thought we were losing. In his book, "The Rise of Christianity" Rodney Stark spends a chapter dealing with how the church responded to a series of plagues that happened in Europe during the 200's to 400's A.D. He says that it was the way that they reached out to minister to the dying, bury the dead and take care of widows and orphans that was primarily responsible for the church's growth during that time period.

When the Moravian missionaries went to Greenland, they were unable during the first year to make any impression whatsoever. Then came an awful epidemic of smallpox in which multitudes were prostrated, and the missionaries went about among them ministering to their bodies and souls in the Master's name. After that the way was clear. The people said, "You have nursed us in our sickness. You have cared for us in distress. You have buried our dead. Now tell us of your religion." It is in the serving the needs of people that God begins to open their eyes to the amazingness of His grace and love at work. They can see tangible evidence that God is at work transforming self-centered people into people who are genuinely willing to "lay down their lives" for even strangers.

The 1999 movie, "Tuesdays With Morrie" was based on the book by the same name. It is the true story of a sportswriter, Mitch Albom and his reunion with his former college professor who is dying with amyotrophic lateral sclerosis (ALS). Mitch's life was that of a very busy workaholic whose life was filled with rushed activities. When he discovers that his former college professor and friend, Morrie Schwartz is in the last stages of ALS he honors a long-overdue promise to visit him.

During those visits Morrie teaches Mitch some very important lessons on what matters most in life and confronts him with some very painful things. In one scene Morrie is very frail and is lying in a recliner in obvious pain. He asks Mitch to rub his aching feet with salve. The following dialogue ensues:

> Morrie: "When we're infants we need people to survive; when we're dying we need people to survive — but here's the secret: in between we need each other even more."
>
> Mitch: (Repeating one of Morrie's favorite quotes) "We must love one another or die."
>
> Morrie: "Yeah, but do you believe that? Does it apply to you?"

Mitch is stunned and defensive as he confesses that he doesn't know what to believe. The world in which he lives doesn't allow for the contemplation of "spiritual" things.

> Morrie: "You hate that word, don't you — *spiritual?* You think it's just touchy-feely stuff, huh?"
>
> Mitch: "I just don't understand it."
>
> Morrie: "We must love one another or die. It's a very simple lesson, Mitch."

An evidence of spiritual maturity is the desire to love people. "We must love one another or die."

Chapter 6

A Desire to Serve

One afternoon I was talking with one of our college students who was working his way through school by working at a local restaurant. He said to me, "You know, it is hard to respect some of the people in our church." I asked him why and he responded by saying, "They look so pious on Sunday but when they come in here, they are very demanding and rude. Many of them never even leave a tip although I try to give the best service I can. I guess just because I am working here as a server, they don't feel they need to treat me with respect."

Our culture tends to look down on people who are in the service industries, the waiters and waitresses, the trash pickup men, the maids in the motels, the store clerks and delivery boys. And yet from Jesus' perspective those who serve are the greatest of all.[119] This is such a difficult concept to grasp that Jesus had to address it at least twice with his disciples. The first time is found in Luke 9:46-48 (See also Matt 18:1-5 and Mark 9:33-37). It occurred just after he had come down from the Mount of Transfiguration and had healed a young man. It says that "An argument started among the disciples as to which of them would be the greatest." The second occasion occurred when they were together during the Last Supper in Luke 22:24-27. After he had taken a towel and wash basin and had kneeled down to wash their feet, it says, "Also a dispute arose among them as to which of them was considered to be the greatest." To me, this is unthinkable that among a group of men who had been with Jesus for the better part of two years there should arise an argument about which of them is the greatest — but such is nature of human nature.

Jesus responded on both occasions by telling them that the one who is greatest among them is the one who serves the others, and why? He said it was because "I am among you as one who serves."[120] Thus one of the chief characteristics of a mature disciple is that he has a desire to serve people.

WHAT DOES IT MEAN TO SERVE PEOPLE?

Both the Hebrew words and the Greek words translated with the words serve, servant, service carry with them the ideas of labor, to wait upon, domestic help, enslaved, to be in subjection to another. Paul called himself a "a servant of Christ Jesus."[121] William Barclay in his commentary on Romans writes about this designation: "He (Paul) calls himself the slave ("doulos") of Jesus Christ. In this word slave there are two backgrounds of thought. (a) Paul's favorite title for Jesus is LORD ("kurios"). In Greek the word "kurios" describes someone who has undisputed possession of a person or a thing. It means master or owner in the most absolute sense. The opposite of LORD ("kurios") is slave ("doulos"). Paul thought of himself as the slave of Jesus Christ, his Master and his Lord. Jesus had loved him and given himself for him, and therefore Paul was sure that he no longer belonged to himself, but entirely to Jesus. On the one side slave describes the utter obligation of love. (b) But slave ("doulos") has another side to it. In the Old Testament it is the regular word to describe the great men of God. Moses was the "doulos" of the Lord (Josh 1:2). Joshua was the "doulos" of God (Josh 24:29). The proudest title of the prophets, the title which distinguished them from other men, was that they were the slaves of God (Amos 3:7; Jer 7:25). When Paul calls himself the slave of Jesus Christ, he is setting himself in the succession of the prophets. Their greatness and their glory lay in the fact that they were slaves of God, and so did his."[122]

The Greek word δουλοσ (doulos) is a word that refers to an indentured slave. But there were times when a slave could earn his freedom. In some of those cases, the slave would so revere their master that they would turn back and ask to continue on as a freedman in their service. He became what was called a "bond servant." When that occurred, the former owner would pierce the ear of the newly freed slave as a symbol that now they are still working as a slave but now they are free and their slavery is the result of a personal choice. This is the case in the lives of those who have given themselves to the Lordship of Jesus Christ.

Speaking at a Founder's Week conference at Moody Bible College, Howard Hendricks told this story. "I was ministering in Fourth Presbyterian Church in Washington D. C. Dick Halverson, my beloved friend, is the pastor there. We had a Thursday morning father-son breakfast at 6:30 a.m. It was to be over by quarter of eight. Many people from the military were there because he has a tremendous penetration into that community in Washington. There were quite a few people from various government agencies and there were some craftsmen, laborers of various kinds. Really, quite a mix.

And after I finished speaking and the meeting was dismissed, I looked over to my right and there was Senator Mark Hatfield stacking chairs and picking up napkins that had fallen on the floor. I said to

Dick, "Man, what a sight." He said, "Howie, he's the greatest model of servanthood we have in this Christian fellowship."

This is the kind of servanthood that Jesus looks for from a mature disciple. Roy Hession gives us five marks of a servant: "First of all, he must be willing to have one thing on top of another put upon him, without any consideration being given him. Secondly, in doing this he must be willing not to be thanked for it. And, thirdly, having done all this, he must not charge the other with selfishness. Fourth, we must confess that we are unprofitable servants. The bottom of self is quite knocked out by the fifth and last step — the admission that doing and bearing what we have in the way of meekness and humility, we have not done one stitch more than it was our duty to do."[123]

Through both the Old Testament and the New Testament, God's chosen people were called "servants."[124] God even called the king of Babylon "my servant." [125] Having a relationship with the true God was called "serving God." [126] One of the apostle Paul's favorite titles for himself was "a bond servant of Jesus Christ."[127] Other writers in the New Testament refer to themselves as servants as well. So seeing oneself as a servant was not understood as a negative thing but a positive title to wear. Servanthood was a position to be held in high esteem and many claimed it as their own. But in our culture and day this is not so. We see servants as lower on the social scale and hence our ambitions seek to raise us away from this title. But from a biblical perspective a mature person is one who has a desire to serve people.

WHAT IS TRUE OF A SERVANT?

1. A servant is someone who lives to do another's bidding. In many of Jesus' parables he describes servants as people whose lives are lived out simply

doing what they are told by their master. The centurion who came to Jesus asking for healing for his servant told Jesus that he didn't have to come to where the servant was because he understood the place of authority. He said to Jesus, "I am a man under authority, with soldiers under me. I tell this one, 'Go' and he goes; and that one, 'Come,' and he comes. I say to my servant, 'Do this,' and he does it."[128] This is the role of a servant. A servant does not have a life of his own and the choices concerning what he is to do are dictated to him by another.

Often they were entrusted with very important matters. Abraham's servant was sent to find a wife for his son, Isaac.[129] Who in our culture today would send an employee to seek out a future mate for one of their children? Joseph was entrusted with everything that Potiphar owned.[130] The only thing he did not turn over to him was selecting what he ate. That is major responsibility and trust. So being a servant does not mean that the work you were called upon to do was not significant work.

2. A servant will be held accountable for what has been entrusted to them. In some of Jesus' parables when he wants his listeners to understand certain biblical principles, he uses illustrations in which servants are entrusted with certain of the master's goods and told to do something with them because when the master returns he will expect a return on what he has given to them.[131] If he has used what he has been given wisely and well, he will be rewarded significantly but if he has neglected to use what has been entrusted to him, he will be justly punished. Jesus used a person's faithfulness with what has been entrusted as a measure of what will eventually be given to them. He said, "…if you have not been trustworthy with someone else's property, who will give you property of your own?"[132]

3. A servant does not expect any special treatment for their faithfulness. In Luke 17:7-10 Jesus said to his disciples, "Suppose one of you had a servant plowing or looking after the sheep. Would he say to the servant when he comes in from the field, 'Come along now and sit down to eat'? Would he not rather say, 'Prepare my supper, get yourself ready and wait on me while I eat and drink; after that you may eat and drink'? Would he thank the servant because he did what he was told to do? So you also, when you have done everything you were told to do, should say, 'We are unworthy servants; we have only done our duty.'" He was saying that a servant has a job to do and that it is expected that he will do it well. Even if he is tired from working, he is expected to keep on working, at times even without being thanked for his faithfulness. Sometimes in our minds we feel like we somehow "deserve" special treatment because of the hard work we have done. But there ought to be no such expectation on the part of a servant. Our attitude is to be that of General Charles G. Gordon. He was an outstanding man of God. When the English government wanted to reward him for his distinguished service in China, he declined all money and titles. Finally, after much arguing, he accepted a gold medal inscribed with his name and a record of his accomplishments.

Following his death, however, it could not be found among his belongings. It was learned that on a certain date he had sent it to Manchester during a famine with the request that it be melted and used to buy bread for the poor. In his private diary for that day were written these words: "The only thing I had in this world that I valued, I have now given to the Lord Jesus."

4. A servant will be rewarded based on his faithfulness to the task assigned. Jesus clearly taught that a faithful servant will be rewarded accordingly. When he was telling the disciples

what they could look forward to in the future,
he told them a parable about three servants who
were given varying amounts of the master's property. He expected them to take what they had been
given and use it during his absence so that his
resources would not sit idle while he was gone.[133]
Two of the men invested the money wisely but the
third simply buried it so that he would not lose
what had originally been entrusted to him. When
they were called to account for what they had done
with the money, the first two reported a two for
one return on his investment. The master said,
"Well done, good and faithful servant! You have
been faithful with a few things; I will put you
in charge of many things. Come and share in your
master's happiness." Not only did they get to hear
words of commendation from their master, but they
were given an even greater responsibility and then
the privilege of being able to share in happiness
of the master. Even the money that was put into
the ground was given to the first servant and when
someone objected the master said, "I tell you that
to everyone who has, more will be given..."[134]

5. In God's eyes, being a servant is the highest
position a person can have. Later in his ministry,
Jesus was very critical of the teachers of the law
and the Pharisees because they taught the Law well
but they didn't practice it personally. He saw
through their outward show of religiosity and the
pretense they displayed as they went about their
religious performances. He told his disciples that
they should not desire to be called "Rabbi" (my
great one, my honorable sir) nor "father" (a term
of authority) nor "teacher" (a guide or master).
These were all terms of respect that the religious
leaders longed for that would add to their prestige or positions of greatness. Rather, he said
they should see themselves as servants because it
is the greatest position they are to strive for.
Then he gives them the reason: "For whoever exalts

himself will be humbled, and whoever humbles himself will be exalted."[135] Paul elaborates on this principle in Philippians 2:1-11. When he thinks about the position a person should long for if the body is to function the way God designed it, he is to "have this mind in you that was also in Christ Jesus." Then he goes on to talk about how he humbled himself and became a servant, even to the point of death. Because he humbled himself in that way, the Father exalted him and gave him a name that is above every name. Exaltation always follows humbling yourself, becoming a servant and leaving the responsibility for being raised up to the God whom we serve.

There is a second reason why this is true and that is that we serve a God who is a servant. Repeatedly the Bible describes God as being a servant to His people. Many of the invitations to prayer are the kind of statements a servant would make to someone he serves. "Call unto me and I will answer you and show you great and mighty things…."[136] "…call upon me in the day of trouble; I will deliver you…."[137] There are many others but they simply indicate that our God delights in being a servant to His people. He is a loving Father, who takes great joy in serving the needs of His children and we are never more like Him than when we are serving people. That is why being a servant is the greatest ambition a person can have.

So we need to be giving God the abilities we have for His use. Oswald Chambers says, "If a man possessing great gifts will not place them at the disposal of God, God is not defeated. He will take a man of lesser gifts which are fully available to Him and will supplement them with His own mighty power."[138]

WHY THIS IS IMPORTANT

There are three reasons why this is a very important attitude to possess:

1. <u>People used by God in significant ways have always seen themselves as His servants.</u> They realized that they were not here to live life for themselves. They were here to serve God in whatever capacity He wanted them to serve. Abraham said to three strangers that showed up at his tent, "If I have found favor in your eyes, my lord, do not pass your servant by."[139] David responded to Saul's inquiry about his ability to defeat Goliath, "Let no one lose heart on account of this Philistine; your servant will go and fight him."[140] God spoke about Moses as "my servant Moses."[141] Joshua asked the commander of the Lord's army, "What message does my Lord have for his servant?"[142] Samuel said to God, "Speak, for your servant is listening."[143]

In the New Testament we find Paul, Peter, James, Jude, and John all referring to themselves as servants of the Lord in their writings.[144] God honors His servants and does great things through those who serve Him. If we want to be used in making a positive impact for Jesus Christ in our generation, we need to see ourselves as servants of the Lord.

2. <u>Servanthood is an essential quality in a leader.</u> One cannot lead others until first they have first discovered what it means to be a follower. Jesus did not say to his disciples, "Listen to me and I will make you fishers of men." Rather he said, "Follow me and I will make you fishers of men."[145] A leader who has not first learned to be a servant follower has all the potential of becoming a tyrant. When God was raising up a leader to follow Moses, he went to Joshua because he saw in him a servant's heart. It says of him, "The Lord would speak to Moses face to face, as a man speaks

with his friend. Then Moses would return to the camp, but his young aide Joshua, son of Nun, did not leave the tent."[146] Joshua watched God's dealings with Moses, observing what he did and said and how he related to God so that when the time came for God to select a replacement for Moses, the responsibility fell to Joshua. Why? Because he had learned how to lead by being a follower.

When Solomon's son, Rehoboam stepped up to take the throne from his father he consulted the elders who had given his father wise counsel. The people had come to him and asked him to reduce the heavy tax burden his father had placed on them and he did not know what to do. The elders answered him, "If today you will be a servant to these people and serve them and give them a favorable answer, they will always be your servants."[147] Unfortunately he did not take their counsel and as a result lost ten of the tribes to another leader. A leader becomes a good leader by becoming a servant to those who he would have follow him.

In the movie, "First Knight" King Arthur is impressed by the fearlessness of young Lancelot. As he takes him toward the room that holds the Round Table, King Arthur shares with Lancelot what Camelot's values are. He says, "Here we believe that every life is precious, even the lives of strangers. If you must die, die serving something greater than yourself. Better still, live and serve." As they come to the great Round Table King Arthur points out to him that the table has no head or foot; they are all equal, even the king. Then Lancelot reads the inscription that is on the table, "In serving each other we become free." A good leader understands this and that is part of the reason he has become a good leader.

3. Serving people is one of the most effective ways of reaching them with the gospel. In his book, "The Rise of Christianity" Rodney Stark evaluates the sociological reasons for why the early church

grew so rapidly during the early centuries of Christendom. One of the reasons he sets forth was that during the second through the fourth centuries there were a series of devastating plagues. Thousands of people died as a result of them. The threat was so great that even medical doctors fled to the mountains in an attempt to escape the possibility of contagion from the diseases. As people suffered and died, the streets were filled with bodies of people both dying and already dead. The only people who made an attempt to minister to these people were the Christians of their day. Their reasoning was that they knew where they were going when they died and so the fear of death was gone. When the unbelievers saw the love and concern they showed for the suffering and their families, there developed a natural curiosity about these people called Christians. They inquired and many of them came to know Christ as a result of that humble service offered by the people of God.

We saw the same kind of focus in our generation from the life of Mother Teresa. Her acts of service are beyond number, but one particular incident reflects the heart from which she served. She was working among the slums of Calcutta dressing the wounds of a leper. An American tourist observed her work and asked if he could take a picture. She granted permission and the tourist framed his shot. Through the camera's lens he could see this world-renowned nun tenderly replacing a bloody bandage that covered a gaping hole where the leper's nose used to exist. The photographer could also smell the stench of this wound as he moved in for a closer shot. After capturing several pictures, the American tourist said, "Sister, I wouldn't do what you're doing for $10 million!" Mother Teresa replied, "Neither would I, my friend. Neither would I!" How could she respond that way? Because of her love for Jesus Christ. She was quoted in an article in Christianity Today as saying, "By blood and origin, I am all Albanian. My citizenship is Indian. I am a Catholic nun. As to my calling, I belong to the whole world. As to my heart, I belong entirely to Jesus."[148]

HOW A PERSON DEVELOPS THIS ATTITUDE:

There are some things a person can do to develop this attitude in their personal life.

1. Develop the right image of Jesus Christ. As was mentioned in chapter 4, one of our attitudes is having a desire to be Christlike. That means we work at developing the attitudes He had as He lived out His life. Jesus made Himself a servant. He was continually being sensitive to the needs of the people around Him and whenever He was confronted with a request to become a servant to someone in need, He always responded by going and serving them even though His disciples didn't understand or even approve. We need to develop that kind of attitude.

Dr. Samuel Brengle was a brilliant American university student. He was the leading orator of his university the year he graduated. Upon graduation he was called to the pulpit of an influential church where he was acclaimed as a "coming pulpiteer." But his heart was not satisfied. He did not feel that he was reaching the people and longed to do more to spread the Gospel. At this crucial time he read of the Salvation Army, then regarded as a rather disreputable organization. But as he read of its achievements among the underprivileged people of Britain and the trophies it was winning from the gutter, he felt that this was the type of work which would satisfy his heart's yearning. He resigned his church, sailed for London and offered his services to General William Booth. He was ultimately accepted for service, but in order to test his caliber he was put in the training garrison with scores of cadets, most of whom, though full of zeal, had almost no formal education.

His first work was to clean a pile of muddy boots belonging to his fellow students. As he brushed away the mud, a battle royal raged in his heart. Was it for this he had renounced his fashionable church and come to London? The Devil pressed the advantages he had gained and Brengle almost succumbed to the tempter's voice when a verse of scripture entered his mind by the Holy Spirit. "He took a towel and girded himself." In a moment he detected the subtlety of his adversary and from his heart he cried, "Lord, if Thou couldest take a towel and wash the disciples dirty feet, surely I can take a brush and clean the cadet's dirty boots." Humility triumphed and he eventually went on to become overall leader of the Salvation Army but the thing that turned the tide was regaining a proper picture of Jesus, functioning as a servant.

Roy Hession writes, "When we understand the humbling and self-emptying that is involved in really being a servant, it becomes evident that only those who are prepared to live quite definitely under the shadow of Calvary, ever contemplating the humility and brokenness of the Lord Jesus for us, will be willing for that position."[149]

2. Change the way we look at ourselves. Since it is true that almost all of the people throughout history that have made a significant impact for God in their generations saw themselves as servants, we need to develop the same kind of self-image. We read a lot today about the importance of having the right self-image. But most of the literature you read in this area speaks to the issue of feeling competent, or seeing yourself as successful. Much of modern education has as its aim helping the people feel good about themselves in a way that will make them successful in their world. But almost no one emphasizes the importance of seeing yourself as a servant to the people who

are around you. Since we are trained in the other direction, it becomes mandatory that we change the way we see ourselves. This is the meaning of the word "repent." Rather than seeing ourselves as "customers" or people to be waited on or taken care of or people of entitlement, we need to see ourselves as those who are here to serve. This will require some major effort to undo and then redo our understanding of success and value. "We shall not enter into more abundant life merely by resolving that we shall be humbler in the future. There are attitudes and actions which have already taken place and are still being persisted in (if only by our unwillingness to apologize for them) that must first be repented of. The Lord Jesus did not take upon Him the form of a bond-servant merely to give us an example, but that He might die for these very sins upon the cross, and open a fountain in His precious Blood where they can all be washed away. But the Blood cannot be applied to sins of our proud hearts until we have been broken in repentance as to what has already happened as to what we already are. This will mean allowing the light of God to go through every part of our hearts and into every one of our relationships. It will mean that we shall have to see that the sins of pride, which God will show us, made it necessary for Jesus to come from heaven and die on the Cross that they might be forgiven. It will mean not only asking Him to forgive us but asking others too. And that will be humbling indeed. But as we crawl through the door of the broken ones we shall emerge into the light and glory of the highway of holiness and humility."[150]

3. Volunteer to serve in some obscure place. There are places of service all around us if we only open our eyes to see them. God might want us to start right at home. Look for some small way to serve your wife, your husband, your children your parents. Wash the dishes, vacuum the house,

mow the lawn, take out the garbage, straighten up a common room, do some repair on the house somewhere, drive someone someplace without having to be asked. The numbers of opportunities are endless when we open our eyes to them. Then turn to the people you work with, or go to school with or play tennis with, or recreate with or talk with across the fence. Stop at a service station and offer to clean their wash rooms. If you hear about someone going through a special time of need, find out any information you can and do something about it. Call your pastor, talk to a school teacher, call the Salvation Army, make an appointment and go see some city official or school principal. Ask them if there are any things you could do to help them. Become a mentor or a sponsor, or a volunteer classroom aid, or help coach some Little League team, etc. The sky is the limit.

Start small and with something for which there will be no open, public praise coming to you. Do it without anyone's knowledge and see what it does for you in addition to what it does for someone else. In his excellent book, "The Spirit of the Disciplines" Dallas Willard talks about spiritual disciplines that if undertaken will bring us into greater conformity to the image of Christ. One of those disciplines is what he calls "service." He writes, "But I may also serve another to train myself away from arrogance, possessiveness, envy, resentment, or covetousness. In that case, my service is undertaken as a discipline for the spiritual life. Such discipline is very useful for those Christians who find themselves — as most of us by necessity must — in the "lower" positions in society, at work, and in the church. It alone can train us in habits of loving service to others and free us from resentment, enabling us in faith to enjoy our position and work because of its exalted meaning before God."[151]

CONCLUSION

Jesus calls us to servanthood. It is not always easy but it is always right. We may not be rewarded for it in this life but that's all right, this life is not the end of our existence. Those we serve may never know we have done it or may never express their appreciation for it — but do it anyway. In fact, you may be mistreated for serving others but so was Jesus.

"Our servanthood to the Lord Jesus is to express itself in our servanthood to our fellows. Says Paul,. 'We preach not ourselves, but Christ Jesus, the Lord, and ourselves as your bond-servants for Jesus' sake.' The low position we take toward the Lord is judged by Him by the low position we take in our relationship with our fellows. An unwillingness to serve others in costly, humbling ways He takes to be an unwillingness to serve Him, and we thus put ourselves out of fellowship with Him."[152]

"O God, help us to be masters of ourselves that we may be servants of others."[153]

Chapter 7

A desire to be involved in Making Disciples

When you give a person a task to undertake, there are three things you should keep in mind: 1) Have you clearly spelled out the responsibility? 2) Have you given them the authority they need to undertake the task? 3) Have you established how you will evaluate their performance? These three words: *Responsibility, Authority* and *Accountability* are essential ingredients in the successful delegating of a task.

In almost the last words Jesus spoke to his disciples in Matthew 28:18-20 He gave them their marching orders. He said, *"All authority in heaven and on earth has been given to me. Therefore go and make disciples of all nations, baptizing them in the name of the Father and of the Son and of the Holy Spirit, and teaching them to obey everything I have commanded you. And surely I am with you always, to the very end of the age."* He had been with them for three years and now He was leaving to return to the Father. He had walked with them, taught them and trained them for the task yet undone when he left. In these words he spelled out for them everything they needed to know for the task ahead:

Responsibility: "Make disciples."
Authority: All authority in heaven and earth
has been given to me, go therefore…." The implication here is that since all authority has been
given to me, I am sending you out with the same
authority. You have all the authority you need to
ask for whatever it is you need to undertake the
task.

Accountability: He did not state this but it is
implied in the statement. They would be evaluated
by whether or not they successfully carried out
this specific responsibility.

WHAT JESUS MEANT BY "MAKING DISCIPLES"

But exactly what did Jesus mean by his statement? Many in explaining this command have said
there are four things involved: 1) Go (evangelism);
2) Make disciples; 3) Baptize; and 4) Teach. But
this is not the language of what he said. In his
command, there is only one main verb and that is
"make disciples." The other three are participles
which are verbs that are dependent upon the main
verb. That means that Jesus said to his disciples
that their job was to make disciples. They would
do it by going, baptizing and teaching but the
goal was to make disciples.

The word translated "disciple" is the verb form
of the Greek word mathetes (μαψητηϖ). It means
"to be a disciple of one, to follow his precepts
and instructions, to teach, instruct." It is not
used in the sense that we use it which would be
more like that of a student. In Jesus' day if
you were someone's "disciple" it meant that you
spent considerable time being with the person,
not just listening to lectures and taking notes
to be regurgitated on a final exam. It meant that
you lived with them, ate with them, went with
them when they lived out their life in the community. A better word in our culture would be the

word "apprentice." Everyone understands what that means. It means you start working with someone as their helper. You spend all day with them on the job. You watch what they do, you carry out tasks the person assigns, he explains to you what he is doing and why he is doing it, he gives you advice and on-the-job instruction, correcting your errors and helping you learn from your mistakes. Eugene Peterson writes, "Disciple (mathetes) says we are a people who spend our lives apprenticed to our master, Jesus Christ. We are in a growing — learning relationship, always. A disciple is a learner, not in the academic setting of a school-room, rather at the work site of a craftsman. We do not acquire information about God but skills in faith."[154]

I recently volunteered to spend three days working with a person doing hiking trail repair in the National Forest near where we live. I had never done that before and so the man who I was going with took me along to both help and learn. I carried some tools, my backpacking gear and every-thing I needed into the campground where we would stay for three days. I had never done trail repair before but he was well trained in doing it so he pointed out what needed to be done, explained exactly what he wanted done and how to do it and then worked alongside of me and supervised the work I was doing. This is apprenticing.

This is what Jesus had in mind when he told the disciples that he wanted them to go and "make disciples." He had been working with them for the past two years. They had watched him, he had given them some specific instructions about how they were to live and work with people and now it was time for them to turn around and do with other people what he had done with them. When he used the word "disciples" it was a word he had used as he described them. Thus they knew what he was describing and how they were to undertake the job. They were to do with others exactly what Jesus had done with them.

The contemporary American church has lost this entire sense of what it means to "make disciples." We have inherited a Greek model of "teaching" which means classroom instruction and up front pulpit lecturing. We have replaced apprenticing with what we call "programs" that are designed to develop workshops, etc. that will attract people and hopefully train them through lecture and teaching how do certain things in their individual lives. It is hoped that if people have enough of the right kind of "information" they will take that and apply it with the result that they will then become "disciples." We have moved away from the simplicity of what Jesus intended and have substituted in its place a very complex structure and program that requires money, facilities, materials and much energy just to keep it running. What Jesus intended was very simple, yet profound in its implications.

The result is that we have lost a true understanding of what Jesus meant when he told his disciples to "Go and make disciples of all nations." When we hear this in our culture we immediately think of church services and programs, committees and facilities, things Jesus never intended us to become involved in. So we engage in these activities and then end up exhausted and frustrated because we watch the decreasing influence of Christianity in our culture. We have forgotten about the impact of one man upon another.

Edward Kimball taught a Sunday School class and was committed to reaching every lost young person in his class. There was one young fellow who had begun working in a nearby shoe shop that was especially on his mind. He was a young backward fellow who was fresh from the farm. One day Kimball went to where he was working and persuaded that young man to give his life to Christ, which he did. Kimball discipled and taught him despite the fact that in Kimball's words, "I have never seen few persons whose minds were spiritually darker when he came into my Sunday School class, or one who seemed unlikely ever to become a Christian of clear, decided views, still less to fill any sphere of extended public usefulness."

The young man Kimball discipled, Dwight L. Moody, went on to become a pioneer in the techniques of mass evangelism. If you follow down through Moody to F. B. Meyer to J. Wilbur Chapman to Billy Sunday to Mordecai Ham to a meeting he preached where some teenagers were won to Christ, and among them was a young man named Billy Graham. Why? All because of the discipling influence of Edward Kimball, a Sunday School teacher, who had a heart for reaching people for Christ and discipling those whom he could reach. This was not a program or a strategy or anything large and well promoted, it was simply one man with a heart to make disciples the same way Jesus did and yet the influence of his life continues strong into our generation.[155]

When we speak about "making disciples" I am not simply referring to evangelism, I am referring to the entire process of seeing a person come to Christ and then following through until that new believer has come to a place of maturity where they can turn around and repeat with another person what has been done to them. It was this that Paul had in mind when he wrote to young Timothy, one of the men that he discipled. He wrote, "And the things you have heard me say in the presence of many witnesses entrust to faithful men who will also be qualified to teach others."[156] And how would Timothy have learned these things? Paul could say to him, "You, however, know all about my teaching, my way of life, my purpose, faith, patience, love, endurance, persecutions, sufferings — what kinds of things happened to me in Antioch, Iconium and

Lystra, the persecutions I endured."[157] And how could Timothy know all these things? He knew them because Paul had taken him along with him and Timothy had learned in the same way the first twelve learned, by observation and apprenticing.

WHY THIS DESIRE IS IMPORTANT

1. Without Christ people are going to hell. Oftentimes in our church activity we forget about this important component of our faith. I don't mean that we don't give mental assent to the concept. It is just something I have observed over the years when I have been in very few church committee meetings where we talked about program and planning to reach people who are going to hell. It does not seem to bother us very much that neighbors, friends, work associates, family members are literally doomed to a God-less eternity unless they come to know Jesus Christ.

Our faith tells us that people without Christ are dying every day and are going to a Christless eternity. This is not just dry doctrine, it is really true. If we believe what the Bible says, there is no second chance for people who go out into eternity without Christ. They are lost for all eternity and will never be able to share in wondrous grace of God that we who know Him have experienced. There is no payment for their sin other than the cross that will enable them to find forgiveness. There is no other religion that offers them anything that will ultimately keep them from hell and this realization ought to compel us take seriously Jesus' charge to us to "Go and make disciples."

I had the opportunity one time to spend time with a man who had come out of an alcoholic background and who God had marvelously saved. He had been transformed by God's grace and had really become a true evangelist even though still working as an auto mechanic. I remember his sharing with me of a dream that came to him in the middle of the night where he had a vision of standing and looking into the depths of hell at the agony and suffering that lost people were going through. He could describe for me the parched throats and hear the cries of those who were perishing and he shared with me that with this was his motivation. He plead with men and women to give their lives to Jesus. Perhaps this is part of the message that God spoke to Ezekiel when He said, "Son of man, I have made you a watchman for the house of Israel; so hear the word I speak and give them warning from me. When I say to the wicked, 'O wicked man, you will surely die, and you do not speak out to dissuade him from his ways, the wicked man will die for his sin, and I will hold you accountable for his blood. But if you do warn the wicked man to turn from his ways and he does not do so, he will die for his sin, but you will have saved yourself."[158]

2. It is the task we have been entrusted with. I recall a time when I was working with a large church staff some of whom were seminary trained and their leading corporate board to get them moving toward reaching their community with the gospel. There were about 30 people there and I gave them an assignment to do, first alone and then we would come back and share together the results of our time of reflection. My question to them was, "What is the task of the church?" After a 15 minute time of reflection I gathered them back together to share what they had written down. As they began to go around the room and share their answers I was floored that not one of them was able to clearly articulate the simplicity of the Great Commission. There were almost as many different answers as there were people. When they finished I was so dumbfounded that I told them we were going to close the meeting because I honestly did not know where to go from there. I had to go

back and regroup because the task we were trying to undertake had to be approached from a different perspective.

It is easy for the church to get off target, especially in this generation. We have so many wonderful "programs" set before us and so much good literature being printed and so many "successful church seminars" that we can attend that it is easy to forget our responsibility and set off in other directions. Our culture is producing an increasing number of emotionally damaged individuals and it is easy to substitute emotional health, financial seminars, building strong families, self-help programs for the task that we have been given. These are all wonderful things and activities in which to be engaged but they are never to be substituted for the main task that Jesus left us with — to make disciples. The leading Christian periodicals and publishers all play up the successful entrepreneurs that have captured the world's headlines and promote those who have seen their church grow from 60 to 5,000 in eight years that it has created an expectation and an image of success that is foreign to the understanding of Jesus.

Our task is to make disciples, not to build large churches or small churches. It is not to increase our membership or sponsor many of the functions and activities that we do. It is to make disciples and we need to return to the simplicity of that.

3. It is the only way we can successfully reach future generations. When Paul instructed Timothy to "entrust to reliable men" he had a four generation vision in his heart.[159] It went this way:

Paul -> to Timothy -> to Reliable men -> to Others.

Paul expected Timothy to train "reliable men" in the same way that he had been trained so that they in turn could do the same to "others." This would mean that not only would Timothy have been won and trained but that some "reliable men" would also have been won and trained to the same degree that Timothy had been. Then they in turn could train "others" who, it is expected, would be able to turn and do the same thing to additional people in successive generations. In this way future generations would have the same sense of God's calling and training as Timothy had gotten and the commission that Jesus had given the original twelve would be carried forth throughout history.

We live in a "large group" world where success is measured by size. For a few years large stadium events were the "thing." They were considered a wondrous success because they could fill the Los Angeles Coliseum with men or create a "Million Man March" that would transform Washington D.C. These events were planned by men who were enamored with size because that is what we are fed in our Christian media. But Jesus did not say, "Go and create large gatherings." He said "Go and make disciples." They may be wonderfully invigorating events that charge men and women and give them a great "feeling" but they tend to then forget that we are charged with developing disciples for future generations. Robert Coleman, writing in "The Master Plan of Evangelism" puts it this way, "And let us remember, too, that one does not have to have the prestige of the world to be greatly used in the Kingdom of God. Anyone who is willing to follow Christ can become a mighty influence on the world, providing of course, this person has the proper training.

Here is where we must begin like Jesus. It will be slow, tedious, painful, and probably unnotoiced by people at first, but the end result will be glorious, even if we don't live to see it. Seen this way, though, it becomes a big decision in the ministry. We must decide where we want our ministry to count — in the momentary applause of popular recognition or in the reproduction of our lives in a few chosen people who will carry on our work after we have gone. Really, it is a question of which generation we are living for."[160]

4. It is the only way which, if taken seriously by every believer, will enable us to reach the world with the gospel. Since we are so enamored by size as our measure of success, we automatically think that bigger is better and that faster is always best. Let me give you some figures that if taken seriously will transform your thinking. It is the difference between addition and multiplication. We will begin with the following assumptions:

1. The population of the earth is 6 billion people. (6,000,000,000)

2. Addition method: That your church or group has designed a strategy that guarantees you can win 2,000 people to Christ everyday so that 14,000 people are added to the kingdom every week. These are not followed up because you simply don't have the resources but at least they have made a decision to follow Jesus.

3. Multiplication method: That to disciple, through multiplication each person won to Christ will be given one year's worth of in-depth teaching and apprenticing. The assumption is also made that by the end of that year both the discipler and the disciple have seen one person come to Christ so they can begin year two each one training a new believer.

How long will it take to reach the world population of 6,000,000,000?

Year	Addition (2,000 per day)	Multiplication (Each one train one)
1	730,000	2
2	1,460,000	4
5	3,650,000	32
10	7,300,000	1,024
20	14,600,000	1,048,576
30	21,900,000	1,073,664,000
33	24,090,000	8,589,312,000

This means that theoretically by using the model of multiplication we could have reached the entire world population of six billion in between 32 and 33 years whereas the method of addition would take 8,219 years to reach the same number and in addition, the people in the multiplication model would have had the opportunity to have one year's discipling. Now based upon experience neither of these examples works in practice the same way it is stated in theory but I wanted you to see that larger is not always better. I wanted you to realize that by going deeper, we may actually be doing a faster job of reaching the world with the gospel than if we simply become enamored with crowds.

But this will never be realized unless we develop a desire to make disciples as Jesus commanded us to do. If we give our time and energy to maintaining and developing church programs, attending countless committee meetings and seminars, occupying our time and talents with traditional church programming we will never see the legitimacy of making disciples nor will we make the time available to engage our time doing this.

Most of the earnest Christian people I have known wrestle with the issue of how they can best invest their time and energy where it will make the greatest return for a life. I try and share with them that it is not in sitting on committees or planning and carrying out elaborate church programming. It will come from catching a vision of the potential impact one life can make if you choose to invest time and energy in one new believer at a time. I advise them to resign many of their responsibilities and begin to ask God to give you one man or one woman that you can begin to invest their life in. If in a year they can point to someone who has gone farther in their walk with Christ than they ever have before and if during that time you will have seen some other people come to Christ as a result of your time together, you could have no greater return for the investment of your life. This is what is meant by "making disciples." Dag Hammarskjold, the past Secretary-General of the United Nations once made a profound, far reaching statement: "It is more noble to give yourself completely to one individual than to labor diligently for the salvation of the masses."

HOW THIS DESIRE IS CULTIVATED

There are five things that come to mind that we can do to cultivate this desire to make disciples:

1. Pray. When Jesus sent out 72 people into the field of ministry, He started them out with this admonition: "The harvest is plentiful, but the workers are few. Ask the Lord of the harvest, therefore, to send out workers into his harvest field."[161] The problem, Jesus said, was not with the abundance of the harvest but with the fact that there are never enough laborers who are willing to be involved in it. It is interesting that He did not tell them to recruit more or to develop pro-

grams for empowering them, he simply told them to pray. The reason is that God, who He here calls "the Lord of the Harvest" is quite able and willing to raise up workers but for some reason, He has set it up so that additional workers will come only as we pray. This deals with the mysterious ways in which God functions that He would limit Himself to the prayers of people but this is what He has chosen to do. So we must pray for He is the Lord of the Harvest.

We need to pray for additional laborers, pray that God's people would see the lostness of their family and friends, pray that they would come to understand what role they can play in this enterprise, pray that they would catch a vision of what can come if we are willing to focus in on one or two individuals, pray that the enemy who blinds the minds of unbelievers would be forced to release his handhold on their eyes so they can come to see the light of the glorious gospel, pray for people around us that God would give us the opportunity to build relationships with them and win their trust and their friendship. None of these things happens without prayer and so our work begins here.

2. Make certain we are filled with the Spirit. It is interesting that Jesus would not send his trained disciples out until they had been baptized with the Spirit.[162] This was something they would experience on the Day of Pentecost which would transform them from people hiding behind closed doors to openly become vocal witnesses to the reality of what Jesus had done. This was not some kind of "emotional high" that made them feel good about themselves but it was a genuine empowering that gave them the internal strength and courage to do what they had been told to do.

The Holy Spirit is probably one of the most misunderstood Persons in modern Christianity. In talking with people, I find they have no trouble conceiving and understanding God the Father. Nor do they have any trouble with Jesus. But, when you start to talk about the Holy Spirit, their minds have trouble perceiving Him as a genuine person. I suspect the words "Ghost" or "Spirit" have something to do with it as we cannot mentally conceive of a ghost or a spirit. And yet He is every bit as much as person as the Father and the Son. His enabling is essential if we are ever to be transformed into the people we have been created to be or do those things that God has called us to do. It was only after the coming of the Spirit on the Day of Pentecost that Peter was willing to stand up and be counted. It was only after the coming of the Spirit that the early church was able to fearlessly preach the kingdom and penetrate their culture in Jerusalem. The story of the expansion of the church in the book of Acts is a living testimony of what happens when God's people clearly understand the task to which He has called them and are empowered to do what before they had been afraid to do.

He is the One who transforms us into the image of Christ.[163] He is the one who reminds us of what Jesus taught so we can have answers and insights when we need them.[164] He is the one who will guide us into all truth and will use what we do to bring glory to God.[165] He is the one who intercedes for us with groanings that are so deep we can't utter them when we are faced with dilemmas we can't handle or need words or courage when we can't find them elsewhere. [166] It is no wonder that Jesus told His disciples that they were to wait in Jerusalem until He had come upon them and <u>then</u> they could start the task of bearing witness to what had transpired in their own lives and in the lives of others.

<u>3. Spend time with unbelievers.</u> In our mobile world it is all too easy when we go through a job transfer or are forced for some other reason to move away from home to simply start attending a church and begin developing friends with only

fellow-believers. If we have lived in one place for a long time it is so easy to settle into the company of people we know and feel comfortable with without sensing any feeling of necessity to reach out and consciously make friends with people who are not believers. Not only are we as busy as people who don't know Christ because our kids are in all the same activities their kids are in but then when you add on top of that we have our "church activities" to do, it becomes very easy for us to simply say we are too busy and thus we don't make the effort to cultivate friendships with people who don't know Jesus. Add to that the issue of foul language, coarse jokes, social habits that may be offensive to us and you have a ready made excuse for not establishing any significant relationships with people who are still searching for answers to life.

But if we are going to make any impact in our communities we are going to have to give up some activities that we feel comfortable in so that we can make time for unbelievers. There are myriads of ways that we can do this: volunteer at your kids schools, look for places of need within your community and go and serve, go talk to city leaders, or school leaders and find places where you can go. Volunteer for the PTA, or some neighborhood book clubs, or coach your kids football teams, etc. But we will never make an impact if we retreat from public involvement because we don't have the time or because we don't want to be threatened by their habits into activities that are not healthy for us. Learn how to participate in events while still maintaining the firmness of your convictions.

I discovered that I never catch any fish if I never go near water. In the same way, we will never see people come to Jesus and be discipled to repeat the process if we never venture forth into territory that is uncomfortable or threatening.

4. Read biographies of people who have made an impact with their life. In my personal library I have an entire section composed of nothing but biographies. Whenever I begin to feel a little lackadaisical or lethargic in my walk with God, I pull out one of them and two things happen: 1) God reminds me of the pain and suffering that others have endured so that I can enjoy the freedoms that I tend to take for granted, and 2) I get challenged to get out of my little world into some new and fresh place where I can live by faith and see God do things that only He can do in those situations. Reading them gives me both motivation and practical ideas about ministry that I find very encouraging and helpful.

I am a person who likes to get on an airplane and hide so I don't have to try and carry on a conversation with a stranger. Walt Henrischen writes, "One day I was traveling in an old DC3 on one of the commuter airlines. I was already in my seat when a rather portly lady, probably in her 60's, came and sat down next to me. She had given the appearance of cheerfulness and friendliness as she made her way to her seat, laughing and joking with others.

When she sat down, I struck up a conversation with her by saying, "My, you are a happy, young lady."

She reached over, put her hand on my arm, and said, "Young man, you have no idea how miserable I really am. I have all the money I will ever need, but my husband is dead, I have no real friends and have no reason for living." By her outward show, there was no way I could have guessed that that woman was a prime candidate for the Gospel of Jesus Christ. Yet there she was, opening her life to me and letting me know that in her own way she was in desperate need of what the Saviour had to offer."[167]

I was deeply humbled by reading that incident and was challenged to rethink my policy of trying to hide when in the company of strangers. I would not have been challenged in that way if I was not reading a book that contained some autobiographical material. The same holds true when I ready biographies. They challenge me to do things I wouldn't normally think of doing. They spur me on to greater heights in areas where I have grown complacent. So read biographies.

5. Look for someone to apprentice. It is my experience that there are countless people within the very church or fellowship that you attend that are hungry for someone to walk alongside of them and help them grow in their lives. I appreciate the story of Dawson Trotman's life. Whenever he was invited to a public event, he always made it a point to look for people who were on the outskirts of the group. These were people who were there by invitation but did not know anyone very well or were just too shy to enter in to all that was going on. He would make it a point to walk over and introduce himself to them and then sit down and talk with them. Invariably the person could always be led into personal conversations that gave him wonderful opportunities to share the gospel or initiate contacts that could later be followed up on. I took to heart what he discovered and have found the same thing true for me as well. I have come upon people in situations like that whom, I have gotten to know and who later turned out to be some of the best discipling opportunities I have had.

Invite people over for dinner, or take them out for coffee or meet them somewhere for breakfast or lunch. Take the initiative and draw them out in the conversation and you will discover that there are numbers of people who are just waiting for someone to open the door into what could be a wonderful discipling opportunity. Make yourself available to them and you will be surprised at what happens.

Recently I talked with a man who had gone to two leaders in his church and asked them if they would disciple him. Both of them turned him down — much to his disappointment. He determined that even though he did not feel adequate to the task he would make himself available to some others who might want to be discipled. I listened eagerly as he shared with me the things that had come as a result of his stepping out and initiating a relationship that could possibly blossom into something that could produce eternal results down the road. If you don't know what to do for certain, there are all sorts of books currently on the market on mentoring that are helpful. Contact the Navigators as they have excellent materials and expertise in this area and ask them for recommendations. But don't let your lack of experience or feelings of inadequacy keep you from what I have found to be the most exciting and fulfilling part of life — making disciples.

CONCLUSION

A mature disciple has a desire to be involved in the mission that Jesus set before His followers. He didn't tell them to get involved in church programming, to serve on boards and committees, or to occupy their time with other non-essentials. He told them to make disciples, to do with others what He had done with them. "Disciples are not manufactured wholesale. They are produced one by one, because someone has taken the pains to discipline, to instruct and enlighten, to nurture and train one that is younger."[168]

As we read earlier, "We must decide where we want our ministry to count — in the momentary applause of popular recognition or in the reproduction of our lives in a few chosen people who will carry on our work after we have gone. Really, it is a question of which generation we are living for."[169]

Chapter 8

How to Develop Attitudes in People

Having now seen the six desired attitudes, the question arises, "How do you develop or change attitudes in people?" According to the Wickipedia encyclopedia, "attitudes come from judgments. Attitudes develop on the **ABC** model (affect, behavioral change and cognition). The *affective* response is a physiological response that expresses an individual's preference for an entity. The *behavioral intention* is a verbal indication of the intention of an individual. The *cognitive* response is a cognitive evaluation of the entity to form an attitude. Most attitudes in individuals are a result of *observational learning* from their environment. The link between attitude and behavior exists but depends on human behavior, some of which is irrational. For example, a person who is for blood transfusion may not donate blood. This makes sense if the person does not like the sight of blood, which explains this irrationality." Having defined attitude in terms of desire the question becomes, "How do you change desires within a person?"

I believe there are five things you can do to change people's attitudes:

<u>1. Help people see their need of the desired attitudes.</u> If someone does not understand the need of a certain kind of attitude they will never purpose to look at themselves and see their personal need for that attitude. The best way to get people to break out of undesirable attitudes or actions in their lives is for them to be brought to the place where remaining as they are is so uncomfortable that they will want to change. This can be done in a number of ways.

a) You can verbally point this out. The Bible refers to this as "admonition" and includes verbally describing both the desired attitudes and some possible ways of developing them. Paul wrote, "Speaking the truth in love we will in all things grow up …"[170]

b) You can put them into situations where they will see their lack. One of the best ways to do that is to take them with you or some other person or team into real life situations in which their lack will become obvious. I recall delivering used furniture one evening to a needy family and when I saw their condition and the abundance they already had I became inwardly critical of them and was tempted to be short with them. The person I was with, on the other hand, was very kind and gracious to them and really ministered to them in a way that I could not at the moment. God used that to point out to me my major lack of love and compassion. He wanted to work on this area and change me. I made it a very serious matter of prayer and God began to help me get rid of my tendency to be critical. He started me really taking time to listen and love.

You can send people on mission trips, schedule them to work alongside of someone whose life demonstrates the attitude they lack, and expose them to people who possess the kind of life posture you see they need. Paul wrote to Timothy, ""Now you have observed my teaching, my conduct, my aim in life, my faith, my patience, my love, my steadfastness, my persecutions, my sufferings, what befell me at Antioch, at Iconium, and at Lystra, what persecutions I endured; yet from them all the Lord rescued me."[171] He took Timothy along so he could be exposed to someone who had the right attitudes in some crucial areas.

2. Putting them with others who have the desired attitudes. I have already mentioned this but it bears its own separate heading. As just mentioned, this was what Paul did with Timothy. Paul admonished the Corinthians, ""I urge you then, be imitators of me."[172] This is the whole heart of apprenticing when it comes to skills but it also works when trying to develop attitudes in people. Work or play alongside a person and trust the Holy Spirit to point out to them the difference the right attitude makes.

3. Expose people to the Word of God. The writer of Hebrews wrote, "The word of God is living and active….it judges the thoughts and attitudes of the heart."[173] The Bible is not just black letters on a white page. It has a life of its own. It is actually alive and like a living organism that we take it into our mind, it will actually work at changing our attitudes even though we are unaware of it. Paul wrote to Timothy, "All scripture is God-breathed and is useful for teaching, rebuking, correcting and training in righteousness, so that the man of God may be thoroughly equipped for every good work."[174] Taking the Word of God into our lives through listening to it, reading it, studying it, memorizing it and meditating on it will single-handedly transform attitudes and thoughts from the inside out. Put together some specific personal Bible studies for a person in the desired areas

of change and then walk through them together and let God's Spirit use both His word and your life to help change the attitudes of another.

4. Help them learn how to "live in the Spirit." By live in the Spirit I am referring to living life in a moment-by-moment walk filled with the Holy Spirit. Since the issue of attitude is an expression of the life of Christ in us that life can only be reproduced as we allow His Spirit to live in and through our lives. He is like the sap that runs through the vine. If the sap runs properly, it brings life to the vine and the fruit that comes as a result is simply the outcome of the vine's allowing the sap to run freely and productively through it. In the same way, as we allow the Spirit access to the inner recesses of our lives and allow Him to bring life to areas otherwise hampered and controlled by our fallen nature, life begins to emerge and our attitudes are changed as a result of the flow of life. This is what Paul is referring to in Galatians 5:16-23 when he admonished the readers to "...live by the Spirit and you will not gratify the desires of the sinful nature......" Rather he says that if we allow the Spirit access, He will produce fruit, which is really changed attitudes expressing the nature of Jesus Christ. This is a hidden work that we can do nothing to effect except remain in the vine.[175] Since He is the agent of our inner transformation, we must make certain that we continue to live in the Spirit and allow Him access into inner recesses of our lives.

5. Pray for people. We are not responsible for people's character transformation. Just like the parent who stands by and watches the physical transformation of their children, helpless to cause it, so too, we can not develop any program or strategy that will automatically change a person's attitudes. All any parent can do is to make certain their children get proper diet, exercise and rest and the body, itself, will do what God designed

it to do. All we can do to change people's attitudes is to provide the right kind of environment in which the desired transformation can happen and then pray that God would use that to bring about the work that only He can do.

It is amazing that there are some things that an omnipotent God can do only as we, His people, pray. One of those things is the transformation of a person's character. Bill's (not his real name) wife had finally cajoled him into coming in together to talk with me about their disintegrating marriage. He had been raised in a home where abuse, both verbal and physical was the norm and he brought some of that into his own marriage. His wife had finally had all she could take and was ready to leave when he consented to come in with her. He was doing so on the premise that he was helping her learn how to cope with the situation they were living in. In the course of the time together, he finally admitted to me that he was abusive and that he did not like it but he did not know how to live life any differently. Together we talked about it and along with some assignments for both of them we started working through the situation. Mostly, we prayed about it individually and together. It was amazing to watch the transformation that took place in his life as he began to face himself and to honestly ask God to change him into the kind of man God had designed him to be. The transformation was nothing short of miraculous because God did what only He can ultimately do, namely to transform people into His own likeness.

God can change people's attitudes. It is true that "if any man is in Christ, he is a new creation."[176] Attitudes can be changed and growth can happen.

Section 2

Skills

Chapter 9

What are Skills?

Charles Blondin was an amazing tightrope walker. When five years old he was sent to the École de Gymnase at Lyon and, after six months training as an acrobat, made his first public appearance as "The Little Wonder". His superior skill and grace as well as the originality of the settings of his acts, made him a popular favorite. He crossed the Niagara Falls a number of times, doing something theatrically different each time. Among them were:

- doing a backwards somersault at the middle of the Falls;
- taking a chair to the middle and sitting on it, balancing the chair on two legs;
- going across it in stilts;
- walking across blindfolded while pushing a woman in a wheelbarrow;
- standing on his head in the middle of the tightrope;
- taking a small stove half-way, he sat down, cooked himself an omelet, then ate it.
- carrying his manager on his back all the way across the Falls

To do this took great skill. He had trained himself so well that he was able to perform these stunts with ease because he did not leave it to natural talent. He worked hard to develop the skills necessary to accomplish them.

Ezra was a descendant of Moses' brother Aaron. He returned to Jerusalem to rebuild the temple after being held captive in Babylon. It says of him, "He was a scribe skilled in the law of Moses which the LORD the God of Israel had given; and the king granted him all that he asked, for the hand of the LORD his God was upon him."[177] He had acquired the skill of being able to understand, interpret and teach the law of Moses and then God used him to do this work because he had developed the skills required.

When we think of skills, we will define them this way: *An ability to do some action well so you can perform it easily and accurately*. My wife's mother died when she was sixteen and it fell to her to step in as the mother figure for her three younger siblings. She had already been doing it since her mother had gone to work when she was eight and left her with the major responsibility of their upbringing. I met her when she was twenty four years old and as we started getting to know each other and then dating, I discovered that she had already developed many of the skills necessary to be a good wife and mother. This made it easier to ask her to marry me knowing that she already had the cooking skills necessary to keep me from starving.

When Paul wrote to the Corinthians he described to them his role in the founding and establishing of that new little church in Corinth. He wrote, "By the grace God has given me, I laid a foundation as an expert builder, and someone else is building on it."[178] What he was saying is that he had developed the skills necessary to plant a new church as a result of his training and experience. When

Solomon was looking for someone to oversee the building of the temple that had been entrusted to him, he sent to the nation of Tyre for a man named Huram. It says that Huram, "whose mother was a widow from the tribe of Naphtali and whose father was a man of Tyre and a craftsman in bronze. Huram was highly skilled and experienced in all kinds of bronze work. He came to King Solomon and did all the work assigned to him."[179] He succeeded in his work because he had developed the skills necessary to undertake the task.

Because of this, we see the important place of skills in a person's life. In the same way, if a person is to develop into a mature disciple of Jesus Christ, there are some skills that need to be developed. Remember our definition of a skill:

Skill is the ability to do some action well so you can perform it easily and accurately.

I will define six skills that are necessary:
1) The ability to hear and follow God's voice
2) The ability to build relationships with other people
3) The ability to build a strong Christian family unit
4) The ability to use one's God-given talents to build the body of Christ
5) The ability to articulate and defend their faith
6) The ability to help others become mature disciples of Jesus Christ

Chapter 10

The Ability to Hear and Follow God's Voice

As I listened to the pastor speak, I became confused. He said, "Yesterday as I was working out, the Lord spoke to me and said….." Then a little later in the message he said, "Last night as I was relaxing the Lord spoke to me about…." Still a little later he said, "This morning as I was driving in to church, the Lord spoke to me about….." The thing that was confusing to me was "What does he mean when he says, 'The Lord spoke to me?'" It sounds as though God spoke to him in an audible voice about something with which he was concerned. To the uninitiated it would seem to imply that this man had an ongoing verbal conversation with God in which he heard God as audibly and clearly as he would another human being.

Yet at the same time, our culture shies away any kind of explanation by a person thinking that somehow they have received a direct communication from God. For many, God is a nebulous concept or a philosophical necessity and to somehow imply that God has spoken directly to you sounds a little presumptuous. But how do we reconcile these two differing ways of thinking? It is crucial that we do so because the Christian faith is built on the premise that God is a Person. Because He is, we as human beings can have a personal relationship with Him which includes being able to communicate back and forth with Him. Since this is true, one of the skills a mature believer ought to possess is the ability to hear and follow God's voice.

What is meant by hearing God's voice?

It means that we have learned how to identify when God is speaking to us and what He is saying. When Jesus was speaking to his disciples he said, "They (my sheep) will never follow a stranger; in fact, they will run away from him because they do not recognize a stranger's voice."[180] Then he went on to say, "My sheep listen to my voice; I know them and they follow me."[181] What he was saying is that his followers have learned to recognize his voice so well that when he speaks to them they will not follow anyone else. He assumed that we would have developed the ability to hear and follow God's voice.

This is a common occurrence throughout both the Bible and the history of God's people. It is not some unique, not often reproduced happening but rather the everyday experience of God's people. He has spoken to individuals and called them to undertake various tasks, He has spoken to them and comforted them in the midst of times of difficulty, He has spoken to them when they have strayed away from Him and He has given them instructions as to what He wants them to do in various situations.

So being able to hear, identify and follow God's voice is a skill that every mature disciple of Jesus needs to develop and master.

Why this is a crucial skill to develop?

1. It is crucial to the development of a strong relationship. Anyone who has seen the movie, "The

Miracle Worker" understands the difficulty of trying to develop a relationship without being able to communicate. It is the story of Helen Keller and Annie Sullivan, her teacher and the struggle that was involved in teaching her how to communicate. Helen became both blind and deaf and her parents had no way of communicating with her. They hired Annie Sullivan, herself a person who had worked her way out of deafness to come and help them with Helen. The movie is the story of the way she began to communicate with her and the breakthrough that came which opened a door to the rest of Helen's life. If one cannot communicate with another it is virtually impossible to develop any kind of a relationship with them.

In the same way, if we do not learn how to recognize when God is speaking to us then all we have left is the memory of our collective history and the development of some theological ideas about what God is like. The Bible becomes a history book with some commands and principles about daily life but the entire thing is devoid of the relational qualities that God so greatly desires to have with His creation.

2. God intended us to understand what His desire for us is. When Paul wrote to the Ephesians, he said, "...do not be foolish, but understand what the Lord's will is."[182] He is not speaking here just about what is written in the Bible. Even though the Bible contains many commands about how we are to live and some additional principles that we can cull from it, it does not cover many of the everyday issues that we face. He doesn't tell me what occupation to pursue, who to marry, whether or not I should get a college degree, etc. These are all things in which we need to work out what His will is for us. They cannot be worked out unless we have learned how to hear His voice. Unless I do that, I will simply be left with the task of figuring out all of these things simply based on the

best of my understanding and I don't believe that is where God wants to leave us.

3. If I don't know how to hear God's voice, I can never be certain that I am accomplishing His purpose for me and my life. The Bible is clear that God has an overarching purpose for His creation. As each of us are born, the sovereignty of God says that individually and corporately we each have a specific purpose we play that enables Him to accomplish His all-over purpose. His purpose is revealed when we are able to hear Him tell us what He desires and where we fit. Otherwise, we would live daily lives of confusion, never being certain of where He wants us or whether we are doing what He desires. One cannot imagine that God would create us, then place us at a particular place geographically and historically and not tell us what that role is and how He wants us to live that out.

In 1 Samuel there is the story of young Samuel who had been brought to the priest, Eli, by his mother to be raised by Eli in the fulfillment of a vow she had made before she was pregnant with her son. God wanted to raise Samuel up to become a leader of His people. One night Samuel heard a voice calling his name. He thought it was Eli and twice he ran to him to inquire what he wanted. The second time Eli realized that it was the Lord who wanted to speak to Samuel and so he told him the next time he heard the voice to say, "Speak, Lord, for your servant is listening."[183] Samuel had not yet learned how to recognize God's voice so when the voice came again a third time he responded by saying, "Speak, for your servant is listening." God then revealed to him what was going to transpire. But Samuel would never have realized the role God wanted him to play if he had not begun to learn how to hear God's voice. In the same way we will not be able to understand the role God wants us to play and the actions He wants us undertake if we do not learn how to recognize His voice.

Much of this becomes very personal and subjective but we need to develop this ability nonetheless. I recall a time when one of the Boards I was working with was working through a very difficult decision that had to be made. We had talked about it for a long time when I finally suggested that we spend some time together being quiet and then praying about the right decision. As we prayed after a while, a simple solution popped into my head that would deal clearly and wisely with the issue and we had not even discussed this possibility in our conversations. I knew it was from the Lord. It had not been an audible voice but I sensed it was God speaking to us. When we finished the time, I shared the thought with the Board and to a man they all agreed that this was the answer God had wanted us to have and we proceeded in that direction. The situation worked out beautifully. If we had not sensed that this was God's voice, we would not have known what to do but God knew what He wanted us to do and so He shared that direction with us as we prayed together.

Vance Havner said, "If we don't know where we are going, we don't know what to do where we are… Blessed is the man who finds out which way God is moving and then gets going in the same direction."[184]

How does god speak to us?

But the question then arises, "How does God speak to us?" The answer is that He speaks in a variety of ways. We need to see this variety if we are to come to be able to hear Him speak. Some of these are subjective and some are objective and will vary from individual to individual and situation to situation. It is assumed that the person seeking this communication is in a right relationship with God and that they are living their lives out of a desire to serve and glorify Him.

1. In an audible voice. There are numerous times throughout the scriptures and history where God has spoken to men in what is described as an audible voice. The incidents are too numerous to list them all here but a few will suffice. In Genesis 3 is the story of the Fall of Adam and Eve. God spoke directly to all of the participants in that story. When Abraham took his son, Isaac up to Mount Moriah to offer him as a sacrifice to God in obedience to God's command, as he was about to plunge the knife in the boy's heart, God spoke to him and said, "Abraham! Abraham! Do not lay a hand on the boy. Do not do anything to him. Now I know that you fear God because you have not withheld from me your son, your only son."[185] When Jesus came up out of the waters of the Jordan River after being baptized by John, it says, "And a voice from heaven said, 'This is my Son whom I love; with him I am well pleased."[186] When Paul was on the road to Damascus to persecute the believers there a light from heaven flashed around him and he fell to the ground and heard a voice say to him, "Saul, Saul, why do you persecute me?"[187]

One can only conclude from reading these and many other instances that what they heard was a audible voice and that if we had been there standing alongside the people in the stories, we would have heard it as well. I have walked with the Lord for 50 years and have never heard an audible voice speaking to me that could be recorded on some kind of tape recorder or electronic device but that does not mean that God has not in times past and still does in the present speak to people in an audible voice.

2. Through angels or supernatural messengers. The word translated angel is "aggelos" (αγγελοϖ) and means "a messenger, envoy, one who is sent,

an angel, a messenger from God." So the primary meaning of the word means "messenger, one who comes with a message." So the primary ministry of angels is to communicate a message to the one to whom they are sent. They perform other ministries as well but their primary ministry is that of bringing messages from God to people. Abraham had three men appear to him on their way to Sodom and Gomorrah. (Genesis 18:1-33) As the story progresses, one of them turns out to be the Lord Himself. But they come to tell him what God is going to do to the cities of Sodom and Gomorrah. Because they came, Abraham was able to intercede for the cities — but to no avail. Daniel was burdened because of the situation they were in and for three weeks he had prayed and fasted. Finally on the twenty fourth day and angel came to him with a message and he described an invisible battle that had taken place in his coming to Daniel from the Lord.[188] He came to tell Daniel what was going to come to pass. Joshua encountered an angel prior to his invasion of Jericho and asked him, "Are you for us or for our enemies?" "Neither," he replied, "but as the commander of the army of the Lord I have now come." And Joshua bowed down before him.[189] There are many other such encounters such as Samson's parents (Judges 13), Zechariah (Luke 2), Paul (Acts 27:23), Philip (Acts 8:26), Cornelius (Acts 10:3, 7); and Peter (Acts 12:7-8). In each of these encounters God used an angel to speak to some one about something that was happening in their lives.

In his book *Angels, God's Secret Agents*, Billy Graham says that the Bible says more about angels than it does about the devil or demons. Drawing from a story originally printed in *Reader's Digest*, Graham tells about an experience Dr. S. W. Mitchell, a celebrated Philadelphia neurologist, had a good many years ago.

Dr. Mitchell had gone to bed after an exceptionally tiring day. Suddenly he was awakened by someone knocking on his door. Opening it he found a little girl, poorly dressed and deeply upset. She told him her mother was very sick and asked him if he would please come with her. It was a bitterly cold, snowy night, but though he was bone tired, Dr. Mitchell dressed and followed the little girl.

He found the mother desperately ill with pneumonia. After arranging for medical care, he complimented the sick woman on the intelligence and persistence of her little daughter. The woman looked at him strangely and then said, "My daughter died a month ago."

She added, "Her shoes and coat are in the clothes closet there." Dr. Mitchell, amazed and perplexed, went to the closet and opened the door. There hung the very coat worn by the little girl who had brought him to attend to her mother. It was warm and dry and could not possibly have been out in the wintry night."

"Could the doctor have been called in the hour of desperate need by an angel who appeared as this woman's young daughter? Was this the work of God's angel on behalf of the sick woman?" Graham asks.

3. Through what people perceive to be supernatural phenomena. Not everyone agrees that certain things people experience are supernatural in origin and yet the real issue is "How does the one to whom they appear understand them?" For example, when Paul had his supernatural experience of seeing Jesus on the road to Damascus, it says of the men around him, "The men traveling with Saul stood there speechless; they heard the sound but did not see anyone."[190] I am not certain they understood that what happened was supernatural but Saul knew that it was and that is all that matters. The three wise men who followed the star to Bethlehem believed that God was showing them something of supernatural significance whether anyone else did or not. (Matt 2:1-12) When Gideon was struggling

with his call to take on the Midianites, he crawled into their camp in the middle of the night and heard a man describing a dream he had to a friend. Gideon took this conversation as God speaking to him about the certainty of his victory and it says, "When Gideon heard the dream and its interpretation, he worshipped God."[191] When Moses was walking by a bush that was burning and not being consumed he sensed something out of the ordinary was going on and he thought, "I will go over and see this strange sight — why the bush does not burn up."[192]

Someone else standing by when these occurred may not have considered them as God speaking to them but those for whom the phenomena was intended certainly did because they had learned how to hear and follow God's voice.

4. Through dreams. Modern psychology has done much to try and interpret dreams from a psychological perspective saying that they are simply the release of your subconscious mind or like a computer doing a defragmenting operation, your mind rearranges itself to get ready for the next day. Admittedly we have many dreams and nightmares that appear to be meaningless but there are times when God has definitely spoken to people through dreams. Joseph was a man who could listen to and interpret dreams. God spoke clearly to him about the coming position he would have and about the coming famine and what he needed to do about it. (Genesis 37-41) Daniel was a man who not only had dreams but was able to interpret the dreams of others. It was through those dreams that God told him about what was to come in both the lives of individuals and in the kingdoms of the earth.

Although there are differing explanations for our dreams, I have found that they play a role in my life. One night I dreamed that a man in one of our congregations was going through a terrible time. He was crying out for someone to help him but no one would come to his aid. When I awoke, the dream was still very vivid to me and so I called him on the phone and asked if I could have an appointment with him. He consented and very shortly after that I drove over to his house. When I got there, I told him about my dream and then said, "Is there something going on in your life that you are in need of help working through?" Immediately he started to cry and after working through his tears he began to share with me what was going on. He said, "I have wanted to come and talk with you about this but I didn't know how to initiate the conversation." Needless to say, God knew his need and was able to communicate that to me through a dream. God still speaks through dreams in our modern day.

5. Through visions. Dreams and visions are very similar happenings. Dreams happen primarily while we are asleep but visions can come to us as we are going through the course of everyday living. In Isaiah 6 Isaiah had gone into the temple to pray. King Uzziah, a godly king had died and Isaiah was not certain about the future state of the nation. It was with that concern that he entered the temple and as he got there he had a vision of the holiness of God in His throne room. Isaiah had just been pronouncing "woes" upon people for various kinds of sins and when he had his vision, his response was, "Woe is me."[193] God showed him this vision to bring him to a new realization of His greatness and of Isaiah's sinfulness. Then when he had things in proper perspective, God called him to go to the nation of Israel with a message.

Ezekiel had numerous visions that started with his vision of the wheels within wheels. Daniel had visions about the coming kingdoms and what would transpire politically for the next hundreds of years. Others of the prophets also had visions of plumb lines, grapes, locusts, etc. Ananias had a vision in which God told him to reach out to Saul who was coming into his town. (Acts 9:10-16) Cornelius had a vision about Peter's coming and what he was to do about it. (Acts 10:3-6) Peter had a vision in which he saw heaven opened and a large sheet coming down with all kinds of things that were "impure" to eat. God used this to speak to him and tell him that he was not to call impure anything that God has made clean.(Acts 10:9-16) This was God's way of telling Peter that the gospel was to go to the Gentiles as well. Paul had a vision in which he saw a Macedonian man standing and begging him to come over to Macedonia and help them. (Acts 16:9-10)

Southwestern Baptist Theological Seminary's Robert A. Baker, professor emeritus of church history, tells about the vision of faith Dr. B. H. Carroll, the school's first president, had as he rode a train passing through the Texas Panhandle in the spring of 1905.

"As I looked out over those plains over which in my youth I had chased the buffalo, there arose before me a vision of our Baptist situation in the Southwest. I saw multitudes of our preachers with very limited education, with few books and with small skill in using to the best advantage even the books they had.

"I saw here in the Southwest many institutions for the professional training of the young teacher, the young lawyer, the young doctor, the young nurse and the young farmer, but not a single institution dedicated to the specific training of the young Baptist preacher. It weighed upon my soul like the earth on the shoulder of Atlas.

"It was made clear to me on that memorable day that, for the highest usefulness of our Baptist people, such an institution was an imperious necessity. I seemed to hear the age-old question of God: 'Whom shall I send and who will go for me?'

"I...was about to dismiss the matter, feeling that I could not do it—when there came to me as clearly as if audibly spoken, the assuring word of our Lord: 'I am he that liveth, and was dead, and behold, I am alive for evermore.'

"When I came to myself I was standing gripping the back of the seat in front of me. Becoming conscious that my fellow passengers were looking at me, some with amusement and some with amazement, I sat down, confused, embarrassed, and humiliated. But from that hour, I knew as definitely as I ever knew anything, that God would plant a great school here in the Southwest for the training of our young Baptist preachers."

6. <u>Through learning how to read your circumstances.</u> As the Sovereign God, He will sometimes manipulate our circumstances to indicate to us the way that He wants us to go. God had used Elijah in a mighty way through his duel with the priests of Baal in 1 Kings 18. When he finished, he was exhausted and when he found out that the Queen, Jezebel, had it in for him, he turned and left. He was feeling tired and discouraged and felt that he alone was the only faithful believer left in all of Israel. God strengthened him to make it to a cave in the wilderness and there caused some mighty violent things to occur, an earthquake, a fire and a very strong wind. When the fire had died down and it was quiet, God spoke to him and gave him instruction in what to do and Elijah was refreshed and struck out on the next phase of his life, all because he had learned how to read the circumstances in which he was and could understand what God was saying. Jeremiah tells of going down to a potter's house and as he stood watching what was going on, God spoke to him out of what he saw and told him that He could do anything He wanted to with Israel. (Jer 18:1-10)

Henry Blackaby in his book, "Experiencing God" talks about learning how to so read your circumstances that you understand what God is doing and then going along with Him in His work. He says that often we put together our plans and ask God to bless them but rather we need to learn how to see God at work in our situation and to go along with Him in that undertaking.

Many times through both Testaments, God has used natural disasters to speak to His people. Sometimes it is to change the course of their lives, sometimes it is to bring about judgment but He uses these different kinds of circumstances to speak to us about the direction He wants us to go. We need to learn how to read our circumstances to determine what God is saying to us about what He wants us to do.

Just before he issued the Emancipation Proclamation, a group of ministers urged President Lincoln to grant immediate freedom to all slaves. He wrote, "It is my earnest desire to know the will of Providence in this matter. And if I can learn what it is, I will do it. I suppose it will be granted that I am not to expect a direct revelation; I just study the plain physical facts of the case…and learn what appears to be wise and right. The subject is difficult, and good men do not agree." He had learned to read his circumstances to determine what he believed God wanted him to do.

Wilson Johnson, the founder of Holiday Inn motels, once said, "When I was forty years old I worked in a sawmill. One morning the boss told me I was fired. Depressed and discouraged, I felt like the world had caved in. When I told my wife what had happened, she asked me what I was going to do. I replied, 'I'm going to mortgage our little home and go into the building business.'

"My first venture was the construction of two small buildings. Within five years I was a multimillionaire! At the time it happened, I didn't understand why I was fired. Later, I saw that it was God's unerring and wondrous plan to get me into the way of his choosing."

7. <u>Through the Bible.</u> The Bible is the written revelation of God to us as His people. But there are two things we need to be aware of if we are going to use it correctly. First, we must be careful not to look to it alone as the only rule to live by. There are many things about which the Bible is silent. It does set down principles of living and then allows us to use those principles to make decisions but the Bible itself does not speak directly to every situation we face. If we limit our decision making to exact quotes from the Bible, we may make some foolish decisions. We have all heard of people who, when looking for direction, randomly open their Bible and point their finger for a "word from the Lord" and proceed accordingly. As Dallas Willard says, "Our reverence for and faith in the Bible must not be allowed to blind us to the need for personal divine instruction *within* the principles of the Bible yet *beyond* the details of what it explicitly says."[194]

Secondly, there are a wide variety of ways in which we can intake wisdom from the Bible. We can listen to it read, we can hear it expounded upon, we can read it ourselves, we can make it a matter of study, we can memorize it and we can spend time meditating on it. In each of these ways, God can speak to us through it. God has spoken to me through listening to the words read on cassette tapes, through diligent study and doing sermon preparation, through memorizing passages and then meditating on them while I hike or work out.

After my retirement at age 66 I accepted a call to be an interim pastor at a church that was larger than any I had ever pastored. We went there with the understanding that I would not be considered for the senior pastor position. After a year and a half, the search team could not find someone they believed was the person God wanted for them and so I talked with the chairman and we wondered together if God was wanting me to step into that position. I felt totally inadequate for the position but said I would pray about it. As I thought about it, I was meditating on God's call to Moses in Exodus 3 — 4. As I reflected on it for a number of days, I poured out my heart to God and told Him it was entirely beyond my ability to do this. I did not want to step back into that kind of responsibility and I asked Him to find someone else. But I could not get away from Moses' encounter. As I reflected on what it was saying, I felt God was saying to Moses, "Moses, it's not about you, it's about Me. If I call you to a task, I will undertake for you and although you are inadequate, I will enable you to do what I ask." As I thought about that, I sensed God was saying the same thing to me and as a result I stayed on an additional three and a half years as the senior pastor and God did exactly what He had promised and sustained me through that time in ways I had never experienced before.

In one of the churches I served, we were facing the great need to do some major renovation of the building because it had been a long time since any work had been done on it. The church was experiencing some financial difficulties and it looked impossible to do. As we met one evening, the man who was our new Trustee chairman shared with us a passage of scripture from 2 Kings about how they were instructed to bring monies into the treasury for the rebuilding of the temple. He had been reading this passage earlier in the morning and as we were having the meeting in the evening everyone at the meeting sensed this was what God was saying to us. We went on to raise the money even though the church was going through financial straits. No one had been able to raise that kind of money before. It all came from drawing on the principles of the Bible and letting it speak to us concerning our current situation.

This was how Daniel responded. In Daniel 9, he was burdened about the situation the Israelites, who were in exile, were facing and he started reading in the writings of Jeremiah. As he read he came across Jeremiah's prophecy that Israel would be in exile for seventy years. He counted the time since they had been exiled and realized that seventy years had passed. He began to pray that God would deliver them as it was written in the Bible of his day. It all came about as a result of God speaking to Daniel through the Bible.

8. Through the voices of other people. God often uses the words of other people to speak to us. This is done in a variety of ways. Oftentimes it happens when listening to a speaker as the speaker shares exactly what one or more of the listeners needs to hear. There have been countless times as a pastor after speaking, someone would come up to me and wonder how I knew what they were going through. One time I had a man come up to me and accuse me of having talked with his wife about their situation because what I had said spoke directly to an issue they were working through. I myself have been the recipient of this as well. I recall one time when I was going through a very difficult time in ministry. I had been asked in a round about way to resign from my position. I resigned with no idea where the next door would open for me. I had left a career in engineering to go to school because I had sensed God's call on my life. Now here I was with no job and nowhere to go. As we went to church one of the following weekends, the pastor spoke on Romans 8:28 and, as I sat there, I began to weep because I sensed that God was speaking directly to me about the fact that He was going to use this for my personal growth and good.

This kind of thing can also come from personally speaking to someone about an issue they are working through. Nathan was the man God chose to come to David following his sin with Bathsheba and to confront him with it through the use of a parable (2 Samuel 2). David immediately recognized the voice of God in what Nathan shared and responded accordingly. Throughout the Bible, various men were called to deliver messages to individuals and the nation with the authoritative, "Thus says the Lord!" This voice can come through what we think is casual conversation or in the midst of a group Bible study. It can come through a wide variety ways and if we are listening for God's voice we will recognize it as such and move on it.

9. Through the use of a renewed mind. God has called us to love Him with "all our minds."[195] Paul admonishes us to "renew our minds."[196] God intends us to use our minds as we serve Him. James wrote to his readers, "If any one of you lacks wisdom, he should ask God, who gives generously to all without finding fault, and it will be given to him."[197] Wisdom is not necessarily a supernaturally inspired insight, but is an insight into things that enables us to understand with our mind factors about the situation we are facing that will make us able to see what to do in this specific instance. Wisdom gives us the ability to analyze and dissect the parameters in a problem and then having done that to reconstruct it in such a way that we can see the way to proceed. Every person has this ability to greater or lesser degrees but because of the indwelling Spirit, the believer has an advantage. The Spirit will look at our situation from a different perspective and bring to mind things that have not occurred to us.

This means that God wants us to use our minds. We need to train ourselves intellectually to be able to gather information, analyze that information and then make wise decisions based upon that information. We need to be careful not to take this too far. Richard Lovelace writes, "If the direction of our lives is reduced to a function of reason alone, however, there is something wanting, something which does not harmonize well with Paul's description of Christians as those "who are led by the Spirit of God." (Rom 8:14) The Christian is then reduced to a closed and isolated rational computer, making decisions without any conscious sense of the Spirit's leading and approval, which does not agree either with the Scriptures of with common Christian experience."[198] This does not mean that we should not use our minds to their fullest extent, it just means there is more to it than a simple matter of logic. John Wesley said, "God generally guides me by presenting reasons to my mind for acting in a certain way."

10. The last way God speaks to us is through an inner, still, small voice. Dallas Willard writes, "The final means through which God addresses us is in our own spirits — our own thoughts and feelings toward ourselves as well as toward events and people around us."[199] Paul writes to the Colossians, "Let the peace of God rule in your hearts…"[200] By this is meant that there are times when we know that what we are about to do or are doing is what God desires us to do. There is a deep sense of inner peace about the rightness of it. This is called "the witness of the Spirit." It does not always give us a direction we should go but can be God's confirmation that they way we have taken is the correct way.

This needs to be confirmed by some of the other methods listed above. Direct commands in scripture are never to be disobeyed or disregarded. There have been times in my ministry when someone has come to me, convinced that what they are doing is the will of God. The only problem with it is that there are direct commands in scripture that contradict the rightness of what they are doing. When I have pointed this out, they have responded with, "Yes, but God has given me peace about it." It is simply their way of ascribing the rightness of their decision to God and telling me that I do not know what I am talking about. All I can do at that point is share with them the scripture they are violating and let the Holy Spirit take it from there.

But there is a very valid place for the presence of the still, small voice in hearing the voice of God. Dr. K. D. Moynagh testified: "I have found that the voice of God has not been heard in the thunder — not in some sensational call from heaven; nor in the earthquake — some extraordinary experience or upheaval in the circumstances of my life. It has been in a still, small voice — a voice of quiet stillness. God beckons us to come near to Him and then He speaks by the quiet, unruffled inner stillness of His peace. This is the umpire in our decisions."

How we develop this skill

There are some things we can do to acquire this skill:

1. <u>Learn how to listen.</u> Forty-three musicians with an average age of 22 were tested by Dr. Rayford Reddell of the San Francisco Hearing and Speech Center. He found that twenty percent of them had the hearing of seventy-year old men. The reason he said was that the sound levels at rock concerts and discotheques sometimes have been measured up to 130 decibels, equal to the scream of a jet fighter's engine and capable of causing irreversible damage.

We live in an age of noise. It is difficult to find many places where some kind of noise is not present. With the new iPods and other electronic means of transmitting sound we are continually plugged in and listening. So if we are ever going to hear the God who often speaks to us in a still, small voice, we need to shut off the noise and learn to listen. In our culture trying to hear God is like receiving a telephone call in a house with the stereo blaring, the television on in a room full of chatting people. It is almost impossible to hear. So we need to learn how to become people who know how to "be still and know that I am God."

There are times when my daughter, in an effort to get her children to listen, literally takes their face in her hands and makes them look into her eyes. When she has their full attention, then she speaks to them and asks them to repeat back to her what she said. When they can do that successfully, she lets them go about their business, confident they have heard what she said. Perhaps we need to let God do the same thing.

2. Gain counsel from others. Until we have some experience behind us, it is always wise, if we are in doubt about the correctness of the course of action before us, to go to someone who is a believer that we know has walked with Jesus a long time and ask their input. Ask them how they would determine the voice of God in this situation. Draw them out and gain from their experience.

3. Read your Bible on a regular basis. I have recently begun a new way of reading my Bible devotionally that has greatly personalized it for me. Each day when I am finished with reading the passage, I write down two things: 1) Those things that stood out to me that God might be saying to me about my present situation. 2) What words God might be saying to me through these insights. I actually start out this section with the words, *"Don, this morning I want to say this to you......"* I have found that it greatly personalizes it and makes me ask exactly what God might be saying. Then on Saturday morning I summarize the lesson for the entire week and come away with one final thought.

You can do topical studies to draw out principles, take notes when the pastor is speaking or when you are reading or listening to messages, read devotional material related to the Bible. I find some of my greatest help has come from memorizing entire paragraphs of scripture and then meditating on it as I memorize. There are things God says to me out of that which are priceless.

4. <u>Be obedient to what you sense God saying to you.</u> A. W. Tozer wrote, "Some Christians walk under a cloud of uncertainty, worrying about which profession they should enter, which car they should drive, which school they should attend, where they should live and other such matters, when the Lord has set them free to follow their own personal bent, guided only by their love for him and their fellow men. On the surface it appears more spiritual to seek God's leading than to just go ahead and do the obvious thing. But it is not. If God gave you a watch would you honor him more by asking him for the time of day or by consulting the watch? If God gave a sailor a compass would the sailor please God more by kneeling in a frenzy of prayer to persuade God to show him which way to go or by steering according to the compass? Except for those things that are specifically commanded or forbidden, it is God's will that we be free to exercise our own intelligent choice. The shepherd will lead the sheep but he does not wish to decide which tuft of grass the sheep shall nibble. God's choice for us may not be one but any one of a score of possible choices."

If we do not obey what God has already shown us, why should He show us anything more. It is like telling your child to mow the lawn and then when he hasn't done it, he comes to you and asks, "Dad, I need to know what will I have to do tomorrow?" Why should you tell him about tomorrow when he hasn't finished doing what you asked him to do today? On one occasion that shrewd saint, George Mueller was approached by a young man who for asked prayer that he might be able to rise in the morning for his quiet time. Mueller replied, "Young man, if you get one leg out of bed I will ask the Lord to help you get the other one out."

Conclusion

We need to develop the skill of hearing and following God's voice. We have listed the ways God speaks to us and talked about what we need to do to develop this skill. Do not just try one method as sometimes they need to be used in combination. Dr. James Dobson wrote about how he deals with decisions he has to make. He said, "I get down on my knees and say, 'Lord, I need to know what you want me to do, and I am listening. Please speak to me through my friends, books, magazines I pick up and read and through my circumstances."

That is good advice.

Chapter # 11

They Know How to Build Relationships With Others

The second skill a mature disciple of Jesus Christ needs to possess is the ability to build personal relationships with other people. We live in a world in which the population is rapidly increasing and one of the issues that is coming with that is the increasing difficulty people are having building significant, long-lasting relationships with other people. Corporations and universities are recognizing that and offering seminars and classes that help people learn how to communicate and build relationships. One of the online universities advertises this as the content of one of their courses:

Course Purpose: Group experiential methods with emphasis on sociometry and psychodrama will be employed to explore the relationships of self with others in terms of initiating, developing, maintaining, and terminating relationships. You will be familiarized with tests measuring various aspects of inter & intra personal relationships. The data will become part of your class file to be used for both instructional and research purposes. The long-range purpose is to improve the effectiveness of interpersonal relationships.

Objectives:
1. To acquaint students with the varied aspects (including gender differences and cross-cultural perspectives) of interpersonal relationship issues.
2. To familiarize students with tests used in measuring various aspects of interpersonal relationships. The data will become part of your class file for both instructional and research purposes. The long-range purpose is to improve the effectiveness of the group-cognitive therapy model for the training of group and individual therapists.
3. To examine factors that affect interpersonal behaviors and relationships.
4. To examine strategies that may aid the process of establishing, developing, maintaining, and terminating relationships.

As additional evidence of this trend, Robert Putman in his book "Bowling Alone" says the following statistics are indicators of the decline in community life in America over the past 25 years: Attending club meetings: down 58%; Family dinners: down 33%; Having friends over: down 45%

Not only is this true in our culture, it is increasingly true in the body of Christ. Over the course of my ministry, I have observed that often the church can become a haven for people who do not have good social skills. The church is one of the few places in our society where a person can find acceptance and be loved as they are. The result is that often people in the body of Christ have difficulty building friendships and developing the kind of solid relationships that will move the body on toward maturity. When Paul wrote to the Corinthians he said, "Brothers, think of what you were when you were called. Not many of you were wise by human standards; not many were influential; not many were of noble birth. But God chose the foolish things of the world to shame the wise; God chose the weak things of the world to shame the strong. He chose the lowly things of this world and the despised things — and the things that are not — to nullify the things that are, so that no one may boast before him."[201] Thus is comes as no surprise that there are times when we have difficulty in building these relationships. It is interesting that Joanne O'Brien and Martin Palmer writing in their book, "The State of Religion Atlas" state that there are 405,000 places of worship in the USA and of those 100,000 have no affiliation with any other church or group. Apparently this difficulty extends beyond the individual. Yet there are more than fifty "one another" statements in the New Testament that deal with the responsibility that we have toward one another within the body of Christ.

We desperately need to help our people learn how to build strong, solid relationships with other people if the church is to survive and be healthy well into the 21st century.

What we mean by "relationships with others"

In Genesis 2:18 we read a very interesting statement by God. He said, "It is not good for the man to be alone. I will make a helper suitable for him." God then proceeds to cause the man to fall into a deep sleep while He removed one of the man's ribs and from it He fashioned a woman and brought her to the man. At the conclusion of every other act of creation it says, "And God saw that it was good." Why was it not good for the man to be alone? The reason is that God created the man in His own image. God is a social being. In our holding the doctrine of the Trinity we say that there is One God who exists in three Persons, the Father, the

Son and the Holy Spirit. This means that God has
relationships as a part of His nature. This "tripersonality" of the divine nature is not merely
economic and temporal but rather it is immanent
and eternal. This tripersonality is not tritheism;
for while there are three persons, there is but
one essence.[202]

Prior to His creation of the man, He said, "Let
<u>us</u> make man in our image, in our likeness…."[203]
This is a statement of one Person of the Trinity
to the other two because they were in an intimate
relationship. If man is created in the image or
likeness of God then a part of that creation is
that he has been created with the capacity for
and the need of social relationships and if we
are going to help people become mature disciples,
we need to help them learn how to build strong
relationships.

When we speak about relationships, we are talking
about connecting with people or forming an alli-
ance or developing the ability to "get along." We
are talking about learning how to meet strangers
and carry on meaningful conversation, about how
to build a strong family, about how to get along
with other people at work or in whatever world you
find yourself. It is the skill that is necessary
to develop friendships or to have intimate conversation with one's spouse. It is a skill that
is necessary for building meaningful small group
involvement or creating a strong, transparent body
of believers. It is crucial to the building of a
strong team of people who are all committed to the
same goal. We have all heard about or read about
sports teams in which the players don't get along
with each other for a multiplicity of reasons.
Despite having outstanding skills when it comes to
dribbling and shooting, if they can't build some
strong relationships between themselves, the team
will never live up to its potential. Without this
skill, it makes it impossible to share personal

thoughts with one another or to hear what is being said or to identify the feelings that are being expressed. In the church the lack of this skill keeps the members on a superficial level and does not allow the body to become the "fullness of him who fills all in all."

Paul sensed this need when he wrote to Timothy. He said, "Do your best to come to me quickly, for Demas, because he loved this world, has deserted me and gone to Thessalonica."[204] Just a little later he writes "At my first defense, no one came to my support, but everyone deserted me."[205] You can hear the loneliness and feelings of abandonment that Paul was feeling and he knew that the only thing that would change that was to have a friend come and be with him in his imprisonment. This is something that we all need in our lives but without the ability to build good relationships, we walk on the empty side of life and never get to experience all that Christian fellowship was designed to accomplish.

Why developing this skill is important

There are some very important reasons why this is an important skill to develop:

1. The culture we are living in is disintegrating relationally. For the past two decades we have watched the divorce rate hover around 50%. This means that for every two marriages there is one divorce. Given that a child's sense of self-worth and self-image comes from the home in which they were raised it means that a growing number of children are being raised in homes where they are unable to watch a mom and a dad demonstrate how to communicate, how to work through issues and how to relate well together. Without role models from which to draw examples of how they are to do this, they are simply thrust into life

with very few skills for establishing and maintaining quality relationships. The consequences of this are increasingly being seen at every level within our society. Not only do the children of divorce carry emotional scars of a variety of sorts, they are unable to establish quality marriages themselves and the pattern simply repeats itself repeatedly, each time going a little deeper and becoming a little more entrenched as a way of life for our culture.

Kids grow up neither knowing how to talk to one another nor how to listen as well. We live on the side of a hill almost at the end of our street. Because it is a good place for people to walk we have all kinds of people walking by our front door. Almost every morning there is a young woman who walks with her dog up our hill and as she does she is constantly talking on her cell phone. She doesn't listen, she only talks and we can hear her as she starts at the bottom of the hill, comes to the top, comes half way down and returns to the top two or three times and all the while she is non-stop talking to someone on the other end of the line. I watch people sitting in restaurants eating together with one on a cell phone, totally ignoring their companion because someone else is occupying their time. You don't build relationship that way and yet it is a way of life for an increasing number of us. Multiply this by the people on cell phones in cars, in grocery store aisles, standing on the streets and you increasingly have a culture where people don't know how to establish quality relationships.

Add to this e-mail, FAX machines, and the countless other ways in which we talk at one another without genuinely communicating and you have a culture that is talking itself into loneliness and isolation. If all of this talk was genuine relation-building, we would be watching the divorce rate decline, a decrease in people with psychological issues and children with increasingly stronger self-worth images. But in fact, exactly the opposite is happening. In a study that was done it was determined that 90% of all failed relationships came about from a lack of honest communication and awareness.

This situation from Louis McBurney illustrates this very well. "I had a delightful, fifteen-minute telephone conversation last Tuesday. Actually I shouldn't call it a conversation. It was more ... well, I'll just tell you about it.

I called a company I do business with. A pleasant female voice said, "Hello, thank you for calling Joy, Inc. If you're on a touch-tone phone, select your choice at any time. If you're calling to check on your credit account, press 1 now. If you have questions about ordering procedures, press 2. If you would like a review of new products, press 3. If you would like to speak to a particular person and you know the extension, key that in now. If you ..."

Well, I was in luck because I knew Joe's number, so I keyed 357 knowing I would soon be chatting away with my rep.

Sure enough, after three or four rings, there was Joe's familiar voice. "Hi, this is Joe. I'm away from my desk right now. But if you'd like to leave a message, you can do so at the tone. If you prefer to wait, my secretary will assist you as soon as possible."

I wasn't particularly pressed for time, so I decided to wait. The tone beeped pleasantly, and since I didn't say anything (I guess) I heard the voice of a pleasant woman: "I'm sorry we can't get to your call immediately, but if you'll hold, your call will be serviced by the first available person. In the meantime, Joy Inc. would like for you to sit back, turn on your speaker phone, and relax to music of your choice. If you prefer classical orchestral music featuring the London philharmonic playing Dvorak, press 1. If you're in the mood for Christian vocalists, enjoy Dawn Rike's new album by pressing 2. If you'd ..."

After several minutes of soothing sounds, Joe's voice surprised me. "This is Joe. Apparently your call hasn't been processed yet. If you'd like to leave a message, you can do so now."

"Joe, this is Louis. I wanted to know about the payment date we discussed a few weeks ago. Please give me a call at home."

Before I could hang up, Joe's voice returned. You can imagine my delight.

"This is Joe. Thanks for calling ... Louis ... I value your business, and you can be assured I'll get back to you soon. It has been a pleasure to bring you Joy."

All in all, the experience could have been worse. Nobody was rude or brusque. All my desires were considered. The music was pleasant. I've done a lot worse with real people."[206]

Sound familiar? This is our culture where quality personal relationships escape us all.

<u>2. It is in relationships that we develop our sense of self-worth.</u> A family had gone to the movies and on the way in the young man of the family stopped by the refreshment stand to pick up some popcorn. By the time he got into the theater the lights were already dim. He scanned the theater and evidently couldn't find his family. The lady who tells the story says she watched him pace up and down the aisles searching the crowd in the near-darkness. As the lights began to go down even further he stopped and asked out loud, "Does anyone recognize me?"

That is the question every generation asks — but especially today. We have discovered that we learn our sense of self-worth through the significant relationships with others in our world. This begins when a child comes home from the hospital and continues all the way through life. It comes from the way our parents respond to us, take time to hold us, or listen to our stumbling attempts at talking. In these things we discover whether or not we are important enough to make time for. This enlarges as our world expands and moves from family members to playmates, teachers, relatives and anyone else we interact with in a personal way. Their responses tell us whether what we think is important or not. They let us know whether anyone recognizes us as significant people. John Trent, writes, "Not long ago, my family and I had the privilege of going on a cruise. As I sat on the deck drinking coffee, I overheard a heartbreaking conversation between a 10-year-old boy and his mother. "But why, Mom?" the boy asked, oblivious to those around him. "Why did he even bother to come?" I could see his mother struggle to frame her answer. "Well," she said, "he's here. And he paid for all of us to go on this trip." "He's not here!" her son shouted. "He's been on the phone or on his computer the whole time!" And then came the shot to the heart: *"Doesn't he want to be with me?"*[207]

What does it say to the companion when the person you are with spends their time on a cell phone when you are together? Is their any higher form of ignoring someone? Is there anything more impolite than this? And yet our culture has come to accept as normal that we have to be available 24/7 to anyone who wants to ring our number. The cell phone indicates the one we truly value. This explains the strength of street gangs. It is here that they find a sense of community, of belonging and of personal worth that goes far beyond that given to them by their families or anyone else. They demonstrate the power of group acceptance and what a driving force it can be.

3. Without this ability the church can never become the authentic body of Christ Jesus died to establish. When Paul wrote to the Ephesians he

said that the body of Christ is "the fullness of him who fills everything in every way."[208] He said ""And in him you too are being built together to become a dwelling in which God lives by his Spirit."[209] Based upon this understanding of the church, he prayed for that "…the God of our Lord Jesus Christ, the glorious Father, may give you a spirit of wisdom and revelation so that you might know him better. I pray also that the eyes of your heart may be enlightened in order that you may know the hope to which he has called you, the riches of his glorious inheritance in the saints and his incomparably great power for us who believe."[210] His writing and praying give to us one of the greatest understandings of the importance of the body of Christ ever written. The body of Christ is literally "the fullness of him who fills everything in every way." But how can the body become all that it has the potential to be if the people within that body don't know how to build quality relationships with one another? It can't! It is in the context of the body that we experience the love of Christ that "surpasses knowledge"[211] but if the individuals in that body are not free to be who God has created them to be and to move in the power that God has given them, how can magnificence ever be realized?

If, because of an inability to develop genuine, in-depth relationships with other believers, we remain strangers to one another, how can we ever become all that God has called us to be in a corporate way? If we can't build these relationships, how can we ever live out the "one another's" that the New Testament sets before us? It is my sense that one of the main reasons the church of Jesus Christ is so anemic and sterile in our generation is in large part due to the fact that we are not willing to invest the time and energy necessary to become all that God has created us to be. When Solomon wrote in Ecclesiastes 4:9-12 about the value of companions who have more together than they could ever experience individually, he was writing about the necessity of being able to build these kinds of relationships that will sustain us when everything in our world seems to fall apart.

4. <u>Without this skill, we will not see new people coming to know Christ.</u> The late Paul Little, then head of evangelism for InterVarsity Christian Fellowship said "Evangelism is the fizz of the Christian life." Evangelism brings excitement. A sense of wonder comes from being able to watch what happens in a person's life when they go from darkness to light. There is nothing that we can be involved in that is any more like heaven on earth than being in the delivery room and watching people being born from above. But we will not be privileged to see that if we don't know how to build relationships with people who are outside of Christ.

Our mobile generation is such that when we move from one location to another for whatever reason, one of the first things we look for as Christians is a church where we can begin to establish "fellowship" with others who share our worldview and values. But therein lies the danger. Getting used to a new environment, getting the children started in a new school, getting acquainted with all the new responsibilities on the job all absorb so much of our time and energy that we do not have time to get involved with non-Christians in our everyday world. We build an entirely new social structure that does not include quality relationships with those who are not believers. The rush of time and the pressures that are upon us prevent us from seeking out non-believers. It involves too much work and energy. Sometimes their vocabulary is offensive and we don't know how to respond to the off-color stories they tell. They may inadvertently ask us to violate some core convictions we hold making it a difficult thing to get involved with them and so we opt out and spend our free time with other believers or family.

Unless we are willing to learn how to build quality relationships with them through activities that we share together in common, many people will never get the opportunity to hear the good news about Jesus and they will die in their sin. All because we have erected a "holy huddle" that we find comfortable and non-threatening and are not willing to get involved with people who are hard to read and relate to. We live in a world that is far more eager to hear about Jesus than we are willing to tell because of all the above. Unless we work at learning how to relate to them on a meaningful basis we will simply not become involved in one activity that reaps benefits that reach into eternity.

For these reasons it is vitally important that God's people develop the skills that enable them to relate to one another and to the world in which we all live.

How we develop these skills in people

Before elaborating on methodology we need to first be reminded that there are many different levels of interpersonal relationships. These relationships vary in their degree of self-disclosure, feedback, and purpose. They vary in the extent to which culture and language are involved. They vary in the degree in which we feel free to ask questions or challenge one another. They can vary in the degree to which both intimacy and sharing occur. So we acknowledge that not all relationships can have the same kind of intimacy, support and sharing.

People who study the dynamics of relationships have identified six stages through which many relationships pass. They start with 1) Contact or initial impressions, body language that one sees when you meet someone for the first time. 2) Involvement comes when we begin asking questions about family, friends, etc. and start getting to know the person. 3) Intimacy comes when the relationship deepens and forms some type, formal or informal of commitment to one another. 4) Deterioration can begin to happen when people decide they don't want to invest the time or energy necessary to sustain the relationship. 5) Repair can occur when both parties are willing to analyze what went wrong with the relationship and are willing to do something to restore it. 6) Dissolution occurs if the two or more people that are involved decide that they are unwilling to work at making the relationship go and turn around and walk away.

So we must understand where we are in relationships before proceeding but the writer is assuming that a mature disciple is desirous of working at building healthy, long-lasting relationships with a variety of people and therefore wants to grow in this skill.

1. We begin by realizing that this skill is only learned in context with other people. You cannot develop this skill by reading a book, or spending time alone in prayer and Bible reading or by memorizing scripture and then taking time to meditate on it. Relationships are only built in concert with other people. This means there must be an investing of time with other people doing whatever is necessary to deepen your relationship with them.

Obviously this begins in the home. It is here that a child develops their sense of self-worth. It is here that they learn how to talk and how to listen. It is here that they learn how to communicate personal, inner thoughts and gain the skill to put them into words. It is here they find the feelings of acceptance necessary to give them the freedom they need to say what they think and feel. If they are not given the time necessary to learn how to express themselves well and to be made to feel important enough to have their ideas accepted as valuable, they will have a difficult time learning how to communicate on a level necessary for building deep relationships.

One of the things I encountered in doing pastoral counseling was the wife or husband who would say to me, "Oh, I could never share this with my husband/wife." My response was always, "Why not?" If the relationship was so fragile that they cannot express their personal thoughts or feelings to one another, then work needs to be done to bring the relationship to that level. What I would usually do was to set up an environment where both were present and then press the issue with them until we could develop the kind of open receptivity that was required to deal with what they were going through. The other person was almost always surprised that their partner did not feel they could share those thoughts with them but for whatever reason this was the impression that had been communicated. If we are going to help couples build stronger relationships it must always be done with both people present. If anyone cannot share internal thoughts and emotions, then the relationship will never go very deep.

One of the ways to help this develop is through strong mentoring relationships where the mentor is open and free to share personal things. If a person can see and experience this kind of sharing in this relationship then they can transfer that freedom to other relationships as well. I have always had a heart to get to know and work with men in a mentoring/discipling relationship. One of the things I have done through my ministry is to simply invite men out to lunch to get to know them and see them in a non-church context. This included asking them about their families, their work situations, their hobbies, etc. It did two things: It deepened my relationship with these individual men and kept me in touch with the workaday world so that my messages and ministry would deal with real issues and not just theoretical things. Naturally, this has brought me a great deal of personal satisfaction as well but its effect on men has been beneficial. I remember one man who I invited to just such a lunch. We met and spent about an hour and a half together just talking. Just as we were about to break up he asked, "Okay, what do want me to do?" It caught me off guard for a moment and I said, "What do you mean?" He replied, "No one ever took me out to lunch without wanting something from me and I just wanted to know what you wanted." When I explained to him my reason for wanting to take him to lunch, just to get to know him so I could better understand his situations and thus to pray for him, he was taken aback. But our culture leaves little time for this kind of relationship building.

We may be able to do some workshops to help people develop this skill but the workshop has to contain a few concrete suggestions and then leave a lot of time for the people at the workshop to work out either one on one or in a small group the suggestions we have made. Relationships can only develop in the context of other people, not in how many notebooks full of information I may have.

2. Build a church atmosphere of transparency and openness. So much of modern church life is built around programs designed with good intentions. But it is the very multiplying of programs and their accompanying activities that keep us from developing the very skills we are trying to grow in our people. The church was never intended to be dominated by "programs." All one has to do is to read the early chapters of Acts to discover that the early church did not have "programs" in the sense we know them today. We read in Acts 2:42-47, "They devoted themselves to the apostles' teaching and to the fellowship, to the breaking of

bread and to prayer. Everyone was filled with awe, and many wonders and miraculous signs were done by the apostles. All the believers were together and had everything in common. Selling their possessions and goods, they gave to anyone as he had need. Every day they continued to meet together in the temple courts. They broke bread in their homes and ate together with glad and sincere hearts, praising God and enjoying the favor of all the people. And the Lord added to their number daily those who were being saved." The only thing here that could even remotely be considered programmatic may be "the apostle's teaching" but even that does not have to be the lecture hall format that we have developed. It all contains the hint of informal groupings of people who come together to share their common life in Christ and to love and support one another. It speaks about the kind of openness and caring that would naturally build deep social relationships.

Norman Grubb writes, "We can liken a man to a house. It has a roof and it has walls. So also man in his fallen state has a roof on top of his sins between him and God; and he also has walls up, between him and his neighbor. But at salvation, when broken at the Cross, not only does the roof come off through faith in Christ, but the walls fall down flat and the man's true condition as a sinner saved by grace is confessed before all men.

"But the trouble soon begins after conversion, and here lies the hindrance to continued revival. Continued revival is continued brokenness, but brokenness is two-way, and that means walls kept down as well as roof off. But man's most deep rooted and subtle sin is the subtle sin of pride: self-esteem and self-respect. Though hardly realizing it, while we are careful to keep the roof off between ourselves and God through repentance and faith, we soon let these walls of respectability creep up again between ourselves and our brethren. We don't mind our brethren knowing about success in our Christian living….But where we fail in those many, many areas of our daily lives — that is a different question."[212]

But this kind of honesty and openness takes time and for most of us, a serious rearranging of our priorities. It means making the time to spend with others, even in addition to our families, in an atmosphere where we can be open and honest and have the time to listen and deal with life issues with one another. Yet it is this very thing that makes our Christian fellowship so appealing to non-believers because they can't find this kind of open honesty and integrity anywhere else in our culture. The unbelieving Greek writer Lucian (A. D. 120-200) wrote after he had seen the warm fellowship of some Christians, "It is incredible to see the fervor with which the people of that religion help each other in their wants. They spare nothing. Their first legislator (Jesus) has put into their heads that they are brethren."

It is in this kind of warm, loving fellowship that self-centered, socially awkward people learn how deeply God loves them as well as how to develop strong, deep personal relationships with others. It is as Roy Hession wrote, "The only basis for real fellowship with God and man is to live out in the open with both."

3. We need to learn how to ask questions of other people. I was raised as a person who was scared to be around people for fear they would discover what I was really like on the inside. One day someone recommended a book to me that started turning my life around. It is the book by Dale Carnegie, "How to Win Friends and Influence People." Although written from the perspective of getting ahead in business it contains some wonderful information about influencing people. One of the main things I gleaned from the book was if you want to become

attractive to people, learn how to ask them questions about themselves and their life. I took that to heart and have found over the years that developing this skill is one of the best things I have ever done to develop social skills. People deeply appreciate someone who is genuinely interested in them enough to ask questions about them and their personal life. Sometimes you are able to help them work through things; sometimes you will just gain information. Other times you open topics of conversation they have wanted to talk with someone about but have not known how to initiate the conversation. I have learned that people love the sound of their own voice and, for people who have never learned how to express themselves, this alone can be a tool to unlock their inner being and give them an opportunity to talk about things they have kept secret for years.

There are two things I would suggest in this area: 1) Purchase the book, "The Complete Book of Questions" by Gary Poole.[213] This book contains 1001 various questions that you can ask in a wide variety of situations. You will not use all the questions but they will prime your pump and get you started. Write some down on a 3 x 5 card and take it with you. Review it before meeting with someone to find one that you think fits and then as soon as can find an appropriate opening, ask the question. 2) Become a reader. As you put new and interesting information into your brain, you will find many opportunities to use it in your relationships with people.

4. Learn how to listen. Some of us have probably had the experience of President Franklin D. Roosevelt. He got tired of smiling that big smile and decided to find out whether anybody was paying attention to what he was saying. As each person came up to him with extended hand, he flashed that big smile and said, "I murdered my grandmother this morning." People would automatically respond with

comments such as "How lovely!" or "Just continue with your great work!" Nobody listened to what he was saying, except one foreign diplomat. When the president said, "I murdered my grandmother this morning," the diplomat responded softly, "I'm sure she had it coming to her."

Listening involves the ability to tune out distracting sounds and personal thoughts and learning how to focus on what the person speaking to you is saying. It involves hearing the words, reading the body language and listening for the emotions that are being expressed. This takes a great amount of time and energy. I will never forget a man who has since become a deep personal friend. I was standing in the foyer of a church at the conclusion of a church service and started speaking to him. When he looked at me, I almost backed away. I had never had anyone stare as intently and listen as deeply to what I was saying as he did at that moment. It was as if there was no one else in the building and that I was the most important person in his world. I have never recovered from that experience. It made such an impression that I vowed then and there to learn how to do what he had done and that dramatically changed the way I relate to people.

This involves what Peter Drucker said, "The most important thing in communication is to hear what isn't being said."[214] There are many excellent books available on learning how to listen and an in-depth explanation is outside the scope of this book. This is an art that will enable us to deepen our relation-building skills. As Stuart Briscoe said, "I'm prepared to be interested in what other people find interesting."[215]

Conclusion

If we do not help people learn how to build strong personal relationship skills then we are dooming them to lives of loneliness and isolation, we are short changing Christ's work in building up His body and we are being disobedient in "teaching them to obey everything I have commanded you." God has created us in His image and ultimately is the One who enables us to accomplish this in our own lives and in the lives of others. All one has to do is to listen to the heart cry of the psalmists as they pour out from the depths of their beings their feelings and emotions and you will discover the absolute need to develop the social skills of communication and expressing emotions. We must help people develop these in our daily relation-ships and then we will be better able to relate to a lost and dying world that is looking desperately for people who care.

Chapter 12

Skill # 3: Building a Christian Home Unit

As I begin to write about this skill, I do so with the realization that we are dealing with family units, broken marriages, blended families and singles. Thus I do not want to limit the discussion to simply nuclear families because that would be to miss a large percentage of our Christian population. I want to focus on what I call a "Christian Home Unit" (CHU). It can include a regular family, a broken family, a newly blended family or a strong unit of singles, bonded together for many of the same benefits that a solid nuclear family can provide. Please read this chapter accordingly and make the necessary adaptations to its message.

A young serviceman and his family were living in a hotel near the military base where he was temporarily assigned. One day his little girl was playing house in the lobby when a lady asked solicitously,

"Isn't it too bad you don't have a home?"

"Oh, we do," the child answered. "We just don't have a house to put it in!"

When I write about the Christian home unit, this is what I am writing about, Christians together in family groupings for love, support, encouragement and mutual growth.

A DESCRIPTION OF A CHRISTIAN HOME UNIT

1. People living together under the Lordship of Christ. The thing that makes a CHU unique is that the unit is not built around common heritage or family roots, economics, or purpose. It is built on the assumption that each member of the unit operates their life under the authority of Jesus Christ. I realize that young children may not have reached that point yet but am assuming that one of the major foci of the parents or guardians is to help them come to that decision as early in their lives as they are able to make it. Through Amos God asked Israel a pointed question in relating to them how He had chosen them out of all the families on the earth. He asked, "Do two people walk hand in hand if they aren't going to the same place?"[216] What He was saying to them is that there is more than just walking together to keep two people on the same path. It is a commitment to the same goal or purpose that enables them to walk together hand in hand.

The thing that keeps a CHU together is the fact that they all function together under the headship that Jesus brings to each individual. In mathematics a basic theorem is "Things equal to the same thing are equal to each other." What that means is that if two plus two equals four and three plus one equals four then two plus two equals three plus one. In the same way, if two or more people are living their lives under the headship of Jesus Christ then they will all be living under the same biblical principles. Their obedience will be together on the major issues of their daily living. This is especially true in two areas:

a. The respective roles each member plays in the unit keeps a CHU together. We live in a day quite different from that of our forefathers. Nearly 53 percent of American women are in the work force in the 1990s, compared with 44 percent 10 years before. Working couples number more than 25.6 million as opposed to 22.3 million a decade earlier. Increasingly, as women gain stature in the workaday world, the dual careers entail high-level positions on the part of both marriage partners. What this means is that the roles each person assumes in the unit have changed in the past few decades. Some people are still living in the kind of home where the husband works, the wife stays home taking care of the children — but many are not. The scriptures are silent about which model, or any other, is right or wrong. It is up to each unit to decide how they want to divide up the responsibilities in the home and roles they are to play. But the scriptures have some strong guidelines about these roles. When Paul wrote to the Ephesians in Ephesians 5:21-6:4 he described in outline fashion the importance of working out what our roles are to be (husband, wife, parent, child, friend). These have to be carefully talked through based upon how each sees their heart, abilities, calling, etc. Having worked with many couples through the years we have had to work out many different kind of working relationships. Few of them came out the same but they each work when all of the people are living under the Lordship of Jesus Christ.

b. How to live under authority. Years ago I heard a psychologist speak about the importance of learning how to rightly relate to authority. He said that if a person does not learn to rightly align themselves under the authorities in their world, they will end up being miserable. I have discovered that he is right. Everyone of us lives constantly under various authorities wherever we are. Even when we think we are in a place where we can be independent from authority we are wrong. Driving alone in your car, walking on a National Forest pathway, sitting alone on a park bench, we are still are under some kind of authority, put in place for the benefit of everyone. I had a mathematics teacher in college who had worked in industry prior to becoming a college professor. He said the time he enjoyed most when he was working in industry was when he was riding the train to and from work. When he was at work, his boss told him what to do, when he was at home he said his wife told him what to do but on the train he was his own boss. He was wrong — he still had to live under the authority of the transportation industry. There is no such a thing as being totally independent.

Where do we learn how to live properly under authority? We do it in our CHU. This is why Paul begins the section in Ephesians 5 with the words, "Submit to one another out of reverence for Christ."[217] This means that one of the most important things a child can be taught in the CHU to prepare them for life on their own is how to relate themselves properly to the authorities in their world. Part of the reason why Paul instructs wives to "submit to their husbands" is that it gives the children a visible example on a very personal level of how a person living under Christ's Lordship responds to authority. If what the child observes and hears is rebellion he will quickly learn that authority is to be defied, disobeyed and disregarded. It will then be left for other authorities later in his

life to teach him how to correctly relate to God-
given authority.

2. The CHU is a place where we look after each
other's interests. One of the things that Paul was
concerned with when he wrote to the Philippians,
was a difficulty some of their people were having
being able to get along together. This is a common
issue wherever two or more people live together
in close proximity. The solution, he says, is to
"Do nothing out of selfish ambition or vain con-
ceit, but in humility consider others better than
yourselves. Each of you should look not only to
your own interests, but also to the interests of
others."[218] Conflict comes where each person in the
relationship is only concerned about what they
want in the particular circumstance. We have all
stood by and watched two people disagree over some
issue that from our perspective looks quite simple
to handle. "Why can't they see how to solve this?"
we wonder. The reason is each one is only interested in the outcome ending in their "favor." Paul
says the solution is for both parties to begin, in
humility, to consider the other better than themselves. This is not to say they are better. We know
from his other writings that "in Christ" he considered all people equal.[219] But for the sake of the
relationship, there are times when we need to take
time to think about the other person before we
begin to think about ourselves. We have a responsibility to look not only at our interests and
concerns but those of the others in the family as
well.

This turns potential squabbles and hurts into
opportunities to think about someone else other
than ourselves and to acquiesce to the things that
are important to them. To do that Paul says we need
to adapt the same attitude that Jesus had when
he didn't think about his superior position but
humbled himself and became a servant to those who
would eventually crucify Him. This is not some-

thing one does naturally. Unless a person lives under the Lordship of Christ and learns what it means to "take up your cross and die daily" this is not something that you will do. Thus the kind of counsel that Paul wrote about when he addressed this kind of situation will not work unless the people living together in close proximity live under Jesus' Lordship. This is what is referred to as "the crucified life."

3. The CHU is a place where biblical values are lived out. A Christian Home Unit lives on an entirely different set of values than do the people next door. When Paul wrote to the Romans, he said, "Do not be conformed any longer to the pattern (lifestyle) of this world, but be transformed by the renewing of your mind…."[220] These values come because as we grow in our walk with God, part of that growth comes from changing the way we understand life and reality. This comes because as we take in the word of God, it begins to change the way we think about things. We begin to see things from more of an eternal perspective rather than a temporal one. God says "My thoughts are not your thoughts, neither are your ways my ways. As the heavens are higher than the earth, so are my ways higher than your ways and my thoughts than your thoughts."[221] We don't naturally think the way God does but as we continually expose ourselves to the Bible, our thoughts begin to change. As a result we begin to transform our minds and part of that process results in adopting a different set of values by which we live.

This affects a great many things. It changes the way we handle our finances. It changes the way we invest our time. It changes the way we look at the worth of a human being as we see that people are more important than "things." It changes our attitudes toward people of different color and ethnicity as well as people from different educational and economic backgrounds. Things that once used to be barriers and issues are slowly being erased because God is changing the way we think. He is "renewing our mind." Because we see people as being made in His image, it changes the way we treat others personally, socially, sexually, and in every other way. We go from being people who carry grudges to people who have become forgiving. We can be patient with others where we couldn't before. And why? Because we are living under the Lordship of Christ.

Thus one of the things that requires much work and communication is in the whole area of what it is that we consider valuable and important. Do we need to own our home? What kind of a car do we drive? How much involvement do we need to have with our church? With our community? How do we want to use our time? How much time does each family member need? The list goes on. But a CHU is a place where these biblical values are lived out.

4. A place where people are free to discover and develop who they have been created to be without the fear of rejection or ridicule. Everyone needs a place where they are given the freedom to grow and develop into the person God created them to be. Venturing out on this path of discovery is a fearful thing because we aren't even certain when we venture forth where the road will take us. One of the things that gives us the courage to step out on such a journey is a family unit that will encourage us as we do. This means we know they will not ridicule us or belittle us when we take our first steps. The Movie "Field of Dreams" is a movie about baseball, pursuing a dream, and choosing life's priorities. Half way through the film, Ray Kinsella (played by Kevin Costner) travels back in time to meet with Doc Graham (played by Burt Lancaster) in the hopes of getting a chance to see his dad again. He would never have had the freedom to do that if his wife had not encouraged him to follow his dream despite the criticism that came from her brother and others.

We all need a family unit like that. For many in our society, they never find a place like that. This is why children get in with the wrong crowds, why people can be coerced into experimenting with substances, practicing lifestyles that they know at the outset are potentially harmful to them. Our young people look to leaders who seem so much more accepting and willing to let them experiment with dangerous things so that the pressure from other friends or family is not enough to refrain them from self-destructive behavior. If only they had a loving home where they could be encouraged to discover and develop themselves without fear, it would keep many young people and adults from ending up ruining their lives.

This doesn't just apply to children. I have known both wives and husbands who have felt very stifled in their marriage simply because the other person was unwilling to allow them the freedom to grow and develop. They are afraid they will find someone else or something else that will become more important and thus they try to squelch their development and growth. If all parties involved are living under the Lordship of Christ, what fear is there? Does God know how He created each of you? Can we trust Him to use the growth and change to build us into an even stronger family unit? This is the crux of the issue. But a CHU must be a place where the people involved are given the freedom to continue to grow and become all God has made them in Christ.

WHY THIS IS AN IMPORTANT SKILL TO DEVELOP IN PEOPLE

1. The Christian Home Unit is one of the two most important basic social units in God's economy. The second is the church but we will look at

that in the next chapter. I have a two year-old grandson who loves to dump out a large container of building blocks and then I can begin to build things with him. I get the privilege of sitting with him on the floor and working along with him in the process. One of the things he is learning is the importance of a solid base if we are going to build anything of height. Unless we lay a strong foundation the building or bridge or skyscraper we build will eventually crumble and fall. (He enjoys that almost as much). But he is learning a lesson that will stand him good for a lifetime. The lesson: It is important to have a solid foundation if you want to build anything of worth and it is worth taking the time to lay the right kind of foundation.

The same thing can be said for a society. A society is only as strong as the foundation on which it is built. A family unit built on the principles of God's word is the only kind of foundation that will give us a strong society and nation. Unless we work to build these strong families the consequences will be far-reaching and eventually destructive. Currently we are watching our culture fall apart because we are moving away from the biblical values that gave us our freedoms and our resultant greatness. We are watching children and adults from broken homes who do not have any idea how to build quality families struggle with the same issues they inherited from their families. Unless we make it a priority to build strong CHU's our society will only continue to spiral downward.

When God created His original couple, part of the explanation He gave was, "For this reason a man will leave his father and mother and be united to his wife, and they will become one flesh."[222] This was before there were such things as mothers and fathers and He was referring to the strong bond that was to become the foundation block of civilization. It is the Judeo-Christian faith that gives the blueprint for what God intended for families and if that family unit is strong, then the resulting civilization will be strong as well. Let the CHU begin to crumble and the rest of the culture will disintegrate very shortly thereafter.

2. It is the place where future generations are taught and trained. There is an interesting statement in Judges chapter 2. Joshua had succeeded Moses and had brought the people into the land God had promised. Joshua had followed God's revelation as he had been commanded in Joshua 1:5-9. Now his work was finished, the land was theirs and they were free to settle down in their new land to begin to take advantage of the abundance they had received. The story reads, "The people served the Lord throughout the lifetime of Joshua and of the elders who outlived him and who had seen all the great things the Lord had done for Israel."[223] They had taught their children the things God had told them to and the result was that they had seen God do great things and their civilization was established on a solid foundation. But then we read, "After that whole generation (Joshua and the elders of his day) had been gathered to their fathers, another generation grew up, who knew neither the Lord nor what he had done for Israel."[224] The next generation did not properly teach and train their children and the result was cultural chaos as recorded in the book of Judges. If the CHU's are strong and doing their job, the next generation will be strong. If they fail to do what they have been instructed to do, the following generation will be rebellious, self-centered and self-destructive.

The family is the place where values, morals, ethics and a proper worldview are taught and internalized. If this does not happen, then the next generation is left on its own to use whatever makes sense to them to form the foundation for their culture. As history demonstrates so clearly, a civilization that is built upon human thought and principles will eventually crumble because it will ultimately be tipped in the direction of self-interest and pure subjectivism. For this reason, it is crucial that we raise up CHU's that are established upon the right foundation and if mature Christians do not know how to do that, the culture in which they live will disassemble itself in very short order.

3. It is in this context that good character gets developed. In his book, "Seven Habits of Highly Effective People," Steven Covey writes about the fact that we as a nation have shifted from being a nation that elects its leaders based upon character to one that selects its leaders based upon image. We have downplayed personal character and have spent millions of dollars on discovering the image that is desirable for a person to become electable and a leader. This means that in the last 100 years we have moved away from quality character as an important element in a person's reputation and now are more concerned about our "image" and way we are perceived. This can be seen in all the "poll analyses" that goes on. Before candidates or leaders make statements or take positions, they first consult the latest polls to see what the people consider important. Once they have ascertained that, then they make their statements. People of character who stand for what is good and right regardless of what the people think or believe are seldom seen. But this kind of character is developed in the context of a strong CHU.

Both Paul and Peter write about the importance of quality character in a believer's life. (Rom 5:3-4; 2 Peter 1:5) Character comes only out of difficulty and personal effort. We are commanded to "add to your faith virtue.."[225] The CHU provides the crucible in which these character qualities are initially developed. Such things as honesty, integrity, respect for people, hard work, diligence, truthfulness, courage, high personal ethics, are learned in the everyday give and take of a strong CHU before they are taken out into the surrounding world to become the modus operandi for their everyday interaction with their surroundings. For this reason it is crucial that we provide our next generation with strong, biblical CHU's so that ensuing generations can experience the same freedoms and privileges that we have come to enjoy.

4. The CHU is a place of refuge and support. God established a six-day work week because He had designed humans to need at least one day in seven in which to be refreshed and renewed for the next six days. We were designed this way. In the same way, God designed us to have places of refuge to which we could flee when the battles of life became so difficult that we are in danger of exhaustion and despair. It is a safe harbor to which we can flee from the storms of life. Without this harbor, we will be in grave danger of shipwreck.

The CHU is a place where I can come to share the burdens with which I struggle. It is a place where I can be accepted and loved and prayed for. No other place on earth will support me like the CHU. It is in such a place that wounds can be healed, that emotions can be worked through, that attitudes can be reaffirmed and renewed, and that personal worth and value can be reestablished. It is in this place of refuge that a person's inner life can be reinvigorated. Here our courage is restored to go back out into the workaday world to make a difference in our culture.

5. The CHU is one of the most effective tools for evangelism God has designed. When Paul spells out the relationship between husband and wife he uses the relationship between Christ and His church as the example.[226] Husbands are to love their wives as

Christ loves the church and wives are to respond to their husbands as the church responds to Christ. This means that husbands and wives can demonstrate a living parable of Christ's love to undeserving humanity through allowing them to watch the inter-relatedness of their home life. It can be done as we invite unbelieving people into our homes for meals, for neighborhood events, as we live out our relationship in the back yard and in the local PTA. People who would never darken the door of a church can observe and understand what a self-sacrificing love God has shown them by watching that kind of love on the part of a husband toward his wife. People can be made to understand how submission can be a sign of strength and independence as they watch a wife who does not sacrifice her identity live in willing submission to someone who loves her enough to lay down his life for her. They can see and discover that there is no fear of manipu-lation or domination in true submission. As they observe these things, they will better understand God's unconditional love for them and realize that there is no fear in submission to someone who loves them to that extent.

As the family unit continues to unravel in our culture, couples are looking for ways to make their marriages work and when they see how God designed it to work in a genuine Christian family they will be more open to the gospel as the source of their hope for making their marriage work. As unbelieving parents, whether single or married, watch the way genuine love exists in a family unit and what that does to the children within their family, they will become desirous of learning what you are doing that makes it work — and they will be open to the gospel in ways they would not have been otherwise. Edgar Guest wrote,

You got it from your father, "Twas the best he had
to give
   And right gladly he bestowed it. It's yours,
   the while you live
You may lose the watch he gave you — and another
you may claim
   But remember, when you're tempted, to be careful
   of his name.
It was fair the day you got it, and a worthy name
to bear
   When he took it from his father, there was no
   dishonor there;
Through the years he proudly wore it, to his father
he was true,
   And that name was clean and spotless when he
   passed it on to you.
Oh, there's much that he has given that he values
not at all
   He has watched you break your playthings in the
   days when you were small
You have lost the knife he gave you and you've
scattered many a game
   But you'll hurt your father if you're careless
   with his name
Its yours to wear forever, yours to wear the while
you live
   Yours, perhaps, some distant morning, to another
   boy to give
And you'll smile as did your father — with a smile
that all can share
   If a clean name and a good name you are giving
   him to wear.[227]

All of this makes building strong CHU's mandatory in our generation. Without them, there is no
hope for our future as a culture and ultimately as
a world.

HOW TO DEVELOP A STRONG HOME UNIT:

1. Build it on strong biblical teaching. Just prior to his death, Moses reviewed with the people of Israel the things God had taught them and what they were to do with it. He wrote, "Hear, O Israel: The Lord our God, the Lord is one. Love the Lord your God with all your heart and with all your soul and with all your strength. These commandments that I give you today are to be upon your hearts. Impress them on your children. Talk about them when you sit at home and when you walk along the road, when you lie down and when you get up. Tie them as symbols on your hands and bind them on your foreheads. Write them on the doorframes of your houses and on your gates."[228] He intended that these people should take the responsibility for teaching their children what they had been given and what they had learned as they had come from Egypt to the Jordan River. He did not say the responsibility for teaching belonged to the priests or the rabbi, the Sunday School teacher or youth pastor but on the parents. He said that this teaching begins by having these things "upon your hearts." They are to be central in the way you think, in the decisions that you make and in the lifestyle that you live. Your children are to be able to see and discern the things that are important to you and what it is that makes you the person you are.

We need to teach self-discipline, honesty, integrity, intellectual content and lifestyle choices as well as all the other positive character qualities that are important to God. Peggy Noonan writes, "In America, our children are born swimming in polluted waters." These are the values and lifestyles in which our children are raised. If they are not taught otherwise in our homes and churches, we will raise another generation who does not know the Lord and what He has done for our country. When Solomon wrote Proverbs he

said, "Listen, my son, to your father's instruction and do not forsake your mother's teaching.
They will be a garland to grace your head and a
chain to adorn your neck."[229] He was writing about
the importance of sound, biblical teaching in the
home and family unit.

The Bible is silent about the correct methodology other than to say that we should be ready to
do it "when you sit at home and when you walk along
the road, when you lie down and when you get up."[230]
This is something that needs to be done continually. There are many wonderful resources available
to us today that will help us do this, both in the
home and in the church.

2. Do everything to be certain that Christ is
the Lord of every CHU member. Although we cannot
guarantee that every member of our unit has been
called by God into His family, we can do everything we need to do to make certain they both
understand the gospel and know what it means to
live with Jesus Christ as the Lord of their lives.
Doing this involves both making the commitment
and then living it out. It is a daily choice in
which we "die daily" as Paul says.[231] Jesus said
that if anyone would follow him they must "take up
his cross daily and follow me."[232] Lordship is an
issue that involves daily decisions to say "No" to
living for ourselves and "Yes" to being obedient
to what He has called us to be. Having Christ as
Lord involves loving God with all one's heart and
soul and mind and strength all the time.

If there is only one adult in the CHU who follows Christ as Lord it can be more difficult to live
that out but it is still possible to demonstrate
His Lordship even in the adversities of life. We
do not live in a perfect world but regardless of
the kind of world we live in we can still allow
Christ to be seen as Lord in that world. As one
reads of the persecution other believers experience in other parts of the world because they hold

true to their faith you come to realize that following Christ as Lord is not conditioned upon the environment in which we live but upon the decision we have made in our heart. We can discover the sufficiency of His grace even in the most dire of circumstances and so it is possible to live out the Lordship of Christ even in the context of a mixed marriage or home unit. But we need to do all that is humanly possible to graciously live out our faith and pray and work that others in that environment may come to do the same.

3. We must model expected behavior, not hypocrisy. Over the course of my ministry the most common hindrance to people being interested in coming to know God is the inconsistent behavior of people who already claim to know Him. Regardless of whether or not people are believers, they always have a certain standard of behavior they expect Christians to have. When that expectation is not met, it becomes an easy focus to keep them from seriously considering the claims of Christ. Children are especially susceptible to this issue. When they hear parents or other significant adults talk with them about certain kinds of behavioral issues and then see them violate their own expectations, they begin to chalk it up to their insincerity and hypocrisy. This gives them an easy out later when facing their own decision about following Christ's Lordship. Ellen Goodman, writing in the Boston Globe wrote, "Americans once expected parents to raise their children in accordance with the dominant cultural messages. Today they are expected to raise their children in opposition to them. Once the chorus of cultural values was full of ministers, teachers, neighbors and leaders. They demanded more conformity, but offered more support. Now the messengers are violent cartoon characters, rappers and celebrities selling sneakers. Parents are considered "responsible" only if they are successful in their resistance. That's what

makes child-raising harder. It's not just that American families have less time with their kids; it's that we have to spend more of this time doing battle with our own culture."

We can not do this kind of battle if we live inconsistently with what we are trying to teach. We must make certain that the values we are trying to teach, the morals we are trying to instill and the behavior we are trying to develop are modeled in the home. If the children can see it modeled and can see the value of that behavior in providing a more mature and successful approach to life they will be all the more apt to want to follow in the footsteps of their parents.

4. We must live by principle and priority. Our Christian faith is not simply a matter of theological content, it is a matter of principles and priorities by which we live. By principles I mean such things as "Seek first the kingdom of God," and "Be anxious for nothing." I mean the principles of "Speak the truth in love," "Forgive those who harm you," or "He who has been stealing must steal no longer, but must work, doing something with his own hands, that he may have something to share with those in need." It means developing certain operating principles by which we live our lives that we will live by regardless of the cost. I have a friend who has two children, a son and a daughter. One day he was talking with his daughter about whether or not she thought her brother was good looking. She responded by saying, "I don't make judgments on family." That's a great principle.

By priorities I mean that we have certain things in our lives that we consider more important than other things. Then we choose to live our lives by things of greater importance regardless of the demands placed upon us by others. We are bombarded by pseudo-demands on our lives that look and feel important but upon evaluation are not that at all. If we live our lives being tossed to and fro by the expectations of others rather than by those things we have determined to be important because of the Lordship of Christ, then we will dissipate our life and our energies without accomplishing what God has designed us to do. The only way to avoid that is to live by priority. Jesus said, "Seek first….." Paul said, "…this one thing I do…." Their lives are examples of people who live by principle and priority. If we are going to develop strong CHU's it will only be as we purpose to do so by making it a matter of priority and then living by our principles.

5. We need to establish mentor families. There are so many people in our culture who have been deeply scarred by the emotional pain of poor family environments that they do not have any idea of how to build their own, strong CHU. They have a deep desire to build a stable home unit but because they have not experienced it nor seen it modeled they do not have any idea where to begin. There are numerous books available on the mechanics of doing this but it is far more than an issue of mechanics. What they need is to be able to see wholeness lived out in the lives of other family units. In studies of children who have come from abusive home situations and then have gone on to lead successful and happy lives, almost all found an adult or mentor outside the immediate family-a grandmother, a minister or some loving person. There was someone who gave them a sense of being loved and important.

One of the most important things a church can do is to establish a mentoring program for families who are in trouble. There needs to be some training but it mostly needs people who are willing to come alongside of another family and begin to treat them as extended family, inviting them to spend time together, go on short trips together, counsel with them in areas of finance and child-rearing techniques and give them a glimpse into how a healthy family functions. In one of our churches an older woman said that someone had asked her daughter what percentage of mothers in their neighborhood worked. She replied, "About 70%." The woman asking the question then commented, "Oh, then about 70% of the children come home to an empty home after school." Her daughter replied, "Oh no, they come over to our home."

Her daughter had understood the important role that mentoring played in the lives of children and had simply opened their home to her children's friends as a place to come and experience what a genuine, Christian home was like. They could catch a glimpse of something they would never see in their own homes and hopefully would be able to use that as a model when they were old enough to begin building their own family.

But, you say that takes a lot of time. Yes it does — but what else is life for if not for giving it away to others? This is the essence of true discipleship and in the area of building strong CHU's it is the only way to make a significant impact for future generations.

CONCLUSION

One of the skills that we need to develop in mature Christians is the ability to build strong Christian home units. It will provide the environment for the establishing of strong families in the building of a strong society for our future. Without this, our nation is doomed to slide further and further along the slope toward ever-increasing selfishness and chaos. It is not an option, it must become a mandate.

Chapter 13

They Know How to Use Their Gifts to Build the Body of Christ

In his book, "Pray at Your Own Risk" Bill Hybels tells of visiting a hardware store that had been in operation for one hundred years. As the proud owner showed him around, he was intrigued by some old tools that had never been sold. There were shovels, sledge hammers, and axes made in the early 1900s. These eighty-year-old tools had never been used. They just collected decades of dust.

As one looks at the modern day church you would find much the same situation. Most of the work is being done by a few of the people while the rest gather dust. Because of the way the church has evolved over the centuries we have developed a mentality that it is acceptable to attend services and even give financially without personally contributing in any other way to the church's life and health and still be considered a growing Christian. The Pareto Principle, developed by Joseph M. Juran and named after Vilfredo Praeto states that, for many events, 80% of the effects comes from 20% of the causes. It is a common <u>rule of thumb</u> in business; e.g., "80% of your sales come from 20% of your clients." The same principle could be easily applied to the church and say that 80% of what happens in the life of the average congregation comes from 20% of the people. The rest sit on the sidelines and applaud the efforts of the twenty percent.

This was not how God designed the church. When Paul wrote to the Romans, he said, "For as in one body we have many members, and all the members do not have the same function, so we, though many, are one body in Christ, and individually members one of another. Having gifts that differ according to the grace given to us, let us use them..."[233] What he was saying is that in the local body of Christ, every member of that body has different and unique abilities that God has given to them to enable the total body to grow and function as it was designed to do. As he says, "Having gifts that differ according to the grace given to us, <u>let us use them</u>..." Therefore one of the skills that need to be developed in a mature Christian is the skill of knowing how to develop the gifts God has given them. The method for determining these gifts will be discussed in Chapter 20 so for now we will only discuss the importance of developing the skill of using those gifts.

WHAT IS MEANT BY "GIFTS?"

The term most often used term related to "gifts" is "spiritual gifts." That phrase is only used once in the New Testament and in that context it refers rather to something that Paul is going to give them that will help strengthen them so that together, both he and they may be mutually encouraged by each other's faith. (See Romans 1:11-12) Other than this one appearance only the word "gift" appears elsewhere even though in many translations, the translators have inserted the word "spiritual" to make it unique and distinguishable.

The word translated "gift" is the Greek word **carisma** (χηαρισμα) and in this usage means "gifts denoting extraordinary powers, distinguishing certain Christians and enabling them to serve the church of Christ, the reception of which is due to the power of divine grace operating on their souls by the Holy Spirit." (W. E. Vine) It is used to refer to eternal life (Rom 5:15-16; 6:23); to divine election (Rom 11:29) and the gift of life itself (2 Cor 1:11). All the other uses of it are used to refer to certain "abilities" that God has given people to enable them to carry out certain tasks or ministries. At times it is unfortunate that the word "spiritual" is attached to the word "gift" because for some it tends to put it into a special, ethereal category that takes it beyond simply a reference to the abilities that God has given to people within the body for the purpose of building up the body and helping it come to maturity. It raises the question of greater or lesser degrees of importance and, when taken improperly, certain gifts give status that other gifts do not possess. This is unfortunate because it introduces something into the body of Christ that God never intended.

Below is a table that contains all the places where gifts are listed and the various gifts that are enumerated.

Passage	Gifts listed
Rom 12:4-8	Prophecy Serving Teaching Encouraging (exhortation) Contributing (Giving) Leadership Mercy
1 Cor 7:7	The ability to remain single or to marry
1 Cor 12:4	Different kinds of gifts

1 Cor 12:7-10	Wisdom Knowledge Faith Healing (Gifts of — plural) Miracles Prophecy Distinguishing between spirits (Discernment) Speaking in tongues Interpretation of tongues
1 Cor 12:28-31	Teachers Miracles Healing (plural) Helps (able to help others) Administration Speaking in tongues We are told to eagerly desire the "greater" gifts
1 Tim 4:14	We aren't told what Timothy's gift was but here Paul is telling him 1) Not to neglect it, and 2) It was given to him when the elders laid their hands on him.
2 Tim 1:6	We aren't told what his "gift" was but 1) He is told to "fan it into flame" and 2) It was in him through Paul laying his hands on him.
1 Pet 4:10-11	Speaking Serve or service

Various authors have enumerated a wide variety of the correct "number" of gifts when that was never God's intent at all. If God would have only given a set number of "gifts" then it seems that the list would have only needed to be included one time in the New Testament or that it would have appeared the same way each time the variety of gifts were listed. This is not the case, however, and so we are led to the conclusion that those listed are only representative of the vast variety of gifts and abilities that God gives to His people to enable them to carry out the building of the local body of Christ.

When I came to this realization it was a very liberating and freeing time. I had been involved in different churches and have been to national seminars on the issue in which I was taught that there were only a certain number of gifts. Upon returning home I would take the listing and try my best to find myself in one of the gift categories that had been set before me. Almost every time I would have to really stretch to find myself in one or another of those categories. When I finally realized that God is simply setting these before us as ideas about the variety of ways He has gifted people in the body it helped me realize that the unique way God had gifted me was because He had a personal role He wanted me to play with the life that was mine. To try and squeeze me into someone else's mould was doing something that God never intended. It was like David trying to fight Goliath in Saul's armor — it wouldn't work.

Having said that, let me point out that the word translated "gifts" has as its root word the word χαρα (charis) which is the word translated "grace." What this means is that God, by His grace and through His Spirit, has given us gifts according to His choosing. This is what Paul meant when he wrote, "We have different gifts, according to the grace given us."[234] He said "There are different kinds of gifts, but the same Spirit."[235] This means that we will each be unique individuals with a gift or gifts that are distinctively ours. When Paul wrote to the Corinthians he tried to help them see that not everyone would have the same gifts.[236] The gifts we have been given are intended to be used by each person. That was why he said, "Having gifts that differ according to the grace given to us, let us use them…"[237] There are some places where there are instructions given to certain of the gifts (Romans 12:6-8; 1 Peter 4:10-11).

Thus we see that every person who knows Christ has become a part of His body and that at the same time he was given certain "gifts" or abilities that God wanted him to have so he could take his part in building up the total body of Christ. Not to learn how to use these gifts and then not to use them correctly is to thwart God's purpose in the giving of the gifts and to leave the church weaker than God intended it to be. The church is described as Christ's "body, the fullness of him who fills everything in every way."[238] If a person does not use the gifts he or she have been given, then the body of Christ loses its fullness and it cannot carry out the task He has assigned it in the specific locale He has placed them in.

WHY IT IS IMPORTANT TO LEARN HOW TO USE OUR GIFTS

There are at least for reasons that I can think of as to why this is an important skill to develop:

1. We are commanded to do it. When Paul wrote to the Romans he said, "Having gifts that differ according to the grace given to us, let us use them." In other words, the gifts and abilities that God has given are expected to be used. In Jesus' parable of the talents in Luke 19:11-27, each of three men was given about the equivalent of three month's wages and was told to "Trade with these until I come." Upon the master's return he called each of them to give an account of what they had done with what they were given. When God gives "gifts" to people, He expects that those gifts will be utilized and returned to Him with whatever increase results from their use. We will each be rewarded based upon how well we used what we had been given.

Since God has given each believer certain "gifts" or abilities that are unique to them, then we are expected to use them to do what He has asked us to do.

2. God has designed each believer to function in a 'body." Paul argues that the body of Christ is like a physical, human body in that it has many members and none of the members are the same but different. Each member is designed to carry out its unique function and when all the people in that body use their gifts properly the body is enabled to do what God has designed it to do. (See Romans 12:4-8; 1 Peter 4:10-11) One of the gaping weaknesses of the modern western church is its poor theology and understanding of the role of the church in the life of a believer. We have so emphasized a "personal relationship with Jesus Christ" that we have overlooked the absolute necessity of the local body of Christ. In talking with people I find many of them have a deep love for God and a desire to grow in their walk with Him but do not have any understanding of their place in or the necessity for the local church. We "church hop" from church to church depending on whoever has the best "program" or the most appealing preacher and feel absolutely no sense of long time commitment to a local body. The result is that people tend not to be around long enough to develop their gifts and discover their place in a local body and hence their gifts go unused and the local church, as well as the universal church, suffers accordingly.

When Paul wrote to the Corinthians, he said, "…..….you are not lacking in any spiritual gift, as you wait for the revealing of our Lord Jesus Christ."[239] The word "spiritual" does not appear in the original language and has been supplied by the translators. What he is saying is that this particular church had all the "gifts" it needed to carry out the ministry that God wanted them to have. Thus the issue is not desiring more or dif-

ferent gifts but working to determine how to uti-
lize the ones that were already there. Since this
is true, it is crucial that we train people how to
use the gifts that God has given them.

3. It is the only way we can "grow up into
Christ." As mentioned earlier, Paul described a
local body of Christ as "the fullness of him who
fills everything in every way."[240] This body is so
great when it comes together to function as it was
designed that God is "able to do immeasurably more
than all we ask or imagine, *according to his power
that is at work within us...*"[241] Because the church
operates on resurrection power she is able to do
far beyond our capacity to think or imagine if the
totality of her people use the gifts with which
they have been entrusted.

In Ephesians 4:11-16 Paul describes how the
body works. He begins by helping them understand
that God has given some people gifts that are
designed to help others in the body discover and
use the gifts they have been given (11-12). As
those gifts are used, we begin to reach the unity
of the faith and we grow in our knowledge of Jesus
and as a result together we become mature. As we do
that, we attain the whole measure of the fullness
of Christ. (13) When we reach forward to that, we
stop being spiritual babies who are unstable and
swayed back and forth by the cunning of men who
desire to mislead. As each member of the body uses
the gifts they have been given it enables all of
its members "grow up into him who is the Head" with
the result that the whole body grows and builds
itself up in love." (14-16) What he is saying
is that individual members as well as the total
congregate of the body will never reach maturity
unless each individual member uses the gifts they
have been given to contribute to the health and
welfare of the body.

The "rugged individualism" philosophy that permeates our culture keeps us from recognizing true

truth about what the body is designed to become. In our thinking, the church is primarily an "organization" that requires people to staff her "programs" and she structures herself accordingly. This makes it possible for the majority of "church members" to be convinced they are growing Christians without feeling any necessity for using their gifts to build the body of Christ. It enables us to focus on our "personal relationships" and to grow in "our walk with the Lord" as individuals without seeing the much larger plan that God has designed for us. God designed the church so that the only way she (both corporately and individually) can grow to maturity is for her members to use their gifts to share with one another and thus become the fullness of Christ that she was created to be.

During the Great Depression, a man named Yates was operating a sheep ranch in the rolling hills of West Texas. His business wasn't generating enough money to pay the principal and interest on his mortgage so he ended up living on a government subsidy. His days were filled with stress over the financial concerns of his family. They lived, dressed, and ate in poverty. One day a seismographic crew asked if they might explore his land for oil. Yates agreed and signed a lease contract. At 1,115 feet they struck a huge reserve of oil. The first well produced 80,000 barrels a day while many subsequent wells generated more than twice that amount. Thirty years after the discovery, one well was estimated to still have a potential flow of 125,000 barrels a day. This vast sea of wealth, known as Yates Pool, had always belonged to Yates. He was a multimillionaire who had spent years in heart-wrenching poverty just because he didn't realize what he already possessed. The church already possesses all the gifts she needs to make a radical difference in her world. She only has to awaken her people to see the need for every member to use their gifts. When they learn to do that, we will begin to see an impact, the likes of which none of us have seen in our lifetimes. We are "the fullness of him who fills everything in every way." We only need to tap our potential to see that worked out in real, tangible ways.

4. It is another way of "laying up treasure in heaven." Jesus told the young man who came to him asking, "Teacher, what good thing must I do to get eternal life?" In his second response to him he said, "If you want to be perfect, (mature) go, sell your possessions and give to the poor, and you will have treasure in heaven."[242] When Paul wrote to the Colossians, he said to them, "Since then you have been raised with Christ, set your heart on things above, where Christ is seated at the right hand of God. Set your minds on things above, not on earthly things."[243] But what are "things above?" I am not certain that I know everything that is "above" but one of the things that is there is the bride of Christ, the church. If I am to lay up treasure in heaven and think about things that are above, one of the ways that I do that is by using my gifts to build the body of Christ. Right now, she is both on earth in the lives of the saints who are here and in heaven in the lives of those who have gone to heaven before us.

One of the ways I can lay up treasures in heaven is by investing those things that God has given me in the building of the earthly body of Christ which, upon the death of her earthly members, goes immediately into God's presence "in heaven." There are a multitude of ways that we can be investing our lives in eternal things and one of those ways is through the building of the eternal body or temple of the living God.

HOW A PERSON DEVELOPS THEIR GIFTS

There are at least five things that can be done to develop the skill of using our gifts to build the body of Christ.

1. Through using them. Whenever we go on vacation, I always try to maintain, to some degree, the workout regimen I use on a regular basis. I cannot do it all the time because the same location and facilities are not always available to me but I do try to find some kind of satisfactory substitute. But when I get back home and resume my regular schedule, inevitably for the first few days, my muscles get sore. The reason they do so is because disuse causes weakness and when I start to reuse them again it takes a while for them to get back into the shape they were before I stopped. The only way I can maintain fitness and my muscles is by using them.

The same thing is true for me as a member of the body of Christ. The only way I can remain spiritually fit is by maintaining my individual walk with the Lord and using my gifts to build the body of Christ. When I stop using my gifts for any reason, two things happen: 1) My gifts begin to atrophy through lack of non-use, and 2) The body of which I am a part begins to suffer because the role I was intended to play stops supplying its contribution to the total health of the body. So if I want to come to maturity and help others within the body to do so as well, I need to be using the gifts God has given me to help the body come to maturity.

2. Through volunteering. Over the years of my ministry I have had numbers of people come to me to complain that no one ever asks them to do anything. My response is almost always the same. I say, "Well, did you ever think about going and volunteering?" It is interesting to see many of the responses. The thought of going to volunteer

never crossed their mind. All they would have to do is to go to their pastor, the church secretary, some member of the staff, paid or volunteer, and offer their services. Yet I have also had people come to me who said they volunteered and no one followed through. Wherever the "blame" falls, the church needs to determine ways of using the gifts of all the members of their body.

I read once about three frogs who were sitting on a river bank on a sunny, hot day. One of them decided to jump into the cool river. How many were left? There were three left. I didn't say he jumped, I just said he "decided to jump." There is a significant difference. There are numbers of people who feel God speaking to them about volunteering for some areas of service as a result of some speaker or incident in their lives. Right at that time they "decide" to do something but it never happens. The result is always the same, the gifts never get used and the work never gets done. The result: the body suffers. The Barna Research Group has determined that only one out of four people who claim to be "born-again" Christians volunteer for ministry in the local church. Somehow we have missed the entire sense of responsibility that goes along with knowing that we are responsible Christians. Perhaps this is the reason that when they asked Americans, "Is the Christian church relevant for today?" only 27 percent of unchurched people said yes and less than half (46%) of the churched said "No."

If you have sensed God speaking to you about some area of service or putting a burden upon your heart about something that you see needs to be done, then go and volunteer your life to undertake the task. You will be amazed at the growth that will occur in your own life and you will get a chance to "lay up treasures in heaven."

3. Through training workshops. One of the things a local church needs to be continually doing is

offering workshops for various gifts that are led by people with that particular gift. A workshop is different from a lecture or a Sunday School lesson. When people come to a lecture or smaller class they don't usually come expecting to do anything with what they hear. It is seen as an "information gathering opportunity." But a workshop on the other hand is a means of training people through practical, hands on instruction and supervised activity. Workshops can be done on church premises or out in the field and are best led by people who are not necessarily teachers but who are individuals that are skilled themselves in a particular skill or gift.

Workshops offer both information plus hands-on experience right at the very time the workshop is being held. I remember having the privilege of conducting a number of Lay Institutes for Evangelism through materials secured through Campus Crusade for Christ. The purpose was to help people gain a grasp of how to share the gospel. They usually were three day events, starting Thursday evening, Friday evening and Saturday all day. They were a mixture of lectures and class role playing. Then after lunch on Saturday, the participants were sent out two by two into the community to go door to door and to practice what they had learned. It was always a fearful group that left the training time to venture forth. But every time, when they returned from their field experience, they were literal times of rejoicing because invariably one or more of the teams had seen someone trust Christ for their salvation The whole group benefitted from the experience.

This is what workshops are geared to do. They are designed both to give some helpful instruction and then to give opportunity to put that information into practice.

4. Through being mentored or apprenticed. Recently I was having difficulty getting connected

to the internet through my personal computer at home. I had tried everything I could think of and had even called a friend who tried to talk me through some things over the telephone. When nothing seemed to work, he came to my home and sat down in front of the computer and started working through his problem-solving procedure. In no time flat, he had discovered the problem, had fixed it and I was once again connected. As he worked, I looked over his shoulder and watched the sequence he went through and the things he did. When it failed again after he left, I sat down and went through the same sequence he had done and was able to get it up and running again without having to call him. This is the process of mentoring or being apprenticed.

A mentor is someone who calls you to work alongside of them to watch and learn what they do. This gives you some ideas as to both what to do and how to do it. Once you have grasped this then they step aside and walk alongside of you as you undertake the same actions. They will then "coach" you through them and correct you as you proceed. In doing this you get the opportunity of both learning and doing under the supervision of someone who is already well trained. Before students, who are getting their college degree in teaching can graduate, they need to work through what is called "student teaching." This consists of sitting in a classroom and observing what an existent teacher is doing and then gradually being brought into the teaching process so that you can begin to practice under the trained eye of a more skilled and experienced teacher. In this way you learn how to do the job in a learning-friendly environment.

In the same way, gifts are developed and used within the context of the body by having people who are already using their gifts in an accomplished way work alongside of someone who thinks they might have certain gifts in an attempt to both determine if, in fact, they do have the gifts and then to train them in proper usage if it is discovered that they do possess those gifts. This provides a safe, open environment in which a newer person can learn a skill from someone who has already developed the skill. This is sometimes inconvenient because it requires trying to coordinate two or more people's schedules but it is a very proven and effective way of developing a person's God-given gifts.

5. By making service within the body a mandatory part of church membership. The average, modern western church membership consists of little more than attending a class or going through some process at the end of which you become a "member." At that point, little more is expected of you than some kind of attendance and financial giving. It is expected that you will come to some of the "special events" the church plans for you but the number and extent is entirely "between you and the Lord."

This is vastly different from the methodology Jesus used. He never spoke about "membership" as we conceive of it today but instead invited his followers by saying, "Follow me and I will make you fishers of men."[244] Implicit in that call was the expectation that following him would cause them to learn from him how to "fish for men" and then they would be able to do the same thing with others. He expected that they would be doing something with the gifts they had been given. This was the mentoring/discipling process in action and when He ascended, the disciples, after Pentecost, eventually began doing the very things he had done and trained them to do.

When people are considering "church membership," a part of that consideration needs to be the expectation that they will use their gifts to enable the organic body to grow to maturity. This may not be the same thing as helping the organization to function and turn out program but it will be the using of their gifts to help other believers work through real life issues and come to fullness of life in Christ. Until this expectation is set before those considering becoming a part of the local church, people will join the church thinking that periodic attendance and some financial contribution is all that is required. When we come to know God, we are called to "love the Lord your God with all your heart, and with all your soul, and with all your strength, and with all your mind; and your neighbor as yourself."[245] This is not a half-hearted kind of commitment. It is an all or nothing kind of love and obedience. Included in that whole-hearted discipleship is the willingness to use the gifts God has given us to build the church of Jesus Christ so that she becomes the "fullness of him who fills everything in every way."[246]

CONCLUSION

God in His grace has "gifted" each believer with abilities that make that individual unique and able to play a specific and vital role in the building up of the body of Christ. A mature believer will have discovered what those God-given gifts are and have developed the necessary skills to be able to use them. In this way, not only will they come to maturity individually but the church will also come to maturity corporately. In this way Christ will live through His people in new and ever-expanding ways both to help them come to maturity and then using them as His arms and legs to make a significant impact upon their world.

Chapter 14

They Know How to Articulate and Defend Their Faith

In the 1970's the late Larry Norman sang a song that contained a line which said, *"If you know a beautiful story, you tell it to a friend..."* He then went on to describe that since we have become the thankful recipients of the story of the grace of God, we have the privilege of sharing that story with others. Arabella Catherine Hankey also wrote a hymn as she began to come out of a serious illness which was so devastating that she had to stop her Bible classes for female factory workers. Her hymn said,

> I love to tell the story of unseen things above,
> Of Jesus and his glory, of Jesus and His love;
> I love to tell the story because I know 'tis true,
> It satisfies my longings as nothing else can do.

God has called us to be a verbal people, who are unashamed to share with other people the message that has been responsible for transforming us and that can do the same for them. Since we are called to be "witnesses" in our world, one of the skills that a mature disciple needs to acquire is the skill of being able to articulate and defend their faith. The reason is simple, no one can act upon something they do not know and no one can know what they need to act on unless someone else shares that information with them. When Paul wrote to the Romans he said, "How, then, can they call on the one they have not believed in? And how can they believe in the one of whom they have not heard? And how can they hear without someone preaching to them? And how can they preach unless they are sent? …. Consequently, faith comes through hearing the message, and the message is heard through the word of Christ."[247]

Therefore, one of the skills that we need to help people learn to develop is the skill of being able to put their faith into words that can be communicated clearly and then be able to give reasons for why they believe as they do and why others should believe that as well.

WHAT IS MEANT BY ARTICULATING AND DEFENDING ONE FAITH

Before Jesus ascended into heaven he clearly commanded his disciples to go into all the world and verbally tell those they met about the gospel of the kingdom of God. In Matthew 28:18-20 we read, "All authority in heaven and on earth has been given to me. Therefore go and make disciples of all nations, baptizing them in the name of the Father and of the Son and of the Holy Spirit, and teaching them to obey everything I have commanded you. And surely I am with you always, to the very end of the age." Mark records it this way, "He said to them, "Go into all the world and preach the good news to all creation." (Mark 16:15) In Luke's gospel Jesus told the disciples, "This is what is written: The Christ will suffer and rise from the dead on the third day, and repentance and forgiveness of sins will be preached in his name to all nations, beginning at Jerusalem. You are witnesses of these things. I am going to send you what my Father has promised; but stay in the city until you have been clothed with power from on high." (Luke 24:46-49) And in John's gospel, Jesus appeared to the disciples behind closed doors and said, "As the Father has sent me, I am sending you." (John 20:21) Then when he stood before them one last time, he said, "…you will receive power when the Holy Spirit comes on you; and you will be my witnesses in Jerusalem, and in all Judea and Samaria, and to the ends of the earth." (Acts 1:8)

He expected them to go forth and verbally share with people the message that He had entrusted to them and then be able to discuss with those who heard the questions they would have resulting from hearing this. They were to do this in a manner that would help them wrestle through the content and implications of what they had heard. There are two parts to this process.

1. Articulating their message. The word that Jesus used with his disciples to denote this part of their task was the Greek word κηρυσσω (kerusso). The word is translated in most translations with the English word "preach." This is most unfortunate because we immediately identify it with the word "preacher" and since only a small percentage of believers are "preachers" the average person excuses themselves from this responsibility. The word translated "preach" is better translated "to proclaim" and is used of a herald who comes to announce some event or happening. The Theological Dictionary of the New Testament says, "The NT uses many words for the proclaiming of the Christian message, e.g., *légein*, *laleín*, *martyreín*, *didáskein*. It is a mistake simply to render such terms, and *kērýssein* itself, by "to preach." Fundamentally

kērýssein is the declaration of an event. Except in Rev. 5:2 we do not find it in the Johannine writings, which prefer *martyreín*, nor in Hebrews. It occurs 61 times in the NT (nine in Matthew, 14 in Mark, 17 in Luke-Acts, 19 in Paul, once in 1 Peter, and once in Revelation.) Its greater importance than *kéryx* or *kérygma* shows that the stress is on dynamic proclaiming." When he sent out the twelve He told them, "As you go, preach this message: The kingdom of heaven is near."[248]

The word does not so much connote preaching in the normal sense that we think of it, rather it means to proclaim or to herald. It is like having some information from a ruling authority that needs to be communicated by whatever means to those for whom it was intended. Thus this is an activity that every believer is expected to take seriously and out into practice in their personal lives. To do this is to "evangelize." The Archbishop's Committee in the Church of England defined evangelism as "To evangelize is to so present Christ Jesus in the power of the Holy Spirit that men shall come to put their trust in God through Him, to accept Him as their Savior and to serve Him as their King in the fellowship of His church."

Since this is a major part of what Jesus asked His disciples to do while He was living among them and since it was also a major part of what He commanded them to do following His ascension, we can conclude that this is something he intended the church to keep on doing until He returns. Therefore, we need to help people develop the ability to articulate this message of the kingdom so that when God presents them with an opportunity to verbally share this message, they can do it with clarity and succinctness.

2. Defending their message. In a pluralistic world such as we live in, there will always be a wide variety of proposed solutions to the human dilemma. These different worldviews each hold dif-

ferent presuppositions and conclusions based upon those presuppositions. That means that as we share this message, we will be challenged as to its content and its exclusivity. When we are thus challenged, it will be necessary for us to be able to "defend" what we have declared. When Peter wrote, he said, "Always be prepared to give an answer to everyone who asks you to give the reason for the hope that you have. But do this with gentleness and respect, keeping a clear conscience, so that those who speak maliciously against your good behavior in Christ may be ashamed of their slander."[249] The word translated "give an answer" is the Greek word apologia (απολογια) and is the word from which we get our word "apologetics." It means a "verbal defense or a speech in defense or a reasoned statement or argument." What Peter is saying is that when people question us as to the source of our strength or challenge the validity of our faith, we are to have an answer to give them that helps explain why we believe what we do and act as we do.

This does not mean that we needlessly argue things or set out to win a debate. When Paul wrote to Timothy he said, "And the Lord's servant must not quarrel; instead he must be kind to everyone, able to teach, not resentful. Those who oppose him he must gently instruct in the hope that God will grant them repentance leading to a knowledge of the truth. And that they will come to their senses and escape from the trap of the devil who has taken them captive to do his will"[250]

Benjamin Franklin put it this way, "The way to convince another is to state your case moderately and accurately. Then scratch your head, or shake it a little and say that is the way it seems to you, but that, of course you may be mistaken about it. This causes your listener to receive what you have to say, and, as like as not, turn about and try to convince you of it, since you are in doubt.

But if you go at him in a tone of positiveness and arrogance, you only make an opponent of him." We are not out to win arguments, we are out to set forth the truth as we understand it from the Bible and then let the Holy Spirit do with that truth whatever He desires to do. We are not expected to have all the answers but when we do respond to questions in the right way, we have God's promise that "As the rain and snow come down from heaven, and do not return to it without watering the earth and making it bud and flourish, so that it yields seed for the sower and bread for the eater, so is my word that goes out from my mouth: it will not return to me empty, but will accomplish what I desire and achieve the purpose for which I sent it."[251] As we do this we need to be aware of the concern that C. S. Lewis voiced when he wrote, "Apologetic work is so dangerous to one's own faith. A doctrine never seems dimmer to me that when I have just successfully defended it."[252] What he meant was as he was exposed to arguments that were contrary to what he believed it raised in his own mind questions he had not thought about before and so he came away with some new, additional things to think through.

So we see that just as we need to develop in a mature believer the skill of being able to articulate their faith, we need to develop in them the skill of knowing how to defend their faith as well. Both involve verbal exchange and every believer needs to be trained in how to do this.

WHY THIS IS AN IMPORTANT SKILL TO DEVELOP

There are at least three reasons this is so:

1. This is what Jesus trained his disciples to do. Jesus used three words to emphasize this part of his command to them: a) Preach. As mentioned earlier, this is the word that means to act as a

herald. A herald is one who has been commissioned to announce or proclaim a message from someone to others. When prestigious awards, such as the Dove award, or the Oscars or other such winners, are to be given usually there is a "presenter" who has been asked to announce the winner's name. Usually you watch them try and raise the suspense and then they open the envelope and announce, "And the winner is……." That is the task of a herald. When Jesus sent his disciples out he told them "As you go, preach this message: 'The kingdom of heaven is near.'"[253] The disciples understood this clearly for we are told that Peter in speaking to Cornelius and those who were gathered in his home, "He commanded us to "preach" to the people and to testify that he is the one whom God appointed as judge of the living and the dead."[254]

b) The second word he used was <u>teach.</u> This is the Greek word διδασκω (didasko). It refers "to hold discourse with others in order to instruct them, to deliver didactic discourses, to impart instruction." It is the word used in Matthew 4:23 when it says, "And he went about all Galilee, *teaching* in their synagogues and preaching the gospel of the kingdom and healing every disease and every infirmity among the people." It is also used in Acts 5:42 where it says, "And every day in the temple and at home they did not cease teaching and preaching Jesus as the Christ." Preaching is the proclamation and teaching is the setting forth in a more systematic, didactic way certain amounts of information. It is not necessarily the classroom style although it can include that. It is any kind of instruction where one person takes it upon themselves to instruct or educate another.

c) The third word he used was <u>witness</u> or <u>testify.</u> This is the Greek word μαρτυω (martus). It is the word from which we get our English word "martyr" and means "one who is a spectator of anything" and is used in both a legal sense as a "witness" in a legal trial or in a historical sense as describing something you have personally witnessed as a part of your everyday life. This is the word Jesus used when he gave his disciples their last command to "be my witnesses in Jerusalem, in all Judea and Samaria and to the ends of the earth."[255] It was the word Peter used when speaking to the crowd that had gathered after he healed a crippled beggar. He said, "You killed the author of life, but God raised him from the dead. We are witnesses of this."[256] When Paul was explaining his conversion to the crowd he spoke about Ananias speaking to him and telling him, "You will be a witness to all men of what you have seen and heard."[257] Being a witness involves verbal skills as we are called on to tell others of what we have seen and personally experienced.

Jesus commanded his intimate followers that they were to articulate their faith and he did so by using these three different words to describe different ways they would fulfill this responsibility. So doing this is important because it is what Jesus called his disciples to do.

2. Unless people hear this message, they will die in their sins. Because of the Fall, everyone born is born spiritually blind and naturally unable to understand the message of salvation and find forgiveness for their sins. Paul wrote to the Corinthians that there is a veil over people's hearts that keeps them from understanding the words of Moses.[258] He goes on to say that "…even if our gospel is veiled, it is veiled to those who are perishing. The god of this age has blinded the minds of unbelievers, so that they cannot see the light of the gospel of the glory of Christ, who is the image of God."[259] This means that the natural man is kept from being able to see the truth of the gospel. Unless God opens their eyes they will be eternally lost. One of the ways that God uses to open the eyes of the blind is through

giving them the message of God. This was why Paul said, "How can they call on the one they have not believed in? And how can they believe in the one of whom they have not heard? And how can they hear without someone preaching to them?"[260] The only way people's eyes can be opened is if we go and speak to them about the kingdom of God. When we do that, the Holy Spirit takes our message and uses it to open their eyes so they are enabled to hear something they formerly could not even hear, let alone understand.

While speaking in London, evangelist D. L. Moody was approached by a British companion who wanted to know the secret of Moody's success in leading people to Christ. Moody directed the man to his hotel window and asked, "What do you see?" The man looked down on the square and reported a view of crowded streets. Moody suggested he look again. This time the man mentioned seeing people—men, women, and children. Moody then directed him to look a third time, and the man became frustrated that he was not seeing what Moody wanted him to see. The great evangelist came to the window with watery eyes and said, "I see people going to hell without Jesus. Until you see people like that, you will not lead them to Christ." Until we see people as lost without this message that we have been given, we will never sense the kind of responsibility we ought to have to go to them and articulate our faith.

3. We live in a world that is rapidly moving away from God's truth. "On an average day in America, twenty-nine new products are introduced, each person is exposed to eighteen hundred commercial messages, and $700 million is spent on advertising. With such a barrage of messages bombarding American people, it is imperative that we make the gospel of Jesus Christ crystal clear. We don't want anybody to miss the most important message of all!"[261] We are deluged with all kinds

of messages in many different forms from early morning to late at night. Research is showing that not only is modern public education amoral, it is anti-moral and distinctly anti-Christian. Our age is characterized by Paul's words to Timothy when he wrote that we are "always learning but never able to acknowledge the truth."[262]

This movement is so well documented by the late Francis Schaefer and many others that I will not take the opportunity here to repeat it. All anyone has to do is to preview the books your children bring home from school, watch the evening news or read newspaper editorials or secular magazine articles to discover that God is not even mentioned in connection with any of what is considered "important news or information." It is as if He did not exist or else has been relegated to an unimportant compartment of life that is the property of those who "need it." As a result we are rapidly moving away from the foundation upon which our western civilization was founded and as we do that we sink ever deeper into mental, moral, social and spiritual decay. The only way to rescue us from that is for God's people to take seriously their responsibility to articulate and defend their faith whether it is in the home, the school, the market place and even in the church. Truth must be reestablished or else we will perish.

HOW WE DEVELOP THIS SKILL

Following are six different suggestions as to what we can do to develop this skill in people.

1. Help each person develop their personal testimony. A testimony is simply a brief statement about how a person recognized their separation from God and how they discovered what needed to happen for that relationship to be restored. Hudson Taylor told of a Chinese pastor who always

instructed new converts to witness as soon as possible. Once, upon meeting a young convert, the pastor inquired, "Brother, how long have you been saved?" The man answered that he had been saved for about three months. "And how many have you won to the Savior? He inquired.

"Oh, I'm only a learner," the convert responded. Shaking his head in disapproval, the pastor said, "Young man, the Lord doesn't expect you to be a full-fledged preacher, but he does expect you to be a faithful witness. Tell me, when does a candle begin to shine — when it's already half burned up?"

"No, as soon as it's lit," came the reply. "That's right, so let your light shine right away."

A testimony is your personal story and cannot be disproved. Every believer needs to be able to share the story of the journey to Christ in either a short or a longer form. It can be passed on in as little as a couple of minutes or can be lengthened to be shared publicly in a longer time. The testimony needs to contain three things: 1) What my life was like before I came to know Christ, 2) How I came to know Him, including the words of your prayer, and 3) What you life is like after coming to know Him. It needs to be shared in such a way that the person(s) listening could walk away and say to themselves, "I could do that because now I know what to do and how to pray." This is probably the single most important thing that a person can learn to get them on the way to articulating their faith.

2. Set up role-playing workshops. The format of the workshop can be designed in two different ways. The first is to help the participants develop their personal testimonies and then give them opportunities to share their testimony with the others in the workshop in one on one settings. The second is to use the teaching part of the workshop as an opportunity to share with the par-

ticipants a simple evangelistic tool such as "The Bridge" or the "One Verse Evangelism" method from the Navigators or "Steps to Peace With God" from the Billy Graham Evangelistic Association or the "Roman Road" to salvation or something similar. Then give them time alone to become familiar with the tool or the message and to memorize its outline or verses. Have them mark their Bibles accordingly as a helpful tool. Then spend the rest of the workshop giving them opportunities to share this tool with each other individually or corporately. This makes them familiar with the tool and gives them some practice in actually sharing the message.

Both of these first two suggestions can also be scheduled with a follow-up session where the participants actually go out into the community to share what they have learned. It can be done through going out door-to-door, or through talking to people on the street or place where people tend to gather. It can be done through a church's follow-up ministry to new attendees or friends of people of the congregation. Some of these are more threatening than others but all are designed to give the person experience in actually doing what they have been trained to do.

You can also have the workshop be an end in itself and be content that you have given the participants the informational know how so when they have an opportunity in the home, on the job or in some other social situation they are able to reach back into their training and use whatever portion seems appropriate. At least now the person has the information and experience necessary so that when God puts them into a situation where they have an opportunity to articulate their faith, they know what to say.

3. Establish some mentors. When Jesus sent his disciples out for the first time without him, he sent them out two by two.[263] He did this for a very good reason; it is easier to go out like they did

with a companion rather than alone. I have done it both ways and believe me going in pairs is much better. I have found out it is very easy to talk myself out of going, to back away from certain doors that don't look friendly, to come up with what I have found were "very good reasons" for not following through — all because I was going alone. But when you go out in partnership I have found that people do things they would not normally do alone because of the presence of a friend who can lend moral support.

Evangelism Explosion trains people in their method of evangelism and then sends them out as a part of a team to call in the homes of people. Watching another person lead in the conversation and then have the experience of leading someone to Christ or answering questions gives the apprentice the opportunity to see that certain questions and techniques definitely work. This gives them the encouragement to try it themselves when it is their turn to share. Such training is very beneficial to someone who is not normally an extrovert and to those who are it gives them a clear, concise format for articulating their faith and responding to questions.

4. Learn the language of our culture. Many Christians of this generation are out of touch with the language and worldview of much of the culture of which they are a part. There are many reasons for this but if we are going to communicate with our culture in language that they understand we must learn to understand what and how they think. This requires hard work and focused thinking. C. S. Lewis wrote, "When I began, Christianity came before the great mass of my unbelieving fellow-countrymen either in the highly emotional form offered by revivalists or in the unintelligible language of highly cultured clergymen. Most men were reached by neither. My task was therefore simply that of a *translator* — one turning Christian

doctrine, or what he believed to be such, into the vernacular, into language that unscholarly people would attend to and could understand."[264]

There are many excellent resources available to us. Personally I would recommend two books, "How Now Shall We Live?" by Charles Colson and Nancy Pearcey and "Total Truth" by Nancy Pearcey. Both of these books are well written and help the reader to think through the issues that we face as we attempt to interact with our culture.

In 1993 I had the opportunity to go on a short term missions trip into central Russia to the town of Irkutsk which is in Siberia. After recovering from the jet lag of traveling across sixteen time zones we gathered together with our translators and friends who were our hosting missionaries. They walked us through some of the cultural issues we would face and explained certain things that would offend the people of this area and how we should conduct ourselves when we were there. After that, I met the young woman who was to be my translator. She was a new believer and a very vibrant person who had served as a translator for other groups of Americans who had come to visit the area. The second evening we had there we were free and so I made an appointment with her just to take the time and get acquainted and ask her some additional questions about the area. We spent about four hours together during which I asked her all sorts of questions about herself and the people of this region. I wanted to understand as much about them as I could so that I could communicate as effectively as possible as an outsider. About three hours into our time she broke down and started to cry. I didn't know what to do so I just waited until she stopped and than asked her if I had done something offensive because I had not wanted to do that. She wiped her eyes and said to me, "You are the first person who has come to us that has shown any interest in understanding who we are as people. All the rest of them simply came because they thought they could solve all our problems. They never bothered to get to know us at all." I could not understand that because how could I communicate with people from a different culture if I did not do as much to understand that culture as I could.

As Christians in western civilization we face much the same dilemma. The people in our culture speak a language that most of us don't understand so if we want to communicate effectively with them, we must learn how they think and live or else we will simply be speaking at them or by them and not with them.

5. Ask God for opportunities to share. When Paul was in Corinth he received some extensive opposition from the Jews in the city. He determined to stop trying to reach the Jewish people there and to rather focus on taking the message to the Gentiles in the city. One night shortly thereafter the Lord spoke to Paul in a vision and said to him, "Do not be afraid; keep on speaking, do not be silent. For I am with you, and no one is going to attack and harm you, because I have many people in this city."[265] What He was saying to Paul was that, although unknown to him, there were man people that God had called to Himself in the city and He was going to reach them through the message that Paul would proclaim.

If God would come to you and me today, He would say the same thing: "There are many people in your city that I am in the process of calling to Myself." We simply need to be asking God to show us those to whom He wants us to speak and then venture forth into our community with our eyes and ears open. John Fletcher of Madeley, Shropshire, England was the saint to whom the rolling drunks in the village doffed their hats and muttered, "There goes the man that loves our souls." He loved them because he spent time asking God for opportunities to share the gospel with the people he met through his day.

Dr. Walter Wilson was a medical doctor who left that profession and became a pastor because he felt the call of God on his life. He was specially gifted as an evangelist. He tells this story: "When I was on a train coming into Philadelphia, I was sitting beside a bald headed man. I said, "Are you a prophet of God?" He said, "Mister, I have been called everything under the sun, but I was never called that. Why did you call me that?" I said, "Because there was a prophet in the Bible who was told, 'Go up, thou bald-headed prophet.' I thought you were going up someday and I could go with you." He said, "Mister, when I go I am going the other way, and it has made me wretched, but I don't know what to do about it." I read to him John 14:6: "I am the way," the way up, and I led him to Christ."

We need to be continually asking God for opportunities to share the good news of the kingdom with the people we are with every day. If we consistently do that, God will open doors for us that will cause us to stand in amazement.

6. We need to experiment by faith with the people who are around us. We never know those people in whose lives God is at work unless we take the initiative by faith and engage them in some way, determined to share the gospel if God opens the door. But we say, "I am not certain what to say or how to start the conversation. And suppose they ask me a question that I don't have an answer to?" Jesus anticipated our concerns and so he said to his disciples, "When you are brought before synagogues, rulers and authorities do not worry about how you will defend yourselves or what you will say, for the Holy Spirit will teach you at that time what you should say."[266] He repeated the same counsel later when he was warning them in advance of the persecution they would experience. He said

"But make up your mind not to worry beforehand how you will defend yourselves. For I will give you words and wisdom that none of your adversaries will be able to resist or contradict."[267]

There was a man by the name of John Vassar, a wonderful soul winner who lived in years past. One evening he returned from a meeting, walked over to the hotel clerk to get the key to his room and there he saw a beautifully dressed woman sitting on a couch. The Spirit of God said to him, "John, go speak to her."

He walked over and introduced himself as a preacher of the gospel. He asked her if she knew the Lord as her Savior. That started the conversation and enabled him to sit down and go through the plan of salvation. The woman was not ready to receive the Lord as her Savior as the seed had not been sown before. So he prayed with her and urged her not to put it off and excused himself.

As he walked away her husband came through the door. Seeing the stranger with his wife he rushed up and asked her, "Honey, who was that man?" She told him. "What did he want?" She said, "He came over to ask me if I was a Christian, if I was saved." Indignantly her husband said, "Why didn't you tell him to mind his own business?" She looked at her husband and said, "If you had seen the tears in his eyes and felt the love in his heart and seen how earnest he was, you would have known that this was his business."

We need to make reaching the lost our "business" because this is what Jesus commanded us to do until He returns. To reach the lost we need to be developing the skill of articulating and defending our faith. This is something that every believer needs to take seriously in their lives.

In the movie "Gettysburg" Colonel Joshua L. Chamberlain of the 20th Marine Regiment learns that his regiment is going to receive 120 Union soldiers who mutinied. He is given permission to shoot any of these mutineers who don't cooperate.

Chamberlin tells the men that he knows about their problem but he admits, "There's nothing I can do today. We're moving out in a few minutes. We'll be moving all day. I've been ordered to take you men with me. I've been told that if you don't come, I can shoot you. Well, you know I won't do that. Maybe someone else will, but I won't. So, that's that." He goes on to describe a little about his regiment's history and about how they started out with a thousand men but that they are down to three hundred now. Then he goes on to say, "This is a different kind of army. If you look back through history you'll see men fighting for pay, for women, for some other kind of loot. They fight for land, for power, because a king leads them, or just because they like killing. But we are here for something new. This has not happened much in the history of the world. We are an army out to set other men free."

The church of Jesus Christ is an army of people out to set other people free. To do that we need to train them in how to articulate their faith and then how to defend it when they are asked questions and confronted with opposition. It is not an easy or always comfortable battle but we must proceed nevertheless.

Chapter 15

Know how to help others become mature disciples of Jesus Christ*[268]

Imagine with me for a moment that you have developed a process whereby you can profitably mass produce "begollies." A begolly is an item that will very quickly become a necessary household item and will be in great demand in the near future. You carefully design each machine so that when they are all working together the begollies will come off the end of the production line made, assembled, packaged and ready for shipment. Now you determine that to operate all the necessary machinery, oversight, etc. you will initially need 163 people so you go out, interview and hire the necessary 163 people. Finally the great day for opening your factory has arrived. You gather all the people in one place, explain what a begolly is, why every household needs one and what specific tasks you want each person present to perform. After a rousing motivational speech, you send them off to get started on this new wonder tool. Everyone cheerfully moves to their assigned place only to discover that no one has trained them in how to operate their machine or run their department. What do you think would happen? Yes, you would have pandemonium.

In the same way, you cannot gather a group of people week after week and motivate them to see the importance of "making disciples" and getting them stirred up to go and do it and then not provide them with the training and skills necessary to carry out their task. Yet this is where the modern church finds itself. We are long on verbal motivation but almost totally lacking in helping our people learn how to be discipled and then in turn disciple another.

WHAT IT MEANS TO "HELP OTHERS BECOME MATURE DISCIPLES OF JESUS CHRIST?"

1. It means that you know how to "follow-up" a new believer. This can be likened to becoming a new parent. Having a new baby is a life-changing experience. You have gone through nine months of anticipation and growing physical discomfort. Finally the day comes when the delivery happens and everyone rejoices when the baby is healthy and well. People may bring in meals, showers happen and people show up to share in the excitement. But eventually life settles back into a normal routine and you are left with the unobserved and difficult task of helping this new life begin to grow to adulthood. Gone is the glamour, the anticipation, the accompanying attention. Now it is the routine of feeding, changing diapers, washing clothing, saying "No," getting up in the middle of the night, talking them for walks, shots, etc. If all it was ended at the excitement of the birth, the new baby would die for a lack of attention and love. But the same thing ought to be true of a "spiritual birth." However, that is not the case in the normal American church. We welcome the new family member, shout or sing at their baptism and then somehow hope that they will keep attending

church or get involved in some kind of small group or serve on some committee and trust that somehow they will come to maturity.

But following-up a new believer is like being a new parent. It means making the time to help them learn what has happened to them, to teach them how to pray, how to establish some kind of devotional life that will enable them to hear God's voice and follow it. There is plenty of material available to help a person do this, but helping someone become a mature disciple starts here.

2. It means knowing how to meet with another person to help them grow to maturity. There are differences of opinion as to when "follow-up" ends and "discipling" begins. Actually it is like moving from infancy into pre-school, there is no definite line. Waylon Moore writes, "All that is done in the life of the believer to bring him to spiritual maturity and Christlikeness is New Testament follow-up."[269] But the emphasis here is on the ongoing need to walk with a new believer for an extended period of time to help them become established in their new life and then to help them learn how to do the same thing with another believer. The length of time this is necessary is dependent upon the individual's background. Jesus spent between two and three years with the twelve men that he trained for ministry. But this involved extended exposure as they spent long hours together in ministry, in walking, in conversation and in personal time with them. This is not the same kind of exposure we can have in our modern day culture but it gives us some idea as to how long it takes to adequately work with a person to enable them to become mature disciples.

3. It means being willing to invest yourself in the life of another. When one becomes a parent, you do so with the realization that before you are finished with the task of parenting, it will take at least 18 years which will include countless hours

of conversation, coaching and mentoring and just being available to teach skills and give wisdom. This is called "investing" oneself in the life of another. We enter into parenthood assuming that we are willing to do this. When one begins the task of helping another person come to maturity in Christ, it involves the same kind of dedication and commitment. We often don't think about this but this is the only way maturity comes. It is something that needs to be seriously considered because this is not some kind of casual program, it is an in-depth, one-on-one relationship in which one person literally gives away a part of their lives to enable another to grow to maturity in Christ.

When Paul wrote to the Thessalonians he said, "As apostles of Christ we could have been a burden to you, but we were gentle among you, like a mother caring for her children. We loved you so much that we were delighted to share with you not only the gospel of God, but our lives as well, because you had become so dear to us."[270] He likened his relationship to them as that of a mother investing her life in her children. When he wrote to the Galatians he said, "My dear children, for whom I am again in the pains of childbirth until Christ be formed in you."[271] When he wrote to the Corinthians he said, "Even though you have ten thousand guardians in Christ, you do not have many fathers, for in Christ Jesus I became your father through the gospel."[272] He saw his task as that of a parent who is willing to invest his life in their children to see them come to maturity. He understood the principle of giving away one's life to save it and so he wrote, "...death is at work in us, but life is at work in you."[273] In order for life to grow to maturity, it takes the death of another, the investing of one's life in the life of another. There is no other way that life and maturity happens.

WHY THIS IS AN IMPORTANT SKILL TO POSSESS

There are at least three reasons why this is a crucial skill for a person to have learned.

1. This is what we have been called to in Christ. Robert Coleman in his excellent book, "The Master Plan of Evangelism" writes, "The Great Commission of Christ given to His Church is summed up in the command to "make disciples of every creature." (Matt 28:19) The word here indicates that the disciples were to go out into the world and win others who would come to be what they themselves were - disciples of Christ. Their mission is emphasized even more when the Greek text of the passage is studied and it is seen that the words, "go," "baptize," and "teach" are all participles which derive their main force from the one controlling verb, "make disciples." This means that the Great Commission is not merely to go to the ends of the earth preaching the Gospel (Mark 16:15), nor to baptize a lot of converts into the Name of the Triune God, nor to teach them the precepts of Christ, but to "make disciples"- to build men like themselves who were so constrained by the commission of Christ that they not only followed, but led others to follow in His way. Only as disciples were made could the other activities of the commission fulfill their purpose."[274]

The modern day church embraces many fine and wonderful activities, Vacation Bible School, Sunday school, small groups, parenting seminars, men's and women's retreats, specialized classes and seminars for a wide variety of purposes. All of these are well-intentioned programs or ministries, but the thing to which Jesus called us was to "make disciples." And how do we do that? The same way Jesus did with the men he trained. When he gave them the Great Commission referred to above, he did not have to give definition to the word "disciple." They knew it because He had trained them to become disciples. Jesus had spent those hours with them training and walking with them and in that process they were becoming mature disciples. When the Holy Spirit came at Pentecost, the power necessary to do what they had been trained to do was made available in and through them. The process was complete. Now they had the power and the pattern and the methodology necessary to undertake what they had been commanded to do. All that was necessary was to start and they would discover in the process the strength and wisdom necessary to complete the task.

Developing this skill in believers is essential if we are to take seriously what Jesus commissioned the church to do. Therefore, this is crucially important for both individuals and the larger, corporate church to both focus on and then do.

2. The modern day church has moved away from this as her primary focus. In his book, "With Christ in the School of Disciple Building" Carl Wilson spends an entire chapter walking the reader through the history of the church to describe how and where we lost this emphasis and methodology.[275] He says it came about because of 1) a vacuum of authority that came when the original apostles had died and the church developed an authoritative New Testament canon to replace them; 2) the indifference of second and third generation Christians; and 3) the rise of four different movements, each with its own emphasis, a) Gnosticism with its emphasis upon special knowledge and learning, b) Montanism with its emphasis upon emotional experiences, c) Clericalism with its tendency for a religious elite, and d) Sacramentalism with its increasing and deadening emphasis upon ritual and ceremony; and 4) Evangelism without adequate discipleship training. He then proceeds to describe

the modern day church where we see the same conditions and emphases.

The modern day church has to some degree lost touch with her original heritage and has rather evolved into a more culturally friendly organization. Nancy Pearcey in her book "Total Truth" describes how the modern American church has evolved into what she has now become.[276] Her analysis helps the reader understand where the issues we are now facing have come from. The modern day church follows far more the modern day organizational thinking that she does the thinking of Jesus. We have developed boards and committees out of necessity and our thinking has come because her main boards are occupied by well meaning women and men who live everyday in the corporate world of modern business. When they make their decisions and develop their plans and objectives in their local churches, they naturally use the thinking processes they bring with them from the corporate world and thus we have moved away from the simple model that Jesus both used and set before his disciples.

This is seen most pronounced in the life style and training of the modern pastor. In seminary he is given classes on Christian education, counseling skills, scriptural exegesis, preaching and techniques of administration that are necessary for running the modern church organization. He is not trained in how to disciple men and women to maturity in Christ. My own training stands as a testimony to this lack. I was a two-year old Christian when I entered seminary. I had been trained as a physicist and a mathematician and so I had to take some additional humanities and history classes to round out my education. Thus it took me four years to complete my seminary education. During those four years the only time any professor invited me into his office was to help me put together my class schedule — one time. One of our professors invited his class over to his home for dinner one evening but beyond that, not one teacher ever took a personal interest in me or went out of his way to help me grow in my walk with Christ. It was an academic experience all the way through. It was not until after I had graduated and begun pastoral ministry that I was confronted with my lack of knowledge in this area. A man who had given his life to Christ at the conclusion of a Sunday morning service called me on Monday morning from his office to set up an appointment for lunch the following day. During lunch, he asked me, "Okay, now what do I do?" I asked him, "Do about what?" He said, "Now that I have started this new life, what do I do next and how do I proceed?" I was dumbfounded. The question had never crossed my mind as to how to answer that. It caused me to quickly scurry about and finally I contacted the Navigators about what to do to follow up a new believer. They sent me their catalog of materials and I ordered every reel-to-reel tape they had (17 in all), and some books. I listened to every tape, read every book and started on a wonderful journey of discipling men that has revolutionized my ministry and the lives of a number of men over the years.

If we are to reclaim the vitality and the world-changing dynamic of the early disciples, we must go back and re-examine the methodology of Jesus and the early disciples. Then we can discover anew the reason for their impact.

3. This is the best way to live your life. In his book, "Disciples Are Made, Not Born" Walt Henrichsen describes what happened to him while he was in college. He wrote, "As I continued my study (to become an engineer), I became even more discouraged. I read, "But godliness with contentment is great gain. For we brought nothing into this world, and it is certain we can carry nothing out. And having food and raiment let us be therewith content" (1 Tim 6:6-8). This picture emerged: I

come into the world empty-handed; I build bridges and dams; God follows behind and burns them down; and when I leave the world, I leave it empty-handed. What a depressing scene!

"So I prayed, 'God, I don't want to give my life to nothing. Why pour 70 years into something and then discover You will burn it, and leave me empty-handed.'"[277] He did some biblical research and discovered there are two things that will not pass away: people and the Word of God. He changed his focus and spent the rest of his life giving away his life to other men to help them come to maturity in Jesus Christ.

My personal story parallels that very closely. I was designing microwave radar antennas as a research engineer when I became a Christian. I continued my work but an unrest began to grow in my heart. One day I was reading in 2 Peter 3:10 where he writes, "But the day of the Lord will come like a thief. The heavens will disappear with a roar; the elements will be destroyed by fire, and the earth and everything in it will be laid bare." One part of a radar antenna system is called the "element" and when I read that the elements will be destroyed by fire it caused me to take notice. I had seen that by the time you design an antenna and get it off the production line for sale, it was already obsolete. Now I realized everything I was going to do was going to be burned up with fire. I started asking the question, "Is there some way that I can give my life to something that will not be destroyed?" I came to the same conclusion Henrichsen did. There are two things that exist forever, people (everlasting life) and the word of God (Isaiah 40:8). I asked God if there was some way I could spend my life putting the word of God into the lives of men and God opened the door for me to seminary and a ministry where I could spend my life helping people get the word of God into their lives. One does not have to go to seminary to be able to do that as in some ways it can be done more effectively by laymen and laywomen individually with other individuals.

This is best done in one-on-one relationships with other people. In his book "The Seven Habits of Highly Successful People" Steven Covey quotes Daj Hammarskjold, past Secretary General of the United Nations as saying, "It is more noble to give yourself completely to one individual than to labor diligently for the salvation of the masses." He recognized that the greatest way to make an impact with one's life is to give it away to individuals who will be changed and do the same for another. J. Oswald Chambers says, "Disciples are not manufactured wholesale. They are produced one by one, because someone has taken the pains to discipline, to instruct and enlighten, to nurture and train one that is younger."[278]

One day I had a successful executive come to me and say, "Don, I am at a place in my career where I have more discretionary time than I have had before. I would like to know where you could use me in the church." What he was asking is was there a committee or board where he could serve in which he could use his business training to make a contribution. I said to him, "The best way you can make an impact for the kingdom of God is to learn how to invest your life helping a younger believer come to maturity." I went on to explain to him what I meant and how that could be done. He had never heard of that before and so he agreed to start meeting with me individually for a while so I could help him learn how to do it. As I walked him through the same process he could use with others, he caught the vision for doing this and continues to do it now, years later. Someday he will stand in God's presence and hear Him say, "Well done, good and faithful servant...." It will not be because he served on boards or committees but because he made a conscious choice to invest his life in individual men.

HOW TO DEVELOP THIS SKILL:

1. It begins with realizing the necessity of doing this. Until we become convinced that this is what Jesus intended His followers to do and the way that He intended them to do it, we will never take seriously His mandate to "make disciples." Until we see that this is the most effective way of reaching all the nations with the message of the kingdom, we will keep trying to devise "newer and better" ways of doing what we have been told to do. Until we return to the methodology that Jesus used in bringing His immediate followers to maturity and training them to do likewise we will continue to "do church" and try to be "relevant" with whatever the latest gimmicks and techniques there are that are used to reach the masses.

When God spoke to Israel through Isaiah, He said, "Since you are precious and honored in my sight, and because I love you, I will give men in exchange for you and people in exchange for your life. Do not be afraid for I am with you; I will bring your children from the east and gather you from the west. I will say to the north 'Give them up!' and to the south, 'Do not hold them back. Bring my sons from afar and my daughters from the ends of the earth — everyone who is called by my name, whom I created for my glory, whom I formed and made."[279] God is making a promise to His people that because they are important to Him, if they are willing to give their lives for the nations, He will give them people from all the points of the globe who will become their sons and daughters. It is these people who have been created for His glory. God makes the same promise to us today that if we are willing to exchange our lives for the lives of others, God will use that "death to self" to literally reach around the world and bring in a harvest of people that will bring Him glory.

Until we see that this is God's promise to His people and that the result of giving up our lives by giving them away daily to walk with and train individuals we will never discover the impact that one life can make upon the course of the world we live in. As long as we continue to look to move large crowds and generate large statistics we are continuing to give away our lives in vain. Robert Coleman says, "Jesus was not interested in the multitudes, but in men who could reach the multitudes" and until we grab hold of the same vision, we will never choose to invest our lives in this way.

2. We need to revise our definition of success. As you read the current Christian periodicals and review the literature that comes out for various seminars held for "successful" churches, you come to the realization that modern "Christian success" is determined by size. Often accompanying the advertisements is the phrase, "Our keynote speaker is ————. His church has grown from 250 to 6,000 in the last —years" or something similar. This is repeated so often that a person comes to the conclusion that success is determined by the outward growth of one's public ministry. The pastors who are interviewed or featured in many periodicals are the ones who pastor the "mega-churches" and the not-so-subtle message that is communicated is that bigger is better and that success is the ability to gather large numbers of people together in one place.

Carl Wilson writes, "The task of building disciples takes longer, is more demanding, and is harder to publicize and sell. People are more impressed with statistics on evangelism than with those on disciple building. Statements such as "We had five hundred at a meeting and eighty made decisions," or "We personally talked to one hundred people and twenty made decisions," are more exciting than, "In the last three months I have spent several hours daily working with ten boys." It is more dramatic to have a baby than to care for a child. But the former is tragic without the latter. The former gives little satisfaction to the parent without the latter. While some may not be easily impressed with disciple building, it pleases Christ to see His children walk in obedience. It should also please Christ to see His children walk in obedience. It should also please Christians. (2 John 4; 3 John 4)[280]

We need to revise our definition of "success" to include this aspect of one-on-one discipleship. The issue is not how many you can count, but how effective we have been in discipling and training those individuals that God has brought our way personally. Coleman writes, "His (Jesus') whole evangelistic strategy - indeed the fulfillment of His very purpose in coming into the world, dying on the cross and rising from the grave - depended upon the faithfulness of His chosen disciples to this task. It did not matter how small the group was to start with so long as they reproduced and taught their disciples to reproduce. This was the way His Church was to win - through the dedicated lives of those who knew the Savior so well that His Spirit and method constrained them to tell others. As simple as it may seem, this was the way the Gospel would conquer. He had no other plan."[281] This is hard work and not always outwardly visible for its initial investment but it reaps the greatest harvest if it is carried through to completion.

3. <u>Make the time available.</u> This kind of life investment takes time and unless we are willing to invest the time necessary for real life change to happen, we will soon become discouraged and think there is some better way to give away one's life. When you "disciple" another it means that you will make yourself available to them 24/7 if they need

the attention. In the same way that your children need your attention at some of the most inopportune times those you are working with will require the same thing. They may hit a snag at work, or in their marriage or other relationship. They may be facing depression or discouragement or the loss of a job or spouse. They may be having a hard time making financial ends meet or making a decision. They need to know that they can call or drop in and that you will make time for them. This has to be done within the right priorities but this kind of availability needs to be there and can not always be scheduled. After all, being a parent is not always the most personally convenient thing — but it is crucial in the child's maturity.

4. Be willing to be a friend. Even though you are considered the "mentor" or "discipler" there must be an equality in the relationship that is found in true friendship. Despite the fact that one person is leading a second one through a part of the process of growth, both of them are growing — just in different areas and probably at different speeds. This means there is a mutuality that exists between the two of them. There needs to be an openness in which both are free to share personal struggles, issues they are wrestling with and needs they wish the other to pray for. Without this mutual openness there will not be an atmosphere of growth from which they both can benefit. If the older person has any kind of an attitude of superiority, it will destroy the kind of relationship necessary for true growth to maturity. This is one of the keys to successful discipleship.

The Christian Herald once carried an article about a senior executive of one of the largest banks in New York. He told how he had risen to a place of prominence and influence. At first he served as an office boy. Then one day the president of the company called him aside and said, "I want you to come into my office and be with me each day."

The young man replied, "But what can I do to help you, sir? I don't know anything about finances." "Never mind that, you will learn what I want to teach you a lot faster if you just stay by my side and keep your eyes and ears open!" "That was the most significant experience of my life," said the now-famous banker. "Being with that wise man made me just like him. I began to do things the way he did and that accounts for what I am today." It is this kind of friendship and vulnerability that enables both of them to grow in Christ.

5. Have a plan. Although some of the discipleship process can never be planned for in advance because of unforeseen issues that will crop up as the relationship deepens, it is good to have a basic plan in mind when one starts discipling another. Part of that plan ought to include the items laid out in this book. In his book, "Disciples Are Made — Not Born" Walter Henrichsen has four chapters devoted specifically to suggested content for doing this kind of discipling: How to Train A Disciple in 1) Follow-up; 2) Imparting the Basics; 3) Conviction and Perspective; and 4) Gifts and Calling. In another book, "The Dynamics of Personal Follow-Up" Gary Kuhne in Appendix 1 gives very detailed plans for ten meetings with a new believer following their decision.[282] In his book, "With Christ in the School of Disciple Building, Carl Wilson spells out seven steps which he believes Jesus took the disciples through and give ideas about how to follow-through with another person using these steps. They are:

1. Repentance and faith
2. Enlightenment and guidance
3. Ministry training and appreciation of benefits
4. Leadership development and government under God
5. Reevaluation and separation

6. Participation and delegation
7. The exchanged life and worldwide challenge[283]

Other authors have given us other different "steps" in a progression to help based upon what they see as of first importance, second importance, etc. A tool that I have found to be extremely helpful is "Lessons on Assurance" and "Lessons on Christian Living" that are available from the Navigators. These are a series of thirteen "fill-in-the-blank" lessons that deal with many of the basic issues of the Christian life. It provides material for at least thirteen sessions and working through these lessons together gives an opportunity for you to build the relationship and develop an atmosphere in which you can learn to share your hearts together built around some lessons. There are verses to be memorized that correspond with each lesson and it gets the person started hiding God's word in their heart.[284]

Related to the plan is the realization that often times the assigned study needs to be set aside for a time of personal sharing and just plain talking. Things will come up in the person's life that are more demanding than the particular lesson you will be working through and thus the lesson needs to be set aside so the issue can be dealt with. Remember: the issue is helping a person grow to maturity, not completing a given set of lessons in a specific time.

6. Take someone along with you when work with another person. In Mark 3:14 we read, "He appointed twelve — designating them apostles (sent ones) that they might be with him and that he might send them out to preach." Jesus called men to be "with him" before he asked them to undertake any kind of ministry. The reason he did this was he realized that skills are better caught than taught. He planned that they would learn all they needed to know simply by being "with him" and watching him

carry on ministry. This is the best way to help someone develop this skill.

A few years ago I was discipling a young man. We were meeting together doing Bible study and sharing with one another. There was a man who had recently given his life to Christ and needed some initial follow-up. I made an appointment with him and took the young man I was working with along with me. We arranged our schedules so that all three of us could be there at the same time. We met in the new believer's home. As Kirk watched me go through "Lessons on Assurance" with Tom, he saw what could be done and how to do it. Kirk went on to eventually go half time with his job and half time with a Christian organization that focuses on discipling students on a local college campus. Eventually he left his secular job altogether and started working full time for a local church doing discipleship with other new believers. It all started simply because I took him along with me when I met with Tom and gave him the understanding of what needed to be done and the confidence that he could do it.

7. Pray. Spiritual growth is a work of the Holy Spirit. We have the privilege of being involved as well. Somehow as we meet together, sharing our hearts, doing Bible study and ministry together, God uses those times to enable others to grow. So we need to develop a prayer list for the specific person we are working with and bring their needs and requests before God. As we pray God give us insights into issues the person is working through and sometimes enables us to see things that we would not have seen in any other way.

CONCLUSION

"Through careful follow-up, a child of God is guided into spiritual maturity. The goal of follow-up in the church is to have every believer walking in obedience to the Word and in victory. This work must be started by those who are mature, the pastor and church leaders, and be expanded until at last every member is actively participating. Leaders must have parent-hearts, and put into effect a program of individual follow-up that provides love, food, protection and training to the immature and to the new babes."[285]

Diagoras, the Rhodian had, in his time, won many wreaths at the Olympian games. He had two boys and he brought them up to the same profession. The day came when he was no longer able to strive for the victory himself, but he went up to the Olympian games with his two sons. He saw the blows they gave and received and rejoiced when they both came out victorious. Another man said to him, "You may die now, Diagoras." The old man seemed to feel the same way for his two sons came to him and put him on their shoulders and carried him through the great assembly to the cheers of those gathered there. The old man was so taken with excitement that he died under the eyes of those who were assembled. He had successfully completed his task.

Someday each of us will stand before our Lord and give an account of what we have done with the commandment He gave us to carry out. Those who have faithfully shared their lives with others to enable them to grow in their walk with God will have the privilege of hearing Him say, "Well done, good and faithful servant" You have been faithful with a few things; I will put you in charge of many things. Come and share your master's happiness."[286] Then we will know that all the time and energy we have invested has been worth it. All because we have developed the skill of helping others become mature disciples of Jesus Christ.

Chapter 16

How to Develop Skills
in People

In Chapter 9 I defined skills in this way: *An ability to do some action well so you can perform it easily and accurately*. We have looked at six skills that I believe are essential if a person is to consider themselves as a mature disciple. When describing each skill we looked at some specific ways of developing that particular skill. In this summation to Section 2 of the book, I would like to review some of those and give a general, over-all description of the best ways to develop skills in people.

1. Through reading about and listening to people who have these desired skills. Sometimes in skill development one of the initial ways of developing them is to hear a person who has the desired skill talk or lecture and describe how they do a certain thing. The same can be said for reading books or testimonies written by people who have developed that skill in their lives. For example, there are many seminars offered by churches who have been effective in building large churches. If that is an ambition that you have, one of the ways to develop the skills to be able to do that is to attend

these seminars and then go back home and attempt to duplicate them. You have exposed yourself to someone who has been affective in developing the skill you desire to have and you have gained from their experience.

There are many wonderful biographies written by godly men and women that describe how they carried out various areas of their lives. For example, if a person wants to learn how to become a person of effective prayer, reading a biography of George Mueller would be a good place to start. If you wanted to learn how to multiply yourself by making disciples, the biography of Dawson Trotman would be a good biography to read. You can also purchase from Campus Crusade for Christ or the Navigators and other organizations many wonderful tapes or CD's that describe how to do various areas of ministry effectively. Listening and reading give you insights into how other people have developed these skills and then it will be left for you to take their examples and try them out in various situations in your own life. This will enable you to learn by experimenting which can be very rewarding as you make mistakes, learn good principles and become more adept at developing that particular skill.

2. Develop workshops for each of these desired skills. Workshops are environments where you are not only taught how to do it but are given opportunity to "practice" the desired skill in a safe and controlled environment. For example I once purchased a tape entitled "The Art of Small Talk." It was a good tape on developing skills in the area of interpersonal relationships. Realizing that some of our people were not at ease in the presence of other people for a variety of reasons, I decided to develop a six-week workshop designed to help people feel more at home talking with strangers and others in their lives. I broke the tape into six sessions and then developed worksheets for

each session. During the session we would listen to a portion of the tape, then there would be a time for questions and answers and then I would put them either one-on-one or in a small group of 3-4 people with specific assignments of things to talk with each other about. For some people it was a very difficult time as they had never had anyone explain to them how to do this. But through the course of the workshop, they began to relax and by the time we finished, even though it was still a little fearful, they were more adept engaging in this kind of conversation.

Campus Crusade for Christ developed a workshop entitled the "Lay Institute for Evangelism." It was a three day training seminar to help people learn how to share their faith using "The Four Spiritual Laws." It was an excellent training tool to help people develop the skills necessary for personal evangelism and raise their confidence level as well. The Navigators had an excellent taped workshop on helping people put together their personal testimony. Many other organizations have similar kinds of tools they have developed to help us develop specific skills in the lives of our people.

One of the best ingredients in any kind of workshop is role-playing. This is where you demonstrate a desired skill in front of the group and then either enlist someone from the group to repeat the exercise or you turn them face to face with each other to "practice" with someone else who is going through the same skill-development workshop. It gives them experience in actually doing the desired skill in a safe environment and gives them confidence knowing that they have done it once or twice. Therefore they feel more at home with it.

3. Apprenticing another. This is probably the most effective way to develop skills in another person. An apprentice is someone who works alongside of an experienced person to watch what they

do in an environment where they can observe and ask questions. When Jesus called his disciples, one of the things he said was, "Come, follow me and I will make you fishers of men."[287] Notice, he took the responsibility for making them fishers of men. Their responsibility was to follow. He knew that by following him around, watching what he did and how he did it, listening to him talk and interact with people they would see and learn how to fish for men. He assumed the role of a mentor and they took the role of an apprentice.

Mentoring (apprenticing) is the most effective way of helping people develop skills. There is not the possibility of misunderstanding either what the expectations are nor how you want the job done. By watching and working alongside of another you can have first-hand knowledge of how to do the job as well as the privilege of having someone critique and guide you as you develop the necessary skills.

In Christian maturity, the same holds true. There is nothing more valuable than having someone who has walked with the Lord for a long time walk with you and help you develop the skills that they have learned through those years. It gives you a chance to interact, observe, ask questions and respond to another who is a little farther along the process than you are.

Many people feel very inadequate having someone look to them as mentors because they do not feel that they have matured to the place where they are ready to have someone else observe them that closely. But this is the same way we all felt when God gave us our first child. The only thing most of us knew was the parenting we had received as a child growing up in our home, and for many that was not the best environment. But ready or not, the child came and we could not wait until we felt adequate. We simply knew that we were older than this baby and therefore we started doing what we knew to do. Naturally, we made mistakes along the way but we assumed that we understood life, God, and principles of living better than they did and so we started. The same is true of mentoring a new or younger believer. We assume that none of us has it all together, but we are farther along than some others and all we are asking them to do is to walk with us for a while as we mentor and share what we have learned with them.

When Paul was writing to the Corinthians, he told them he was writing to them as their spiritual father. As such, he felt no embarrassment to say to them, "Therefore I urge you to imitate me."[288] He could say that because as he wrote later in this letter, "Follow my example, as I follow the example of Christ."[289] He reiterated the same concept when he wrote to the Philippians. He said, "Whatever you have learned or received or heard from me, or seen in me — put into practice. And the God of peace will be with you."[290] These are not the words a person with a strong ego saying that he is better than anyone else, they are simply the heart of a man who understands what mentoring through a good example is all about and recommending that people follow his example as he tries to follow the example that Jesus set before him.

Each of us as believers who have walked with the Lord for a while ought to be able to say to someone who is newer or younger in the faith, "Let's get together for coffee or lunch or for dinner at my home" and offer them the opportunity to walk with us for a while as we help them grow to maturity in Christ. It may begin with nothing more than meeting regularly to share the contents of our quiet times or daily Bible reading and then sharing prayer requests. There are plenty of materials available to help us in that process and you can locate such through denominational publishers or para-church publishers.

Section 3

Knowledge

Chapter 17

What is meant by Knowledge?

As we move into the third section of the book, "Knowledge" we need to understand what this is and why it is important. The dictionary defines knowledge as "acquaintance with facts, truths, or principles, as from study or investigation." I would define it: *"Knowledge is a working familiarity with certain information and facts that can be applied to everyday situations."* There is a danger in certain kinds of accumulated knowledge because as Paul warns us, "Knowledge puffs us."[291] He is not saying a lack of knowledge is preferable but rather that if we accumulate information for information's sake we can become proud because of the amount knowledge we have amassed. But certain kinds of knowledge are essential if we are to be mature believers.

A few years ago we purchased a good used pickup truck. It had been previously owned by the daughter of the service manager of an auto dealership and so it had been maintained very well. Because I was new to the vehicle there were some things that I didn't understand about it. I took it back to the dealership to ask about a CD player that I did not know how to work. After the manager explained it to me, he pointed out that the owner's manual was in the glove compartment and that perhaps it would be good if I took time to familiarize myself with it. When I got home, I took the manual and sat down to read it. I was amazed at some of the features the truck had that I was unaware of. I kept saying to myself, "I didn't know that" as I read it. I had been driving the truck without being aware of some features that made operating it much easier and better. I discovered that it is true, "You cannot operate on what you do not know."

We have heard the old maxim, "Ignorance is bliss." There is only one problem with that statement, it is not true. Ignorance can be dangerous and even fatal on occasion. Therefore if we are going to be complete in our definition of a mature disciple, we must think about the information we want them to have in order to be able to live adequately. In explaining why many believers fail to live the new life that is theirs "in Christ" Miles Stanford says, "The most prevalent factor is that many Christians do not know the truth concerning their union with the Lord Jesus in His death, burial, resurrection and ascension."[292] What he is saying is that a major reason people live such anemic spiritual lives is that they do not know who they are in Christ and what the resources are that have been made available to them now that they are "in Christ."

The apostle Paul shares his concern. Numerous times in his writings he uses the phrase, "Do you not know….."[293] to try and answer a question he has raised or to deal with a situation he is addressing. What he is doing by asking that question is helping them to see that the answer to what they are going through comes from something that they ought to know but don't. That is why he is writing this particular thought in the letter. For example, when he writes to the Romans he writes about the extensiveness of God's grace. (Rom 5:20-21) He says, "But where sin increased, grace increased all the more."[294] Then he anticipates that someone will think about that and come to the conclusion, "Since the greatness of God's grace is seen when He forgives sin, it makes sense that if I want people to see His grace in action, I should sin in even greater ways." But he realizes that there is a fallacy in this kind of logic and that fallacy comes from the fact that the person coming to that conclusion does not understand a certain piece of information. So he writes, "We died to sin; how can we live in it any longer! Or *don't you know* that all of us who were baptized into Christ Jesus were baptized into his death?"[295] He then goes on to explain (Romans 6:4-11) that far from purposely sinning that grace might abound, when we became Christians we actually died to sin's power over us because were made partakers of His resurrection power. Since we have died to sin's power, how can we even think about continuing to sin and in so doing give God a chance to display His grace? For him, the solution to their question is to give them knowledge of what happened when they were justified by faith in Jesus' sacrifice on their behalf.

You cannot operate on what you do not know! Paul understood this and proceeded to give them some additional knowledge they needed that would enable them to come to a greater maturity than they had currently attained.

But what does a disciple need to know to grow to maturity? That is the question before us. To answer that I will set forth the following six things I believe a person needs to know if they are to become "mature in Christ." They need to know:

* Who they are "in Christ"
* Basic Christian doctrine
* Their unique temperament and gifting
* A general overview and understanding of the Bible
* What a Christian worldview is

* 54 verses of scripture from memory that teach these 18 areas of maturity we have been defining

Chapter 18

Who we are "in Christ"

One of the things I enjoy doing is amateur photography. The freedom that the new digital cameras give allows me to take as many pictures as I like without costing me a small fortune to get them all developed. In order to increase my ability to manipulate the pictures, I purchased a special program that will enable me to do that. When I installed it, I realized it was so complex that it would be good for me to purchase an additional book so I went out and purchased one of the "...for Dummies" books. As I started reading and trying it on the computer I realized there was much more to the program than I had ever imagined. I discovered that I can do many different manipulations I never knew were possible. If I had not purchased the companion book, I would probably never have known what I could do and would have never used the program to its maximum potential simply because I did not know what I had.

The same thing is true when a person becomes a Christian. The moment we invite Jesus to become our Lord and King and entrust our lives to Him, two things happen to us instantaneously. They are not necessarily accompanied by any emotion but may be as well. But the presence or lack of emotion or feelings has nothing to do with the two changes that have taken place.

1. The first thing that happens is that Christ comes to live in us. Jesus said, "Whoever eats my flesh and drinks my blood remains in me, and *I in him.*"[296] This is not a reference to communion or the Mass because that had not been instituted when the Lord said this. Rather is a statement that refers to the indwelling presence of Jesus in the believer. He would later say, "Because I live, you will live also. On that day you will realize that I am in the Father, and you are in me, and I in you."[297] He went on to say, "If anyone loves me, he will obey my teaching. My Father will love him, and *we will come to him and make our home with him.*"[298] Paul wrote, "...Christ in you, the hope of glory."[299] And again, "I have been crucified with Christ and I no longer live, but Christ lives in me. The life I live in the body, I live by faith in the Son of God, who loved me and gave himself for me."[300] There are numerous other references as well but they all teach the same thing: when I invite Jesus Christ to become my Lord and King, in a way we don't fully comprehend, he comes to live inside of me.

We can't totally understand the process nor do we comprehend all of the implications but it is a supernatural work done in such a way that my physical body becomes the residing place of the living God. Paul refers to the believer's body as the "temple of the Holy Spirit"[301] How to distinguish between God the Father being in us (John 14:23), Jesus the Son being in us and the Holy Spirit being in us is an impossible task for the human mind but it is true nevertheless. Being a Christian means having the living God dwelling inside your physical body and living His life out through that body. It is an amazing reality!

2. The second thing that happens is that God places us "in Christ." This is a term describing a

new relationship with God or what some call a "new position." This term "in Christ" is used 85 times through the New Testament and is the most common description of a believer that is found. This is an act that is so fundamental yet revolutionary that it alters everything about a person except perhaps the temperament or social style with which we were born and the body in which we live. Because it is so revolutionary it is important that a believer understand this new position or else they will be like me trying to use a new software program that I don't understand. They will continue living this new life without understanding the extent of the transformation that has taken place or the resources that have become available to them. This results in anemic and ineffective lives.

WHAT IT MEANS TO BE "IN CHRIST"

"In Christ" is the main term in the New Testament that describes what it means to be a Christian. Paul says, "Therefore, if anyone is *in Christ*, he is a new creation; the old has gone, the new has come."[302] The word "new" here refers to a new substance and means "of a new kind, unprecedented, novel, uncommon, unheard of." They are a completely new entity. But from what perspective? They still have the same body, they think the same thoughts, their temperament has not significantly changed. Sometimes there has been a major change in certain habit patterns or responses to life. So in what sense are we a "new creation?" We are new in the sense of our position before God. Before becoming a Christian I was a member of the human race who had inherited the genes from my parents and along with that a sinful nature that insists on wanting its own way. God looked at me not as one of His children but as a self-willed human being trying to live his life by his own wits and cleverness. I may have even been religious but that religion was mostly of my own making with some biblical or "religious" ideas and concepts thrown in. As such I was trying to somehow earn God's favor by my own effort and as a result was dead in my "transgressions and sins in which you used to live when you followed the ways of this world and the ruler of the kingdom of the air, the spirit that is now at work in those who are disobedient."[303]

But when a person comes to see that this is a dead end street and does not work, the realization comes that the only way life works is if I invite Jesus to become my Lord and King. He made that possible through his death on the cross. This death was responsible for cleansing away the things that had kept me from knowing God all along. When this is done a person goes from being in the position of a "created human being" to being in the position of being a "child of God." I go from being an outsider to being a member of God's family and that makes all the difference in the world.

Perhaps the best illustration of this is to think about the position of an adopted child. When a child is put up for adoption, it means either the natural parent or parents are dead or that for some reason they do not think it is in the child's best interests for them to raise him. Another family, for whatever reason decides they want to adopt a child. They begin a search and locate the child that is looking to be adopted. After going through all the legal process necessary for the adoption, the child is placed in the custody of the adopting family. On the day the adoption is final, the law begins to look upon the adopted child in exactly the same way it looks at a natural child that has been born into the family. Legally, it is as if the adopted child has been "born again" only this time into a new family. Now he is "in the family" and has the same position as that of a natural born child. He has the same legal rights in every way as any natural children. In short, he is in a new position with all the benefit and rights that this new position brings.

Paul uses this word analogy when he writes, "In love he predestined us to be *adopted* as his sons through Jesus Christ, in accordance with his pleasure and will…"[304] When he writes to the Romans he says, "For you did not receive a spirit that makes you a slave again to fear, but you received the Spirit of *adoption*. And by him we cry, "Abba Father." The Spirit himself testifies with our spirit that we are God's children."[305] And when he writes to the Galatians he says, "But when the time had fully come, God sent his Son, born of a woman, born under law, to redeem those under law, that we might receive the *full rights* of sons. (adoption as sons) Because you are sons, God sent the Spirit of his Son into our hearts, the Spirit who calls "Abba, Father." So you are no longer a slave, but a son; and since you are a son, God has made you also an heir."[306] All of these verses speak to the fact that believers have been "adopted" into God's family. It means that prior to being adopted no one in the whole human race was a part of His family but when God put them "in Christ" they became a part of His family. Before that moment, God was not their Father but when they were adopted, their immediate response was to cry out, "Abba, Father." Being adopted into the family means that before the transaction they were simply slaves with no inheritance or rights but once they were adopted into His family, they became joint heirs with Christ, being in the position to inherit everything that God's only "natural" Son inherits.[307]

This means that the adopted person has been placed under a new "head." Adam is the first "head" of the human race. Since we are all descended in one way or another from Adam, he is the head of our natural heritage. When he sinned, he sinned as our "head" and as a result we all were affected by his sin. We "inherited" a sinful nature as a result of what he did. Through Adam sin entered into the world and death and condemnation followed not only in his life but in the lives of every descendant save one from that time until this.[308] Because he was the head of the human race, it affected every human being born from that day on. This is because we were "in Adam." The Jewish people considered that whatever happened to the one through whom they were descended happened to them. When Christ comes in, He becomes our new "head" and whatever has happened to Him has happened to us as well.

The author of Hebrews makes this argument when he is writes to demonstrate that the priesthood of Jesus is greater than that of Aaron, Israel's first high priest. He uses as his example, Melchizedek, the king of Salem and a priest of the Most High God.[309] When Abraham was returning from defeating Kedorlaomer and the kings who had united with him (Gen 14:1-20) Melchizedek, king of Salem, came out to meet him. He brought out bread and wine and blessed Abraham and Abraham gave him a tenth of everything he had taken in battle. Because the Levitical priesthood had not yet been established but because he was directly descended from Abraham through Isaac, and then Jacob, the writer said that Levi was "in Abraham." What he meant was that because Abraham as the "head" did what he did and because Levi was "in Abraham" therefore Melchizedek is greater than Levi because "in Abraham" he offered the sacrifices and tithes. This is referred to as "identification." It means that what happens to the head or representative happens to those descended from the head. It is somewhat like the hometown people cheering for their local football team. If the team wins the game, the people of the town say, "We won" even though they did not play in the game. The players were acting as their representatives so that when the team won, they won. They "identify" themselves with the team.

When God places us "in Christ" Jesus becomes our head or representative. If He wins, we win. When He died on the cross, we died (Gal 2:20). When he was buried, we were buried (Rom 6:3). When he rose from the grave because we were in him, we rose from the grave(Rom 6:4). When he ascended to be seated at the right hand of the Father, we rose with him and are seated at the right hand of the Father (Eph 2:6). This explains why Paul sees the believer as already "glorified" (Rom 8:30 — the verb "glorified" is in the past tense indicating that it is something already past — we were pre-destined, we were called, we were justified and so we were glorified). Why is this so? Because God put us "in Christ" and whatever happened to Him has happened to us because he is the head of a new race of people called Christians. Just as we were once "in Adam" with all that being descended from him brings to us, so now we are "in Christ" with all that this new relationship brings with it.

Watchman Nee writes, "Many a time when preaching in the villages of China one has to use very simple illustrations for deep Divine truth. I remember once I took up a small book and put a piece of paper into it, and I said to those very simple ones, 'Now look carefully. I take a piece of paper. It has an identity of its own, quite separate from this book. Having no special purpose for it at the moment I put it into the book. Now I do something with the book. I post it to Shanghai. I do not post the paper, but the paper has been put into the book. Then where is the paper? Can the book go to Shanghai and the paper remain here? Can the paper have a separate destiny from the book? No! Where the book goes the paper goes. If I drop the book in the river the paper goes too, and if I quickly take it out again I recover the paper also. Whatever experience the book goes through the paper goes through with it, for it is in the book."[310]

This is what it means to be "in Christ." It means that God has placed us "in Christ" upon our regeneration and that being in Him means that what position He is in, we are in also. The ramifications of this truth are far reaching in terms of their implications.

WHY THIS IS IMPORTANT

1. We need to learn to see ourselves from God's perspective. This is especially true for those who became Christians as adults or for people who were raised in difficult environments where parents or other significant people in our world ingrained in us a poor self-image. When Paul wrote to the Corinthians, he told them, "Therefore, if any is in Christ, he is a new creation; the old has gone, the new has come!"[311] This means more than just having our sins forgiven. It means that we have become entirely new entities. That means we need to begin looking at ourselves from a new perspective. If, as referred to above, God sees the believer as already glorified, I need to begin to look at myself as already glorified.

The Emancipation Proclamation, issued by Abraham Lincoln on January 1, 1863, during the American Civil War, declared that all "slaves within any State, or designated part of a State … then … in rebellion, … shall be then, thenceforward, and forever free."[312] Thus these slaves were no longer simply pieces of property, they were free people with all that that implies. Yet for someone who had been born a slave, raised a slave, worked as a slave they had seen themselves as a slave all their lives. It would take time before a person who had grown up to see themselves in that way could change the way they looked at themselves. But it would begin by starting to see at themselves as free people. It would also take more than a century for others who were not slaves in their world to see them differently as well — but it would have to begin by their change of self-perception.

The same is true of the believer. To someone who has been raised to look at themselves as "stupid" or "foolish" or worthless or unable to do anything significant it requires time for them to begin to see that this self-perception is wrong. We are "new creatures" in Christ and we need to begin to look at themselves from God's perspective with all that this new position implies. If a person is ever going to become mature in Christ, they need to learn how to see themselves in Him.

2. When God placed us in Christ, He gave us everything we need. Paul says, "For in Christ all the fullness of the Deity lives in bodily form and you have been given fullness (πληροω pleroo - to render full, to complete, to fill to the top: so that nothing shall be wanting to full measure, fill to the brim) in Christ, who is the head over every power and authority."[313] The KJV translates this as "Ye are complete in him..." It means that in Christ we have everything we need, we have been filled with full measure of His presence and power. Peter puts it this way, "His divine power has given us everything we need for life and godliness through our knowledge of him..."[314] This means that "in Christ" there is nothing we lack that is necessary for us to be all we have been recreated to be.

From time to time there are people and movements that come along that state that your rebirth or conversion is not enough. In order to really have power, you need to have a second experience or encounter or knowledge before you can fully experience the abundance of the Christian life. This comes from an improper understanding of what it means to be "in Christ." Either a person has been made complete in Christ or they have not. Either they have everything they need for life and godliness or they do not have it. It is not a matter of not having all of it because all of it comes when

God places me in Christ. The issue is not whether or not I have everything I need but it is a matter of seeing all I have and then learning how to "reckon" on that and live my life accordingly. I do not need a second experience and nowhere in the New Testament are believers commanded to seek such an experience subsequent to the outpouring of the Spirit on the Day of Pentecost. The reason some in the book of Acts had a subsequent experience was because they had not been fully taught concerning who they were in Christ. It was not because they were lacking part of their full salvation. All of God's Spirit comes to indwell an individual when they become Christians.

3. It enables us to do battle with Satan. Satan is a deceiver and the methodology he employs is deception. He is the one who will come to us and suggest that we have committed some sin that is so great that perhaps God has not forgiven it. He is the one who comes and reminds us that we are failures. He is the one who comes and tries to tell us that what we are doing is really so insignificant that maybe we should invest our energy elsewhere. He is the one who comes and says to us, "Who do you think you are? Look at your background. You can't do that. You are so unworthy that you can never do that." All of these are true — if how we see ourselves is still in Adam. I have been a failure. I am unworthy. My little bit does appear to be insignificant. But I am no longer in Adam. I am now in Christ. In Him I have been totally forgiven. In Him I can do all the things that God sets before me to do. In Him I know that my labor is not in vain regardless of how insignificant it might seem to the world around me.

It is in reminding Satan of what is true of me in Christ that I am able to do spiritual warfare and thwart the "accuser of the brethren."[315] The primary way that I do my daily battle with the enemy is by reminding myself and Satan that "...though we live in the world, we do not wage war as the world does. The weapons we fight with are not the weapons of the world. On the contrary, they have divine power to demolish strongholds. We demolish arguments and every pretension that sets itself up against the knowledge of God and we take captive every thought to make it obedient to Christ."[316]

WHAT IS TRUE OF US "IN CHRIST"

The following is a brief summation of those things that are true of <u>every believer</u> in Christ:

* We will never face condemnation. (Rom 8:1) Our forgiveness is so complete that we will never have to see or face our sins again.
* We are a "new creation." (2 Cor 5:17; Eph 2:10) The person I was before in Adam has been undone and God has made me a totally new creation.
* We have died with Christ. (Rom 6:5, 8 — past tense) To die means for something to lose its power. It means that the power that something held over my life has been crucified, it has lost its power. I have died to the following things:
  a. To sin — Rom 6:2
     1) We are dead to sin but alive to God — Rom 6:11
     2) We have been "set free" from sin — Rom 6:22
  b. To the Law — Rom 6:14; 7:1, 4, 6
     1) We have been set free from the demands of the Law — Gal 2:4
* We have been raised with him from our death (Rom 6:4; Col 2:1-2 - this is past tense).
* We have been "made alive" (Rom 6:11; Col 2:13 — this is past tense). This made alive comes because the Holy Spirit has come to dwell in

us and has given us a new life that we did not have before.

* We "will be" united with him in his resurrection. (Rom 6:5) One day we will experience the same kind of physical resurrection that Jesus did because we are in him. (1 Cor 15:22)

* We are no longer slaves to sin. (Rom 6:6) Because we have died to sin which held us captive in Adam our bondage to sin has been broken. A person who has died is no longer affected by the laws that once controlled them. (Rom 7:1)

* We are sanctified. (1 Cor 1:2) To be sanctified means to be set apart from ordinary things to be used only for a special purpose. Our lives are no longer "common" but God has set us apart for a special role or calling in life.

* We have been sealed with the Holy Spirit. (Eph 1:13-14; 2 Cor 5:5) This is a seal that God puts on each believer that only He can undo. His seal is eternal.

* We have been adopted as sons. (Eph 1:5) God has done the adoption therefore it will not be undone. It means that we are "joint-heirs" with Jesus so that everything he inherits we will also inherit.

* We are "complete" (πληροω pleroo). (Col 2:10) There is nothing we lack to be able to function effectively and be "overcomers" in our faith.

    a) We have been given "every spiritual blessing" in Christ. (Eph 1:3)

* We have been given the ability to understand the mystery of God's will. (Eph 1:9) A person cannot understand this without divine revelation but In Christ God has opened our eyes and enabled us to see and understand things

we could never comprehend while we were in Adam.

* We have been raised up and seated with Christ in the heavenly places. (Eph 2:6) This speaks to the issue of authority since God has seated Christ at His right hand and put all things under his feet. (Eph 1:19-23)

* We have the promise that God will supply our every need. (Phil 4:19) In the same way that the Father supplied Jesus with everything he needed, He will supply our need in the same way.

* We have been circumcised (past tense and passive meaning some one else did it to us) with a circumcision not made with human hands. (Col 2:11) This is an Old Testament concept of having a heart that is circumcised and speaks to an entirely new nature that God changes the believer into.

* We can "stand firm." (2 Cor 1:21) This is a present tense verb which indicates something that is ongoing. To "stand firm" means "to make firm, establish, confirm, make sure" and indicates that in Christ God will continually give us the strength to enable us to stand and withstand anything that will come our way.

* We have found our righteousness in Christ. (Phil 3:9) Righteousness refers to the state of being in a right standing before God. In Philippians 3:7-11 Paul describes how as a Jewish Pharisee he had tried to earn his standing before God but found that he could not do it. When he came to Christ, he realized that Christ had died to atone for his sin and that righteousness could only be found in Christ, not his own effort. This gave him a wonderful sense of release and peace because he could stop trying to earn something that could never be earned.

* We have been given an "upward call." (Phil 3:14) This speaks to the issue of signifi-cance and purpose. In Christ God has given us an "upward call" to live out in our lives and the living out of that call we will dis-cover the purpose for which we have been created and find the satisfaction that comes from knowing that there is a purpose for my life.

This is not the total statement about our posi-tion in Christ but from the above list, you can understand why it is so important that a believer know who they are in Christ. There is confidence and assurance that comes from knowing this and gives us a true picture or who we really are from God's perspective.

WHAT WE CAN DO TO GAIN THIS KNOWLEDGE:

There are two essential things we can do to acquire this knowledge and one skill we need to develop to help us apply it.

1. Do a Bible study on the "in Christ" passages. This not only includes the phrase "in Christ" but also other "in" statements as well. These include "in the beloved," "in him," "in me," etc. The fol-lowing passages would be a good place to start:

John 14-16
Romans 5-8; 10:11
1 Corinthians 1:5, 30; 15:18-24
2 Corinthians 1:20; 2:14-17; 5:17-21
Galatians 2:16-17; 3:26-28
Ephesians 1:3-20; 2:6-13; 3:6, 11, 21
Philippians 2:5; 3:9-14; 4:7, 13, 19
Colossians 1:16-19, 28; 2:9-11
1 Thessalonians 4:16
2 Timothy 2:1; 3:12, 15

This may not be an exhaustive list but it is a good place to start. As you do the study, focus on what it says about our position in Christ. Make a list of everything that it says are true about you now that you are in Christ. As you do that, you will be impressed with you will discover and it will begin to enable you to see yourself as God sees you in Christ.

2. Read books that deal with this topic. There are a number of excellent books that deal with this subject and I have included many of them in the bibliography. There are two especially that stand out to me. The first is "The Normal Christian Life" by Watchman Nee. When I left the engineering field to go to seminary, a friend gave me the book. I was about three years old in the Lord when I worked as a lifeguard for the summer in my hometown and because some days my job quite slow, it enabled me to work my way through the book slowly. The book revolutionized my life in terms of understanding and the way I looked at myself. It helped me see I truly was in Christ and it started me on the road to changing the way I saw myself and who I was in Christ and what was available to me as a result of that. I cannot recommend this book highly enough.

The second book is "The Complete Green Letters" by Miles J. Stafford. It is a pulling together of five small books he had written into one volume and is a very practical book in terms of helping a person gain a grasp of who we are in Christ and how to realize that in our everyday lives. It is divided into five parts: 1) Principles of Spiritual Growth; 2) Foundations of Spiritual Growth; 3) The Ground of Growth; 4) The Realization of Spiritual Growth; and 5) A Guide to Spiritual Growth. It will help the reader catch a fresh glimpse of who they are in Christ and how to make that real in your Christian life.

3. A person needs to learn how to "reckon" the things that are true into their lives. Reckon is

the Greek word λογιζομαι (logizomai) and it is a mathematical accounting word. It means "to count, compute, calculate, count over." It can best be understood by use of an example. Recently we sold a house that we owned in northern California. When the sale was complete and recorded, the title company transferred by wire a sum of money to my bank account. They notified me of the transfer and when I went online to check the truth of what they had said, I found that the exact amount they told me had been credited to my account. Now I was faced with a decision. I had not handled the money nor endorsed a check nor had I even seen it being transferred. All I had to go on was the word of the title company and what my online bank information had told me. Was it there or wasn't it? There was only one thing to do: I had to begin to treat that money "as if" it were there even though I had not seen it. When I started doing that, I discovered that what I had been told was true even though I had not seen nor felt anything with its transfer. This is called "reckoning." It means that I took the information I had received to be true and acted on it. In the acting on it I discovered that what I had been told was true. That's what it means to reckon.

If we are going to become all we are in Christ, we have to "reckon" that what we are told is true. Then we need to be living by faith in what is true and move ahead "as if" what God says about us is true. When we do that, we discover to our amazement that what we have been told is true of us in Christ is really true. Only then do we begin to see we really are "new creations" and that in fact the old truly has passed away. This is living at its highest.

CONCLUSION

We have seen what it means for us to be "in Christ" and what some of the ramifications of that are. We have seen why it is important that we know what we are in Christ and exactly what some of the things that are true of us in Christ really are. Now we need to search out these things for ourselves, become convinced of the truth of that and then reckon ourselves to indeed become all that we are.

Chapter 19

They Know Basic Doctrine

The second thing that a mature believer needs to know is certain basic doctrines which will form the basis of their lives and ministry. The reason why this is such an important area of focus is that the damage that can be done in a person's life when they lose the truths upon which life is built is disastrous and sometimes fatal. An illustration of that is an article that appeared a while back in *Redbook* magazine. The publishers hired one of the top pollsters in the nation to survey a full representation of our seminaries which are supposedly preparing men for Christian service in the Protestant churches. Here are some of the results: Of the ministers in training, 56 percent rejected the Virgin Birth of Jesus Christ. 71 percent rejected that there was life after death. 54 percent rejected the bodily resurrection of Jesus Christ. And 98 percent rejected that there would be a personal return of Jesus Christ to this earth. When this happens in the pulpit, the destruction that occurs in the pew is devastating.

WHAT IS MEANT BY DOCTRINE:

The word translated "doctrine" in the New Testament is the word διδασκαλια (didaskalia). What it means is "teaching, instruction, that which is taught, doctrine." It is from the root word διδασκαλοῶ (didaskalos) which means "in the NT one who teaches concerning the things of God, and the duties of man."[317] It is used to describe the basic truths that are foundational to Christianity.

In Paul's thinking, there was a set of teachings or information that he was concerned about getting his listeners and readers to understand. When he wrote to Timothy he said that the law was good for helping people settle on "sound doctrine."[318] He told Timothy that there was a time coming when people would forsake good doctrine and thus he should give himself to the teaching of "good doctrine."[319] He also warned him to "watch your life and doctrine closely."[320] The doctrine that he was to teach was found in the divinely-inspired scriptures that had been given to him. This would help people be fully prepared for the good works God had called them to.[321] Paul was also concerned that the people in positions of leadership in those early churches are able to instruct and exhort others by using sound doctrine.[322] His concern was that the doctrine "not be slandered"[323] but rather that they "may adorn the doctrine of God our Savior in all things."[324] Timothy and Titus were young men that Paul had discipled and nurtured so his exhortation to them was deeply concerned that they both hold to and teach good doctrine because he knew it would form a lasting foundation in people's lives.

This doctrine Paul had passed on to his followers had come to him by special revelation from God and thus was to be maintained and passed on with great care. In Galatians 1:11-24 he describes how this revelation came to him and what he did after he had received this. In 1 Corinthians 2:6-16 he writes about how the Holy Spirit searches the mind of God and then comes and reveals it to man so that we can have a sure word that we can build on. Then when he writes to Timothy he says that "All scripture is inspired by God (God-breathed) and is useful for teaching, rebuking, correcting and training in righteousness, so that the man of God may be thoroughly equipped for every good work."[325] Peter confirms this when he writes, "Above all, you must understand that no prophecy of Scripture came about by the prophet's own interpretation. For prophecy never had its origin in the will of man, but men spoke from God as they were carried along by the Holy Spirit."[326] Then he tells them that some of these Scriptures are hard to understand and as a result some people distort them to their own destruction.[327]

Before proceeding we must remember that there are three different kinds of truth: 1) *Research truth*. This is the kind of truth that comes because we observe, study, do investigation and write down what we discover to be true. We start this as infants and follow it all the days of our lives. 2) The second kind of truth is *reasoned truth*. This truth we discover because we take the research truths we have found and use that as the basis for conclusions we can come to as a result of logically thinking and reasoning with them. We use inductive and deductive reasoning skills to arrive at additional truths. 3) The third kind of truth is *revealed truth*. This kind of truth can not necessarily be known by research or reasoning. It can only come if someone chooses to reveal something to you that you could not otherwise know. This is primarily the area of personal things although it can relate to other things as well. For instance, how do we know that murder is wrong? We could study and research it and come to conclusions about the damage it does and then try to prevent it from happening by passing laws, using police force, etc. But the only way we know it is wrong is because God revealed to us that it is sin and by inference that it is wrong. The doctrine we are thinking about in this chapter is teaching coming from the truths revealed in Scripture that we could not otherwise know either by research or reason.

WHY DOCTRINE IS IMPORTANT

1. It builds a strong foundation When Paul wrote to the Ephesians he wrote about the fact that they were "built on the foundation of the apostles and prophets with Christ Jesus himself as the chief cornerstone."[328] He was writing not only about the men themselves but about the teaching ministry they had been called to. He also told them that if the church was functioning as God designed it to function, that they would "no longer be infants, tossed back and forth by every wind of doctrine and by the cunning and craftiness of men in their deceitful scheming."[329] Good doctrine forms the foundation upon which we build a strong individual and church. Although a person might not understand every implication of the basic issues, they will have a solid structure upon which to build further growth. Without a strong foundation, people are easily led astray as history amply illustrates. As C. S. Lewis writes, "Doctrines are not God: they are only a kind of map. But that map is based on the experience of hundreds of people who really were in touch with God."[330]

2. It moves people on to maturity. The writer of Hebrews was greatly disturbed at the immaturity of those he was writing to. He wrote, "We have much to say about this, but it is hard to explain because you are slow to learn. In fact, though by this time you ought to be teachers, you need someone to teach you the elementary truths of God's word all over again. You need milk, not solid food! Anyone who lives on milk, being still an infant, is not acquainted with the teaching about righteousness. But solid food is for the mature, who by constant use have trained themselves to distinguish good from evil."[331] He desired to help them understand

some "deeper things" but was unable to because they had not yet grasped some of the basics. My son is a high school mathematics instructor and one of the things that is difficult for him is having to deal with students who did not grasp certain things when they were younger and thus were unable to go on into trigonometry and geometry in the later years.

Without having a good foundation it is impossible to help a person move on to maturity but if they have learned to grasp certain fundamental things then they can go on to grow ever deeper in their understanding and in their walk with the Lord.

3. There is a natural tendency to move away from absolute truth. History records repeatedly the move away from truth to apostasy. There is something about the natural mind that causes it to be easily moved away from holding revealed truth to moving toward philosophical reasoning which takes it increasingly away from truth. The writer of Hebrews wrote, "We must pay more careful attention, therefore, to what we have heard, so that we do not drift away."[332] When Jesus confronted the Pharisees and teachers of the law, he quoted Isaiah 29:13 to explain this very kind of drift. He said, "They worship me in vain; their teachings are but rules taught by men."[333] He was pointing out the tendency to substitute man made rules and insights for the revealed word of God and to build intellectual systems upon that rather than strong doctrine.

When Paul wrote to the Colossians, a people he had never visited but who he had learned were starting to drift away from the basic truths of Christianity, he wrote, "Since you died with Christ to the basic principles of this world, why, as though you still belonged to it, do you submit to its rules: "Do not handle! Do not taste! Do not touch!"? These are all destined to perish with use, because they are based on human commands and teachings. Such regulations indeed have an appearance of wisdom, with their self-imposed worship, their false humility and their harsh treatment of the body, but they lack any value in restraining sensual indulgence."[334] This tendency is always away from revealed truth. It is evidenced in the so-called "Ivy League" schools. Each of them was founded upon strong biblical principles but now many of them have slipped into disbelief. Harvard permitted freedom in matters of theology and made no religious requirement of college officers; Yale drifted partly in concern for academic excellence amidst an environment of agnosticism and unitarianism; Dartmouth and Columbia only had a statement in its charter about the great principles of Christianity and morality in which true Christians of each denomination are generally agreed. It had no strong statement of faith. Princeton yielded because of pressure from alumni. Princeton's charter insisted on a saved faculty, but did not require this of its students. As time went on there were more and more non-Christian alumni who could give or withhold donations, it finally succumbed to their demand for a voice in the management and educational policies with the result that they moved away from the foundation upon which they were built. Each of these schools drifted from the foundation on which is was laid and allowed themselves to be taken in by other philosophies because they did not lay down and keep a strong doctrinal foundation.

Toronto-born Dr. Charles Templeton, a man who was a graduate of Princeton Theological Seminary and at one time drew crowds of 40,000 people as an evangelist. When he left his calling and became a television producer he gave the following as his explanation: "If you're going to preach effectively," said the 42-year-old Templeton as he left for Rome and Cairo to secure personality interviews for TV, "you have to have conviction. My convictions as to some aspects of Christian doctrine have become diluted with doubt. I don't say I'm right and all others are wrong. But feeling as I do, I could not go on in the ministry. So I left."

"The decision to change my vocation was a slow and painful one," said Templeton. "I could continue to preach, with mental reservation, or accept the alternative and leave the ministry. It became clear to me that I had no other choice."

This is a natural tendency of the human heart and an inclination that is in the heart of every believer. In order to deal effectively with that predisposition, one must set down certain basic doctrines as true and from which you determine not to waver.

4. There is coming a time when there will be a wholesale move away from revealed truth. Paul especially writes to Timothy about this coming day. He writes, "The Spirit clearly says that in the later times some will abandon the faith and follow deceiving spirits and things taught by demons. Such teachings come through hypocritical liars, whose consciences have been seared as with a hot iron."[335] He writes in 2 Timothy, "For the time will come when men will not put up with sound doctrine. Instead, to suit their own desires, they will gather around them a great number of teachers to say what their itching ears want to hear. They will turn away their ears from the truth and turn aside to myths."[336] All one has to do to see that this is true is to study church history and you will discover that this has been the natural tendency from the beginning.

There is only one thing that will sustain a person who will be tempted to move with the majority at such a time as this and that is the foundation that sound doctrine brings. Unlike research truth and reasoned truth which continues to change as new discoveries are made, revealed truth does not change and thus to find stability in one's life there must be the basic structure of sound doctrine.

5. Sound doctrine brings hope. A *Peanuts* cartoon pictures Lucy and Linus looking out the window as a steady downpour of rain. "Boy," said Lucy, "Look at it rain. What if it floods the whole world?"

"It will never do that," Linus replied confidently. "In the ninth chapter of Genesis, God promised Noah that would never happen again, and the sign of the promise is the rainbow."

"You've taken a great load off my mind," said Lucy with a relieved smile.

"Sound theology," pontificated Linus, "has a way of doing that!"

Linus was absolutely right, sound doctrine brings hope and stability to a person's life. When Paul wrote to the Romans he said, "For everything that was written in the past was written to teach us so that through endurance and the encouragement of the Scriptures we might have hope."[337] Again, as he was writing to Titus to describe for him the kind of leaders he should look for to bring strong leadership and stability to the church, he said, "He must hold firmly to the trustworthy message as it has been taught, so that he can encourage others by sound doctrine and refute those who oppose it."[338]

THE DOCTRINES THAT SHOULD BE TAUGHT

The following is a list of the doctrines that I consider important enough to form the basis for teaching people. The list is not complete and only contains a brief description of each doctrine along with some Scripture to validate it. The reader is encouraged to fill this out in whatever way is beneficial to those you are leading.

1. The Bible

The Bible is the book out of which all the other doctrines come. For a person's belief system to be strong, it begins with the right view of the Bible and its authority.

    a. It's inspiration.

        1) Revelation. Revelation is the manner in which God made known His mind to men. He revealed certain things that we could never discover or reason to on our own. (1 Corinthians 2:6-16)

        2) Inspiration. Inspiration is the way that God worked so that the authors wrote down what had been revealed accurately from His mind. (2 Timothy 3:16-17; 2 Peter 1:20-21)

        3) Illumination. Illumination is the way that the Holy Spirit enables those who read the Bible to understand precisely the way God intended it to be understood. (1 Corinthians 2:12; 1 John 2:27)

    b. Its eternality. The Bible is eternal and eternally true. Other ideas and philosophies will come and go but the word of God remains fixed eternally. (Isaiah 40:6-8; Psalm 119:89)

2. God

    a. Existence. God is the only uncreated being in the universe. He does not owe His existence or power to anyone other than Himself. (Genesis 1:1; Exodus 3:14; Isaiah 44:6)

    b. Trinity. God exists as three Persons yet there is only one God. This is true because there are three Persons in the Bible who are referred to as God and yet there is only one God. (Matthew 29:19; 1 Corinthians 12:4-6; Ephesians 4:4-6)

c. Sovereignty. For God to be sovereign means
that He is in absolute control of the universe He created.

Because this is true, He can do whatever He wills.
(Psalm 115:3; Isaiah 14:24-27; Daniel 4:35)

3. Jesus Christ

a. Deity. Jesus Christ is God in the flesh. He
is as fully God as He was before He became
man. (Matthew 1:22- 23; Philippians 2:5-11;
Colossians 2:9-10)
b. Humanity. Jesus Christ was fully human yet
without the sin nature inherent in man. He
faced the same temptation Adam did in the
Garden of Eden. (Philippians 2:6; Colossians
2:9; 1 John 4:2)
c. Ministry. Jesus was clear about the primary
reason for His incarnation. He came to be
the perfect sacrifice or atonement for the
sins of man. (Matthew 1:21; Luke 19:10; 1
Timothy 1:15)

4. Holy Spirit

a. Personality. The Holy Spirit is a Person in
the same sense that any other person is. He
is not an "it" or a "ghost." He is a person
who thinks, feels, and has a will. Jesus
referred to Him as "he." (John 14:26; 16:7-
15; Romans 8:15-16, 26-27)
b. Deity. The Holy Spirit is referred to as God
and is given the attributes and abilities
that only God has. (Acts 5:9; 1 Cor 2:9-11)
c. Ministry. His primary ministry is to glorify Jesus, to bring about the new birth in
the lives of people and to teach and comfort
those who are believers. (John 3:5; 14:16;
16:7-11)

5. Creation

   a. How creation occurred. God created the uni-
      verse which we observe. He spoke what was
      invisible into visible existence. (Genesis
      1; John 1:3; Colossians 1:16; Hebrews 11:3)
   b. How it is sustained. God created the uni-
      verse and built it on certain laws that He
      alone fully knows. He uses these laws to sus-
      tain the universe. (Colossians 1:17; Hebrews
      1:3)

6. Fall

   a. Man in his original state. Man in his orig-
      inal creation was created without sin. As
      such there was unbroken fellowship with God
      and unlimited use of his created facilities.
      (Genesis 2:15-25)
   b. The Fall. When tempted in the Garden Adam
      succumbed to the temptation and as a result
      he was cast out of the Garden. (Genesis 3:1-
      19; Romans 5:12-19)
   c. Man as a result of the Fall. His fellow-
      ship with God was broken, sin entered into
      the human race and every part of his cre-
      ated being was affected. (Genesis 3:16-19;
      Jeremiah 17:9; Romans 3:9-18)

7. Redemption

   a. How it was accomplished. Jesus Christ ful-
      filled every demand of the Law and as a sin-
      less sacrifice gave His life as a ransom for
      the sins of man. (John 3:16; 2 Corinthians
      5:14-15; Ephesians 1:7)
   b. How it undoes the Fall. When a person is
      redeemed his relationship with God is
      restored, his sins are forgiven and he can
      begin to recover those things that were lost

due to the Fall. (Romans 5:12-19; 8:9-11; 2 Corinthians 5:17)

c. How it is received. Man is given this redemption as a gift to be received by faith. It cannot be earned by any religious ritual or good works. (Romans 1:17; 4:1-25: Ephesians 2:8-9)

8. Future Things

a. The Second Coming. Jesus Christ ascended into heaven following His resurrection with the promise that one day He would return to earth. (Matthew 24-25; Acts 1:10-11; 1 Thessalonians 4:13-18; Revelation 22:12)

b. Judgment. Every human being will be held accountable for their lives. There will be two judgments, the Judgment Seat of Christ for believers and the Great White Throne Judgment for unbelievers. (Romans 14:12; 2 Corinthians 5:10; 2 Timothy 4:1; Revelation 20:12)

c. Heaven & Hell. Just as there are two judgments, there will be two real, literal destinations. Heaven is the destination of believers and Hell is the destination of unbelievers. (Matthew 6:9; 1 Thessalonians 1:10; Matthew 5:29; 2 Peter 2:4)

HOW THESE DOCTRINES ARE ACQUIRED:

1. By the proper training of pastors and teachers. When Paul was describing the kind of men he looked for in those who would be involved in leadership, he wrote, "He must hold firmly to the trustworthy message as it has been taught, so that he can encourage others by sound doctrine and refute those who oppose it."[339] Many of the modern seminaries are changing their curriculum to train future pastors to be professional leaders of orga-

nizations, teaching them the principles of church growth and church management rather than helping them become people who focus on teaching sound doctrine. The result is church leaders who see themselves as CEO's rather than men who "Preach the word; be prepared in season and out of season, correct, rebuke and encourage — with great patience and careful instruction."[340] We need to challenge our seminaries to train people who can become people of the word, teaching sound doctrine and knowing how to instruct people in doctrine rather than knowing how to manage the modern church organizations whose origins are in the business world model rather than in the word of God.

2. Teach sound doctrine from the pulpit and in the classroom. I would call pastors and teachers back to the art of dynamic expository preaching. Part of the direction of the modern church is toward religious psychology where we focus on people's emotional problems and give them the "how to" messages that are people-centered. When sound doctrine is properly taught and sound Biblical exposition is done, God by His Spirit uses that word to lay foundations for mental, spiritual and physical health that can not be laid in any other way. Paul's admonitions to Timothy and Titus can not be improved on and we do so to our own peril. If a person is gifted as a teacher, then they should teach (Romans 12:7). To see Paul's heart for this the reader is encouraged to read 1 Timothy 1:3; 4:6; 2 Timothy 2:15 and Titus 1:9 as well as the entire Pastoral Epistles.

This teaching can be done from the pulpit with good, strong biblical exposition. It can be done in smaller classroom settings where the content is teaching oriented and not just coffee/fellowship oriented with a little "lesson" thrown in. It can be done by teaching people good personal Bible study skills and enabling them to correctly interpret and apply the Scriptures for themselves.

Unless this is done, we will continue to set the stage for the cults to draw away our people by their appearance of being good Bible students.

3. Use well-designed Bible studies. There are valuable and excellent study materials available on the market that wrestle with solid doctrinal material and work to give the participants a solid biblical foundation for their faith. We need to train and qualify the small group leaders to be men and women who know how to understand and teach good doctrine so that when questions come up in discussion the people involved can be led to relevant sections of scripture that give authoritative answers rather than simply having everyone share their opinions.

Some of these materials are produced by denominational publishing houses or by others genuinely desirous of giving people a solid foundation. Through the course of my ministry I have used many different sources for this kind of study but the two places I keep coming back to are Intervarsity Press and NavPress. I have also greatly appreciated those publishers who are increasingly making the works of some of the Puritan fathers available for us in updated English language.

4. Help people learn how to "adorn" the doctrine. Paul wrote to Timothy and told him to admonish those who were living in slavery to live in such a way toward their masters that their lives would "not blaspheme" the doctrine of God.[341] When he wrote to Titus he admonished him in almost the same way to live in such a way that they would "adorn" (make attractive) the doctrine of God.[342]

What he is saying that there is more to doctrine than simply a body of information. The doctrine has significant implications for the way we live. It is not only something for our intellectual stimulation or to be used to win arguments, it is something to be lived out in our daily lives. Doctrine has applicational value and we need to teach it in such a way that people are challenged to go out and live their doctrine.

CONCLUSION

God wants His people who are mature to have a certain knowledge of doctrine and teaching. It is usually true that what we understand determines how we live and conduct ourselves in every day life. We need to help people become people who think deeply about the things of God and who come to some solidified conclusions about what they believe and who they are.

Chapter 20

They Know Their Unique Temperament and Spiritual Gifts

David was a young man with limited experience in the issues of warfare. When he came to the battlefront to bring the food from his parents for his brothers who were in the army of Saul, he had no idea that he would become involved personally. After watching Goliath put forth his challenge and then having seen the trembling response of the soldiers, he realized that God could defeat this giant with ease and so he asked the question, "Who is this uncircumcised Philistine that he should defy the armies of the living God?"[343] Saul recognized a man of courage and after talking with David realized that he might be the one who could defeat Goliath. Seeing that David was just a simple shepherd boy and that he had no armor with which to fight, he did what any good commander would do, he had him put on the "proper" coverings of protection. David felt obligated to try them on because, after all, what did he know about fighting a war? He had only fought against the wild animals who came to attack his sheep.

After trying on the armor of another, he realized that he could not do battle in another man's equipment and so he took it off and said, "I cannot go in these because I am not used to them." The rest is history. He went on to use the implements with which he was familiar and well practiced and went on to defeat Goliath and to win the victory for the "armies of the living God."

Even though he was young, David realized that he could not work effectively if he tried to be someone else or if he carried out his ministry wrapped in the dress and mannerisms of another. This is a lesson that a mature believer needs to learn early on or else they will continually struggle against the pressure, both internal and external to try and live life the way someone else does it. To do that a person needs to understand their own unique temperament, experiences and gifts or abilities.

WHAT IS MEANT BY THIS

It is said that there are no two snowflakes that are exactly alike. As a youngster growing up in southern Minnesota I had ample time to ponder that statement walking to and from school on cold, blowing days. Even though it seemed impossible, the "experts" said it was true and who was I to question their conclusions?

It is also true that there are no two sets of fingerprints that are exactly alike. And why is this so? It is true because that is the way God has made us. Each one of us are unique individuals, with different combinations of natural abilities, temperaments, learning styles, personalities, spiritual gifts, bodies and life experiences. Therefore if we are each one a unique creation, we need to not be afraid to honestly face that and sort through who we are and how we have been created so that we can find the liberation that comes from being free to become all that we have been created to be.

In Psalm 139, David wrote, "For you created my inmost being; you knit me together in my mother's womb. I praise you because I am fearfully and wonderfully made; your works are wonderful, I know that full well. My frame was not hidden from you when I was made in the secret place. When I was woven together in the depths of the earth, your eyes saw my unformed body. All the days ordained for me were written in your book before one of them came to be."[344] This is a statement of the wonder David felt when he meditated on the fact of God's superintending presence and ministry in his formation while he was still inside his mother's womb. Jeremiah felt much the same when he wrote, "The word of the Lord came to me, saying, 'Before I formed you in the womb I knew you, before you were born I set you apart; I appointed you as a prophet to the nations."[345] Isaiah also wrote, "Before I was born the Lord called me; from my birth he has made mention of my name."[346] Each of these men had come to the realization that God had created them uniquely even before their birth and had designed them for a special place in His purpose.

This is true for every human being. Since we each play a different role in God's divine plan it is important that we come to understand who we have been created to be and the role that we have been designed to perform. That way we can focus our time and energy in carrying out that role and not be detracted by trying to be someone else. Just like David realized he couldn't enter into battle in someone else's armor, we need to see that we will be most effective in life if we discover and acknowledge who we are and how we have been created. Then we can invest our lives in more specifically focused efforts so we can say with Jesus, when we face the end of our lives, "I have brought you glory on earth by completing the work you gave me to do[347]" and know we have lived out to the full our designed place in the economy of God.

WHY THIS IS IMPORTANT

Aside from the obvious implications from the above, this is important knowledge to possess for the following reasons:

1. Our ministry flows out of our being. In his book, "The Making of a Leader" Robert Clinton makes a strong case for this truth that what we do flows out of who we are.[348] This truth is emphasized in many books for a very obvious reason: Who and what I am determines what I will succeed in doing. In the activism of western civilization this does not appear so obvious but from God's perspective it is a crucial realization. To many in our culture personal worth comes as a result of achievement. To be successful in the work place or on the athletic field or in the halls of academia is said to bestow a deep sense of personal worth. So many people strive for personal achievements in these areas in an attempt to gain a sense of self-worth. Yet we know that our worth comes from the price God was willing to pay for our salvation. God made us in His image and because of that fact alone we have great worth. The way we acknowledge and enjoy that is by making what we do to be an honest expression of who we are, who we have been created to be. If this is not the case, then we can work and work and work at things in which we are not proficient or successful, and derive no joy or satisfaction whatever in the performance of the task. God never intended that to be the case.

God desires that what we do should flow out of who we are and who we have been created to be. Therefore, it is extremely important that we take the time necessary to evaluate our strengths and weaknesses, our innate capacities and the abilities God has bestowed on us, our temperament and our physical capabilities. To do this is the same thing that a good manager does when she surveys her resources before proceeding with a project to make certain she has all the personnel and equipment she needs to see the project to completion. If she does not, she is wise to either move in another direction or else reevaluate the project in its entirety before thinking about proceeding.

2. It keeps us from trying to be something we are not. Early in my walk with the Lord, I started reading Christian biographies. I had a fascination with what godly men and women had seen God do in their lives. I did it because I wanted to be used in every possible way I could with what God had given me and I felt that I could learn from them. Not having anyone who would mentor me and walk with me, I thought the next best thing to do was to see what other men and women had discovered about the ways of God. So while I was attending seminary and pastoring on weekends, I also read biographies. But an unexpected thing began to happen to me. The more I read, the more discouraged and unloved I felt. I was feeling like a failure in God's eyes and that I could never possibly measure up to what God desired of me.

But upon reflection, I discovered what the source of my feeling was. When I would read a biography of someone like George Mueller, I would use him as the standard for my prayer life. When I read the biography of John Wesley I would use him as the standard of for my open air witnessing. When I read the story of James Kennedy and Evangelism Explosion I unconsciously felt that he was the measuring stick for me in the area of personal evangelism. What I was really doing was building an ever-increasing model of the "ideal Christian" that was impossible for anyone to live up to. Then as I compared myself to this "idol" I always came out short and thus felt discouraged and guilty. It was not until listening to a message one day that I realized what I was doing and saw that God did not want me to be anyone but me and that the ministry that He would give me was one that was based upon who He had made me to be, not the composite I had erected from all these other men. When I finally faced what I was doing and gave myself to God just as I was, it was like getting out of prison. I realized that it was a prison I had built for myself and that the enemy used that impossible standard to keep me discouraged and down on myself. It was like someone said, "I was trying to play the piccolo in the tuba section."

God has created each of us uniquely and wants us to come to grips with who we are so that we can be satisfied with who He has made us. Then we can give Him all that we are for whatever ministry He has designed for us. When Paul wrote to the Romans, after his long presentation of who they were in Christ (Romans 5-8) he calls on them to "present your bodies as a living sacrifice."[349] Following that he tells them, "For by the grace given to me I say to every one of you: Do not think of yourself more highly than you ought, but rather think of yourself with sober judgment, in accordance with the measure of faith God has given you."[350] The word translated "sober" means "to put a moderate estimate upon one's self." The word translated "think" means to direct your mind seriously to something and so what Paul is telling them is that after they have given God their bodies and have begun the process of transforming their minds, they need to start thinking seriously about themselves, who they are and how they have been created. It is not specifically stated but to think "more lowly" of yourself is just as wrong as thinking "more highly" of yourself. By writing this, he is helping us understand the importance of honest self-appraisal. In fact Romans 12:1 begins the practical application of this letter and before he writes about loving one another and accepting one another, or anything else, he focuses on the necessity of a honest self-appraisal. God does not want us to be someone else. He created each of us uniquely and would want us to see that and come to the place where we can appreciate that and give thanks to Him for the wonderful way He has created us. When Paul wrote to the Corinthians he warned them against this danger of comparing ourselves with one another. He said, "We do not dare to classify or compare ourselves with some who commend themselves. When they measure themselves by themselves and compare themselves with themselves, they are not wise."[351]

3. Our greatest joy will come from being who we are and letting our service flow out of that. There is an interesting word play that is found in this regard. The Greek word that translates to "rejoice" is the word χαιρω(chairo). It is the word that means to rejoice, be glad, be joyful or to be full of joy. One of the derivatives of this word is the Greek word χαρισ (charis) which is the word translated by our English word "grace" and is used to describe the grace of God by which deals with us in ways we don't deserve. One of the other derivatives of that word is the word χαρισμα(charisma) which is the word "gift" and is used of to describe what we have come to call "spiritual gifts" (abilities given to believers by the Holy Spirit to carry out various forms of ministry).[352]

The conclusion of this brief word study is this: God by His grace (charis) gives us spiritual gifts (charisma) which, if used in the power of the Holy Spirit, will give us joy (chairo). When we carry out ministry by using the gifts that God has given us, we will find a deep sense of joy that cannot be found elsewhere. Opposite to that, when we carry out ministry in areas that we are not gifted, we will find that not only will the work become drudgery and tend toward discouragement and resentment but we will not see the results we would were we to function with the God-given abilities we have.

For these reasons it is very important that a mature believer discover their uniqueness as a person and come to embrace that as God's design for them. This will free them to be what they have been created to be and allow them to say "Yes" to areas of ministry for which they are gifted and to say "No" to opportunities that present themselves for that which they do not have the necessary abilities or temperament. It will enable the local church to stop comparing herself with other congregations and let the Holy Spirit develop in them the corporate uniqueness for which He has brought them together in that place.

HOW WE HELP PEOPLE DISCOVER THEIR UNIQUENESS

I am going to list six different tools or activities a person can use or engage in to help themselves come to grips with who they are and discover their uniqueness in Christ. This is not meant to be an exhaustive list but a starting point.

1. The use of spiritual gifts tests. A number of different publishing houses and denominational offices have developed a wide variety of written tests that a person can take that will help them narrow down the possible areas of gifting they may have. I would suggest going to your nearest Christian book store, or going online to locate them. There are a few of things to take note of as you use them. First, they tend to be academic. The end result of the test gives the person an intellectual list of some possible areas of gifting depending upon how they answered the questions. Second, each of these tests is based upon some conclusions the authors of the tests have arrived at prior to writing the test. They have each limited the number of gifts based upon their particular

theological conclusions about spiritual gifts. Some may say there are seven, others twenty one and these are based upon some specific conclusions they established before assembling the test. I do not say this to be critical but simply to point out the importance of understanding the underlying assumptions before using the tool. I recall taking a test that believed in a limited number of spiritual gifts. I came away from the test with the feeling that I did not fit the description of the gift I was "supposed" to have. I remember trying to force myself into the mould only to eventually realize the harm of what I was doing.

Thirdly, because they are academic they tend not to motivate people into ministry. I have found that giving people such tests gives them a certain sense of satisfaction with seeing how they gifted without necessarily moving them into some type of ministry as a result. They go forward from the experience with the thought, "I have the gift of mercy" and then they do nothing about it. Thus when you give or take these tests it is highly recommended that there be some immediate experience or ministry into which they can be placed that will allow them to experiment with and confirm the new information.

2. Construct a personal timeline. Clinton says, "A time-line is an important tool for analyzing the life of a leader, for it reveals the overall pattern of God's work in a life."[353] A time-line is simply the constructing of a visual picture of the experiences a person has gone through in their life time to help us understand how God has worked and to give the person a better general feel for how they have been made.

To do a time-line do the following:

* Draw a long line on a sheet of paper. It may take two or three pieces taped together before you finish

* Divide it into significant seasons
    Childhood; Grade school; High School; College, etc.
    Any other breakdown that seems significant to you
* Ask the following questions as you spend time with each individual section. Write them in the timeline where the sequentially occurred.
    What memories make me smile?
    What would I do over again if I had the chance?
    What got my attention so that I made a conscious change in my behavior or attitude?
    What memories stab my heart?
    Who has made a big difference in my life?
    Who has hurt or disappointed me?
* Review the lifeline and ask the following questions: (Write these on a separate piece of paper in journal-like form)
    Why do I remember that?
    What did I learn?
    How did it change my life?
* Now look for God in your past by asking the following questions:
    What part did God have in the season, event or relationship?
    What did I learn about Him?
    How is my life different?
* Take some extended time when you have finished and ask these questions:
    What does this tell me about the way God made me?
    What does this tell me about the way God has used me?
    Based on this how may God want to use me in the future?

Some people recommend getting a large sheet of cardboard and some small "Post-It" notes of different colors. Divide the sheet into the above mentioned sections and then place the different colored Post-It" notes in the sheet where the events occurred. This way you can easily recognize the different way that different people or events affected your life. This is a commonly used tool and others may have other ideas but this gives you a general overview of creating a time-line.

3. Determine your temperament or social style. There are many different kinds of temperament evaluators available. You can purchase the Taylor-Johnson Temperament Sorter, you can find someone to give you the MMPI (Minnesota Multiphasic Personality Inventory) or use the Meyers/Briggs test as well.

The one which I have found the easiest to use and interpret and then apply is what is called the "Social Style" inventory. It is found in a variety of forms (the DiSC profile, the animal evaluator — lion/otter/golden retriever/ beaver — Driver/ Expressive/Amiable/Analytical — etc.). These came initially from the research and work of David W. Merrill and Roger H. Reid in their book, "Personal Style and Effective Performance." They say "All people exhibit patterns of behavior that can be identified and responded to, and if we can describe and adjust to these behaviors, we can achieve more satisfactory relationships."[354] These behaviors are called "social styles" and can be measured and described. They are based on two different measurements. The first is "Less Responsive/More Responsive" and the second is "More assertive/Less assertive." A person who is a "More Responsive-More assertive" is called a *"Driver."* A person who is a "Less Responsive/More assertive" is called an *"Expressive."* A person who is a "More responsive-Less assertive" is called an *"Amiable"* and a person who is a "Less responsive-Less assertive" is called an *"Analytical."*

The reason this is such a helpful attribute to identify is that it describes with great accuracy how others see you respond in various social situations. Understanding this enables a person to determine ways to change their behavior to get different results out of certain situations. It develops "Versatility" which can be purposefully planned and executed. According to their research, a social style is something each individual is born with and will probably carry with them throughout their entire lives. The styles are neither good nor bad, they simply describe the way a person responds to life. To try and determine which style is better or worse is futile. But understanding this helps the individual and those around them to know how they will most likely respond to life situations unless they make a strong effort to respond differently.

The reason this kind of measurement or understanding is important is because we can know how we will naturally respond in a variety of circumstances. Then through the filling of the Spirit and walking in that power a person can choose to alter the behavior if it will lead either to sin or to a foolish way of handling them. This is invaluable insight if we want to grow to maturity and come to respond to life as Christ living in us would.

For further help in this area, please consult the bibliography at the back of the book.

4. Examine your own heart. Each of us has a good knowledge of who we are and what we can do well. Some times, especially in the Christian world, we have trouble honestly acknowledging for ourselves those things we inwardly know to be true about us. We are afraid to do so may indicate pride. Humility is wrongly understood and a person feels that to claim to be able to do something well carries with it the connotation of pride. But the simple realization is that if God has made us the way we are, and we do not admit the truth about ourselves we

are actually denying the truth about the person God made us to be.

Each of us knows those things we do well and those things we do not. We know what brings pleasure in the doing and what does not. To simply take time to think through and list those things that we believe we do well and those things we know we do not do well will probably take a good afternoon but it may be one of the best investments of an afternoon we will make. Think through the following things:

* Roles you play: mother or father or child, employee, student, volunteer, etc.
* Hobbies you enjoy or extracurricular things you enjoy doing.
* Things you have done in your life that have given you the greatest pleasure. Why were they enjoyable?
* Things that have been the most difficult. Why were they difficult?
* What are my greatest strengths?
* What are my greatest weaknesses?
* Places where you have experienced your successes.
* Places where you have experienced your failures.

As you do this, write them all down on sheets of paper and then take a week or two to ask yourself,

* What does all of this tell me about myself?
* What kinds of things do I think I would be best qualified for?
* What kinds of things do I know I should stay away from?
* How do I think God could best use the rest of my life?

295

Proverbs 14:10 says, "The heart knows its own bitterness, and no stranger shares its joy." What it means is that there are things about a person that no one else can share. Only you know the bitterness you feel inside at times and there are times of joy that can never be completely shared with anyone else. So too, there are things about ourselves that no one else will ever know and so we need to take some time to simply work through what we know in our heart to be true.

5. <u>Talk with friends or people who have had extended opportunities to observe you in action.</u> These may be members of your own family, close friends, work associates or anyone else who has had a chance to watch you work and interact in a variety of social situations. You may want to make a list of questions you want to ask them and make notes while they are talking. Use some of the questions listed above or put together some others in more specific areas than those already listed. What you are trying to do is to understand how they perceive you as a person and what they see you been good at.

Some times we think we should focus on our weaknesses and try to make them strengths because we unconsciously think that is the way to do the best we can with what we have. Buckingham and Coffman in their delightful book, "First Break All the Rules" have an insightful thought in this regard. They put together a four stage statement about what great managers know:

People don't change that much.
Don't waste your time trying to put in what was left out.
Try to draw out what was left in.
That is hard enough.[355]

Solomon wrote, "Let another praise you, and not your own mouth; someone else, and not your own lips."[356] Other people can see things in us

that we often are blind to or unwilling to admit
to ourselves. Most of the time they are reluctant
to share them with us unless they are invited to,
either as a job appraisal or as a result of a personal invitation on our part. So do not be slow in
inviting some people that know you well to share
with you what they see to be true about you.

6. Being involved in different forms of ministry.
Nothing helps you more in coming to know yourself
like volunteering for a variety of things. In this
way it will become obvious to you the things that
you do that you enjoy and that come easily and
those things you do that are pure drudgery and
that are a burden to undertake. They will help you
discover what you do well and what you don't do
well. Since God gives people gifts and abilities
to be used for His glory, it stands to reason that
we will discover those gifts and abilities in the
midst of carrying out ministry for His glory. He
will see to it that our understanding of ourselves
and of others will come into clearer focus as we
are undertaking various forms of ministry. Then,
as it becomes clear what we succeed at and where
we fail, we can more clearly understand who we are
and how God has designed us.

Someone has said that it takes more than twice
as much energy to turn the wheels of a car that is
standing still than it does one that is in motion.
God can direct us more easily and with greater
clarity when we are at least undertaking some form
of ministry than He can when we are simply sitting
on the sidelines trying to increase our intellectual understanding of who we are. Go to your
pastor, a friend, someone whom you trust, a board
member of some group that is doing something you
think you would enjoy and ask them how you can get
involved. They will help you at least get started
on the wonderful journey of discovering who you
are and where God wants to use you in the best way
possible.

Chapter 21

They Have A General
Overview of the Bible

In his book, "30 Days to Understanding the Bible" Max Anders relates this story about Charles Steinmetz. Charles Steinmetz was an electrical engineer of towering intellect. After he retired, he was asked by a major appliance manufacturer to locate a malfunction in their electrical equipment. None of the manufacturer's experts had been able to locate the problem. Steinmetz spent some time walking around and testing the various parts of the machine complex. Finally, he took out of his pocket a piece of chalk and marked an "X" on a particular part of the machine. The manufacturer's people disassembled the machine, discovering to their amazement that the defect lay precisely where Steinmetz's chalk mark was located.

Some days later the manufacturer received a bill from Steinmetz for ten thousand dollars. They protested the amount and asked him to itemize it. He sent back an itemized bill:

```
Making one chalk mark                    $1
Knowing where to place it            $9,999
```

It is the same way for followers of Jesus. Having an answer for people's questions is good but knowing where to show it to them from the Bible is even better. God's people are expected to have a working relationship with the Bible. It is the source of their ultimate truth, a book that gives them light upon their daily path, a foundation upon which they can build their lives, a book that reveals the true God to them and a place to which they can turn for solace that will help them discern the correctness of their deep intents and motivations. Therefore a mature Christian should have a working knowledge of the Bible that gives them a general overview of the places where things are found and to which they can turn.

Not having this overview is like an English professor who teaches Shakespeare and yet doesn't know one of his writings from another; like an insurance salesman who doesn't know her way around her rate book; like a policeman giving a ticket who can't locate in his book what the violation code is for the specific law they are breaking. When God gave Joshua his instructions prior to leading Israel into the land He had promised them, He said, "Do not let this Book of the Law depart from your mouth; meditate on it day and night, so that you may be careful to do everything written in it. Then you will be prosperous and successful."[357] God expected him to be familiar with everything He had told Moses because this would become the foundation of how He was going to lead and direct him.

WHAT IS MEANT BY A GENERAL OVERVIEW OF THE BIBLE

1. It means that a person knows the names and locations of the 66 books of the Bible. It used to be a common practice in Bible-believing churches that in their childhood children were taught to memorize the names and locations of all the books

of the Bible. This was repeated through their upbringing so that by adulthood they could easily recite them. Many churches no longer see that as important. The result is that a high percentage of average church goers can no longer repeat their locations.

I remember as a new believer I was sitting in a young adult Sunday School class and the teacher asked us to turn to a certain biblical text. I had just received a new Bible but did not have a clue as to where the books were located. I held my Bible close to my chest, looked around to see approximately where everyone else had turned in their Bibles and turned there myself. When the teacher started reading, I quickly turned to the index, looked up the location and found the actual passage. I vowed that I would not go through that embarrassment again and set about to learn all the books of the Bible. That was better than fifty years ago and that has proved invaluable to me through the years.

2. It means that a person understands how the Old Testament and New Testament are laid out. Not all the books of the Bible contain the same kind of content. In the Old Testament the books are broken into these categories:

* History books of the nation of Israel
* Wisdom literature written to help the reader gain greater wisdom in living
* Poetry that could be read and sung on a variety of occasions
* Prophecy that both pointed out the sins of Israel and helped them understand their future

The New Testament is broken down into the following categories:

* History books that tell of the life of Jesus and the early church
* Letters written by early Christian leaders to various churches and individuals about the Christian life
* Prophecy written for encouragement and to help them keep life in perspective

A mature person ought to understand these divisions and which books belong in each category. It will help them know where to turn when looking for answers and help in their daily living.

3. It means that a person has a brief understanding of the content of each book of the Bible. This content does not need to be a detailed outline or a totally comprehensive understanding but it needs to grasp the central message or theme of the book. For example, Genesis is the book of beginnings: Creation, Abraham, and Israel. Matthew is the story of the life of Jesus told from a Jewish perspective. Roman's is a logical explanation of the Christian life from start to finish.

In this way the believer can have a mental understanding of generally where to look when they are trying to understand something specific or when they are trying to prepare an answer to a question someone has asked them.

4. It means that they have an understanding of the thought flow and themes through the entire Bible. This is important so that when mature Christians are reading in any specific book, they understand where that particular book fits in the total picture of the Bible. For example when they read the book of Isaiah, they realize that it was written late in the history of Israel as a nation in the land so that Israel could understand why God is saying certain things to them at that point in their history.

WHY THIS GENERAL OVERVIEW IS IMPORTANT

1. <u>Because there is an appalling ignorance among God's people concerning the truths in the Bible.</u> Jay Leno frequently does a "man-on-the-street" interview, and one night he collared some young people to ask them questions about the Bible. "Can you name one of the Ten Commandments?" he asked two college-age women. One replied, "Freedom of speech?" Mr. Leno said to the other, "Complete this sentence: Let he who is without sin . . ." Her response was, "have a good time?" Mr. Leno then turned to a young man and asked, "Who, according to the Bible, was eaten by a whale?" The confident answer was, "Pinocchio."

When the Barna Research Group completed a study for the Tyndale House Publishers, they discovered the following. More than 90 percent of American households have one Bible and better than three out of four have two or more copies. 80 percent of Americans said the Bible is the most influential book in world history. Unfortunately, much of this respect for God's Word is superficial. Barely one-third of adults read the Bible in a typical week and just one in five will read every page of Scripture in the course of their lifetime. Additionally, the most popular strategy for choosing a passage to read is simply flipping through the pages until spotting something that sounds intriguing, rele-vant, or interesting. This method of random selec-tion is used by nearly half of all adults who read the Bible. These findings may explain why 56 percent of Americans think the Bible teaches that taking care of one's family is the most important task of life (See Deut 6:5 and Matt 22:37), 72 percent believe that people are blessed by God so they can enjoy life as much as possible (see Gen 12:1–3), 42 percent claim the Bible says Jesus sinned while on earth (See Heb 4:15), and four out of ten people think "all individuals will experience the same outcome after death, regardless of their religious beliefs." In America, the Bible seems to be widely respected, but not seriously studied.[358]

This ignorance is there despite the fact that so many people say they believe the Bible and build their lives on it. This is also true despite the fact that in 1992 the Associated Press evaluated four thousand self-help books that had been written over the last year. They concluded the best self-help manual was not penned that year or any year recently. AP put the Bible on the top shelf for self-help.[359]

2. It gives us a foundation for truth and living. The Bible is the one single book that has been inspired by God and if used correctly will develop people who are "thoroughly equipped for every good work."[360] George Washington recognized this when he said, "It is impossible to govern rightly without God and the Bible." Thomas Jefferson served as President of the Washington, D.C. school board during his tenure as President of the United States. One of his duties on the school board was to select the textbooks to be used by the students. He selected the Bible as the primary text with this rationale: "I have always said, and always will say, that the studious perusal of the sacred volume will make us better citizens."

Francis Schaeffer repeatedly said that if we forsake the authority of the Bible then all we have left is morality by majority vote. What is right and wrong will not be determined by an authoritative word from God but rather by what 51% of the people think is right at any given time. But if we do not have a working knowledge of the Bible, then even though we might say we have been born-again, our values and morals are simply determined by the accumulated information we have gathered through our upbringing, our education and whatever other exposures to "truth" we might have experienced.

   3. The Bible is where God reveals Himself to us most clearly. When David wrote Psalm 19 he started out by describing how the creation bears witness to its Creator. "The heavens declare the glory of God and the skies proclaim the work of his hands."[361] Then he goes on to describe how the heavens are continually pouring forth a kind of language that describes the greatness of its Creator and there is much we can learn about Him from just studying its majesty. But he realizes that as wonderful as this revelation is, it is not complete and so he goes on to write, "The law of the Lord is perfect......."[362] In so doing he acknowledges that the natural revelation found in the universe is insufficient and that we need the written "law of the Lord" to further understand the greatness of God.

   In the Bible we have specific statements where God describes Himself. He said to Moses, "I am the Lord. I appeared to Abraham, to Isaac and to Jacob as God Almighty, but by my name the Lord I did not make myself known to them."[363] He gave Moses a greater revelation of His nature than He had done to anyone else prior to that. As one continues to read the Bible we come across increasing self-revelations of God that enable us to understand Him in an even greater way.

   Not only that, but we see God in action and in those actions we discover things about Him we could find out in no other way. God said, "For my thoughts are not your thoughts, neither are your ways my ways," declares the Lord. As the heavens are higher than the earth so are my ways higher than your ways and my thoughts than your thoughts."[364]

   A. W. Tozer said, "The Bible is among other things a book of revealed truth. That is, certain facts are revealed that could not be discovered by the most brilliant mind. These facts are of such a nature as to be past finding out."[365] Having a general knowledge of the Bible enables us to come to a deeper and clearer understanding of the nature of our God.

4. We need this to be able to give answers to people who ask us. When Peter wrote to "God's elect strangers in the world" he said, "Always be prepared to give an answer to everyone who asks you to give the reason for the hope you have. But do this with gentleness and respect, keeping a clear conscience…"[366] If we are living lives of integrity and honesty before people in our world, inevitably when the circumstances are right, someone will inquire about some aspect of our faith. When that happens we need to be prepared to share with them a good answer. That answer will always be founded in the word of God because this is the foundation of our faith and the source from which we draw our worldview and responses to life. If we do not have some kind of a working grasp of the scriptures when we engage in such a conversation, then all we are left with is our opinions and point of view. In their mind, our opinion carries no higher authority than their does. But when we are able to use the Bible and show people what the foundation for our opinion is, it carries much more weight and authority.

5. We have been told to put God's word in our hearts. As mentioned earlier, when God spoke to Joshua prior to his leading the people into the land God has promised Abraham, He said, "Do not let this Book of the Law depart from your mouth; meditate on it day and night, so that you may be careful to do everything written in it. Then you will be prosperous and successful." [367] The thing that would bring the people success as they took over their promised land was to live according the word of God and the way to do that was to talk about it, meditate on it and then do it. This was why the psalmist wrote, "I have hidden your word in my heart that I might not sin against you."[368] This was also why the book of Psalms opens with

the admonition about the man whose "… delight is in the law of the Lord and on it he meditates day and night."[369]

With the word of God stored permanently in our minds or hearts, it serves as a constant Global Positioning System to show us where we need to be going and to warn us when we get off the right path. Charles Garfield wrote, ""This book of the law shall not depart from your mouth, but you shall meditate on it day and night, so that you may be careful to do according to all that is written in it" (Joshua 1:8). New Agers have stolen and perverted the concept of meditation so that many contemporary Christians seem uneasy with the term. Joshua noted the need for it centuries ago. Liu Chi Kung placed second to Van Cliburn in the 1958 Tchaikovsky Competition. A year later he was imprisoned during the Cultural Revolution in China. For seven years he was denied the use of a piano. Soon after his release from prison he was back on tour, and the critics were astonished that "his musicianship was better than ever." The obvious question was, "How?" One critic said, "You had no chance to practice for seven years." Liu replied, "I did practice, every day. I rehearsed every piece I had ever played, note by note, in my mind." Meditating on God's Word allows us to live above our circumstances."[370]

<u>6. It helps us understand our internal motivations for doing what we do.</u> One of the things that is difficult for us is to always understand the reasons behind doing what we do. Counselors are taught to ask their clients, "Why did you do that?" in an attempt to get them to think through why they responded as they did to a given circumstance. Often times, this is a very difficult, almost impossible thing to do. Who can truly say they understand the real motives behind what we do?

Yet the writer of Hebrews said, "For the word of God is living and active. Sharper than any double-edged sword, it penetrates even to dividing soul and spirit, joints and marrow; it judges the thoughts and attitudes of the heart."[371] What is it that enables us to judge the thoughts and attitudes of our hearts? It is the word of God. If I allow the word of God to remain in my mind and thinking as I pray about certain decisions I need to make or how to handle certain circumstances I will face through the day, God promises me that His word will help me understand not only what to do but why that is the best course of action. Nowhere does the Bible encourage us to become involved in introspection. But God promises that His word will enable us to understand our thoughts and attitudes so that we can move forward confident that our motives and attitudes are right.

HOW TO HELP PEOPLE OBTAIN THIS KIND OF GENERAL OVERVIEW OF THE BIBLE

1. By training and encouraging our pastors and teachers to focus on expository preaching and teaching. Expository preaching and teaching is that kind of method in which the preacher/teacher immerses himself in an extended passage of scripture and then comes to the people to enable them to understand both what it says and how it relates to life in the here and now. Expository preaching often works itself through a book of the Bible in such a way that the hearers not only understand the meaning and application for a smaller portion of a book but also understand it in its larger context.

Ezra was an example of such a teacher. It says of him, "For Ezra had devoted himself to the study and observance of the Law of the Lord, and to teaching its decrees and laws in Israel."[372] Then when the opportunity presented itself to him to use what he had learned, it says, "Ezra opened the book….They read from the Book of the Law of God, making it clear and giving the meaning so that the people could understand what was being read."[373]

We live in a generation of preachers who have forsaken this calling and are instead raising a generation of people who are being entertained by videos, cute stories and techniques that find their root more in the theatre than in the prayer closet. Our generation has bought into a philosophy that has said we need to address "felt needs" and try to combine ideas from the Bible with insights from modern psychology and preach to the hurts of people. We have laid aside the majesty of the word of God and have led our people to drink from wells that do not quench thirst. It is like it was during the day of Ezekiel when God said, "Son of man, prophesy against the shepherds of Israel, prophesy, and say to them, even to the shepherds, Thus says the Lord GOD: Ho, shepherds of Israel who have been feeding yourselves! Should not shepherds feed the sheep? You eat the fat, you clothe yourselves with the wool, you slaughter the fatlings; but you do not feed the sheep."[374]

When Jesus uttered his final words to Peter, his admonition to him was "Feed my sheep!"[375] This so mightily impressed Peter that when they were confronted with a situation that tempted them to spend their time ministering to the physical needs of widows, they came to the congregation and asked them to select some other men who could give themselves to the feeding of the widows in their midst so they could "…give our attention to prayer and the ministry of the word."[376] This was not to say that giving attention to the needs of the widows was not deeply spiritual work, he was just repeating the priority that Jesus had given him and was determined not to be side-tracked from it.

It is time for the leaders of the modern church to return to the priority of the word of God. Many of the churches that I have attended recently do not even encourage their people to bring their Bibles. They rather put the words up on the screen and in so doing excuse the people from locating these words in their Bibles and train them to be observers rather than participants. The results are devastating. If I could say one thing to pastors and teachers, it would be Paul's words to Timothy, "Preach the Word, be urgent in season and out of season, convince, rebuke, and exhort, be unfailing in patience and in teaching."[377] Seminaries need to stop helping pastors in training become experts at the art of administration and program and instead help them become modern day Ezra's who "devoted himself to the study and observance of the Law of the Lord, and to teaching its decrees and laws in Israel."

Mahatma Gandhi spoke forcefully to Christians when he said, "You Christians have in your keeping a document with enough dynamite in it to blow the whole of civilization to bits, to turn society upside down, to bring peace to this war-torn world. But you read it as if it were just good literature, and nothing else."

2. Motivate people to learn all the 66 books of the Bible and to obtain an overall grasp of its message. One of the principles I set down in Chapter 17 was "You cannot operate on what you do not know." This especially applies here. If a person does not know where the books of the Bible are located or what their titles are, they will not be encouraged to go beyond an elementary approach to its wealth. There are songs that can be learned that teach the books of the Bible in sequence as well as little poems that can be quoted. Granted, this does not appear to be too "sophisticated" or "relevant" but it does help people get to know their Bibles and that must be a major focus of our

attempt to help them come to maturity. We need to be less concerned with how we appear to the "educated" world and more concerned with how mature in Christ our people are becoming.

Noah Webster's name is synonymous with his most famous work, Webster's Dictionary. His dictionary graces the shelves of countless libraries, offices, and schoolrooms. Even though Webster is remembered for his book of definitions, he did not believe his dictionary was the preeminent project of his life. He also produced, The Noah Webster Bible. He called this edition of the Bible "the most important enterprise of my life." The man of many words claimed there is no word more important than the Word. Maybe that is why he said, "Education is useless without the Bible."

<u>3. We need to provide classes, seminars and other teaching tools to help people develop this kind of knowledge.</u> These can not be strictly lecture classes because studies have shown that people do not remember a large percentage of what is delivered purely by lecture or direct presentation. There are a wide variety of excellent seminars and tools that are available to help people do this:

* "30 Days to Understanding the Bible" by Max Anders is an excellent tool to help people either individually or corporately come to have an all-over grasp of the Bible. In it he covers three main sections: The story of the Old Testament; The story of the New Testament; and The Ten Great Doctrines of the Bible. He was one of the original team members with Walk Thru the Bible Ministries and has taken much of that material and incorporated it into this book.
* Walk Thru the Bible seminars. They have developed two excellent overview seminars that present the Old and New Testament with clever signs and memory devices for easy recall.

Their one day seminars are exceptional in giving the attendee an simplified overview of the Bible and helping them feel confident in their ability to recall the information. See the bibliography for their address.

* Bible Study Fellowship does an excellent job with helping people understand overviews through a combination of lecture and small group participation.

* Many publishing houses have book study materials that focus on one book of the Bible or give an overview. A word of caution here: It has been my experience after years in church ministry that a Sunday School class does not necessarily provide an educational environment. I have worked with people who have sat for years in traditional classes doing individual book studies who do not have the slightest grasp of some of the books they have studied. There is something about the traditional classroom experience in a church that causes people to engage in conversation but not develop lasting understanding of an entire book or section of the scripture.

* Many other individual teachers have developed their own study materials that others find helpful. Beth Moore and Kay Arthur, Henry Blackaby, John MacArthur are names that come to mind as well as others. These materials can be helpful but care must be taken by the teacher to make it become more than just a fill-in-the-blanks type of study. Our purpose is not to get through the materials, good as they may be. Our purpose is to help the people gain a working knowledge of the Bible so they can grasp its meaning and then apply it to their lives and worlds.

4. Teach them how to study the Bible for themselves. One of the best things we can do for helping

people become mature in Christ is to teach them how to study and apply the word for themselves. This seems so elementary that it should go without saying but when was the last time your church or fellowship helped you learn how to study the Bible for yourself?

Perhaps the most helpful method of personal Bible study is the inductive study method. It is broken into four steps with each step asking certain questions of a passage or making you do certain things to the passage. The steps are:

Step 1: Observation (What does it say?) This is
determined by asking:
Who are the persons involved?
What is happening?
Where is it happening?
Why is it happening (Does the passage tell you?)
When is it happening?
How is it happening?

Step 2: Interpretation (What does it mean?)
Determine definitions of words
Mark out the relationships of words, ideas, people
Think through the implications

Step 3: Application (What does it mean to me?)
Write down the principles
Determine the principle that is most applicable to your present situation
Determine which specific relationship in your world you need to work on with that principle
Make a specific application beginning with "This week I will…….."

Step 4: Correlation (Where does it fit?
Setting it in its context
Fitting it into the total picture of scripture

This method of Bible study when taught and practiced can lead to becoming a good Bible student who is able to work through the scriptures by oneself but then to go on and become a strong group leader as well. For more information on this, please see the bibliography.

The Navigators have developed an easily remembered way of talking about five different ways of in-taking the Bible into one's life. They refer to it as "The Hand." The first way is to hear the word of God. The second way is to read the word of God. The third way is to study the word of God. The fourth way is to memorize the word of God and the fifth way is to meditate on the words of God. For more information, contact them (See bibliography)

The word of God forms the foundation of all that a mature believer is and does. Thus we need to give people a good overview of the Bible so that it can become a tool that enables them to gain wisdom, perspective, conviction and encouragement.

Chapter 22

Have Developed a "Biblical Worldview"

INTRODUCTION

Our youngest daughter is a very organized, disciplined person. She lives by her cell phone and her daily schedule. When she graduated from college she had the privilege of spending three months in some central African countries, working a couple of organizations on various projects. Fortunately we could e-mail back and forth and it was interesting to see her reaction to these other cultures. For them, a 1:00 p.m. appointment could mean anything from being there at 1:00 p.m. or starting to think about getting there. The way people looked at their schedules and lives was very different from how she had learned how to handle life. It took her quite a struggle before she could finally understand how they looked at life and how they handled living by their schedules.

Anyone who has spent any amount of time living and interacting with people from different cultures has experienced this phenomenon. It is because there is a difference in worldviews.

The same is true with the way a believer looks at reality. This is especially noticeable if one comes to Christ later in life after having been conditioned to look at life from a naturalistic perspective in all your education and training. But when one becomes a Christian, one of the things that begins to change is the way we look all of life. This is to be expected because when Paul begins his application section in the book of Romans, chapter 12 after having set forth our position in Christ, he says, "Do not be conformed to this world but be transformed by the renewing of your mind."[378] What he admonishes us to is the work of changing the way we think about life and the world that we live in. When we love the Lord our God with our entire mind, it changes our perspective on almost every part of life. As we do this we are building a "biblical worldview" so that as we mature we are developing an ever increasingly biblical way of looking at and living life.

DEFINING A BIBLICAL WORLDVIEW

The word "worldview" comes from the German word "Weltanschauung." "Welt" is the German word for "world" and "Anschauung" is the German word for "view" or "outlook." James Sire defines a worldview as "a set of presuppositions (assumptions which may be true, partially true or entirely false) which we hold (consciously or subconsciously, consistently or inconsistently) about the basic makeup of our world."[379] He goes on to say, "We should all think in terms of worldviews, that is, with a consciousness not only of our own way of thought but also that of other people, so that we can first understand and then genuinely communicate with others in our pluralistic society."

Colson and Pearcey write, "The term *worldview* may sound abstract or philosophical, a topic discussed by pipe-smoking, tweed-jacketed professors in academic settings. But actually a person's worldview is intensely practical. It is simply the sum total of our beliefs about the world, the 'big picture' that directs our daily decisions and actions. And understanding worldviews is very important."[380]

Nancy Pearcey in her book, "Total Truth" writes, "To say that Christianity is the truth about total reality means that it is a full-orbed worldview. The term means literally a *view* of the *world,* a biblically informed perspective on all reality. A worldview is like a mental map that tells us how to navigate the world effectively. It is the imprint of God's objective truth on our inner life."[381]

A worldview then is the way that a person understands and explains the world that is around them. It is the mental grid that we have constructed and through which we view and explain our personal world. It is a model of reality that we have in our head through which we interpret everything we see. A biblical worldview is the way we look at life through our understanding that comes from our study of the Bible.

From my perspective, there are at least three assumptions we make when establishing a biblical worldview:

<u>1) God exists as a personal, sovereign Being.</u> God is a person in the same sense that we are persons. He (I use the masculine pronoun because that is how He chose to reveal Himself to us in the Bible) can be known in the same way that any other person can be known, through personal relationships. He is sovereign in that He created our universe according to a purpose or plan that He had predetermined prior to that creation and through which He is currently working out that purpose. As a sovereign God, He does what He chooses to do simply because He is God. What this means is that the universe in which we live has been created by a personal God who is working through what He has created to bring about the purpose for which He

created it. The result is there are some aspects of life and reality that will be understandable by the human mind and some that will be beyond our ability to ever discover or comprehend.

2) God has spoken to us primarily in the Bible. The Bible is a unique book in that it has been given to us through the intervention and ministry of the Holy Spirit (1 Corinthians 2:6—16; 2 Timothy 3:16). He used the unique temperaments and minds of different authors to communicate different kinds of information in such a way that when they had finished their writings what had been written down was the exact mind of God in those areas.

Because this is true, the truth contained in the Bible represents divine, absolute truth about morals, ethics, law, and about the way He wants us to live. It gives to us a worldview from God's perspective and it is this worldview that He wants us to understand and adopt as His description of reality, of the way things truly are. We know that Satan is a liar[382] and that he wants to get us to adopt alternative worldviews to the one we find in the Bible. This is called "the wisdom of the world"[383] and it comes to us in many different forms depending upon the age in which we live and the environment in which we have been raised. In order for us to come to a biblical worldview we must come back to the Bible and understand what God's perspective on reality is so that we will not be "conformed to this world."[384]

3) There is both a visible and an invisible dimension to reality. Our worldview can not be complete unless we understand that we are living in a reality that can both be seen and quantified and a reality that cannot be seen which must be accepted and dealt with by faith. The writer of Hebrews wrote, "By faith we understand that the universe was formed at God's command, so that what is seen was not made out of what was visible."[385] This statement does not come out of some anti-

quated, uneducated mind that was simply accepting a superstition that was commonly held by primitive people. It is a statement about the way the universe actually came into being.

It is this invisible world that Paul wrote of when he stated, "For our struggle is not against flesh and blood (the visible world) but against the rulers, against the authorities, against the powers of this dark world and against the spiritual forces of evil in the heavenly realms."[386] It was this invisible world that Elisha was able to see that he asked God to reveal to his servant in 2 Kings 6:15-17. It was this invisible world that Daniel saw when he looked up and saw a "man" before him who told him about a battle he had endured after having started to come to Daniel to respond to his prayer in Daniel 10:1-21. The reality of a battle that is going on unseen by human eyes is as much a part of a biblical worldview as the part that we can see and interact with on a visible, human level.

Every part of these three assumptions is valid and important if we are to construct a biblical worldview that enables us to understand and explain the reality of what we observe going on in the world around us. This constitutes a biblical worldview.

WHY IS A BIBLICAL WORLDVIEW IMPORTANT? It is important for the following reasons:

1. It gives us the grid through which we can correctly understand and interpret reality. I recall driving one day with my wife in the car and becoming aware that it looked a thunderstorm was rapidly approaching. I turned to her and remarked about how dark the clouds were becoming and that perhaps we needed to think about pulling off the highway and looking for a place of safety. She looked at the sky and then turned to me and said, "Honey, perhaps you better take off your sunglasses. I don't

think it is as dark as you think it is." Imagine my surprise when I followed her advice. She was right and I was wrong. I was looking at what I thought was reality through darkened sunglasses and it affected how I defined reality.

Unless we have developed a biblical worldview we will do the same thing as we try to understand and interpret what we see going on around us. As we watch the newscasters and read the newspapers and books written by modern day authors, we need to be aware that their worldview is probably quite different from ours. Their perspective on what is occurring in our world will probably be very different from what a biblical worldview would say about it. From our understanding of the way God has worked with His people and with the sur-rounding nations in the past will give us some understanding of how God could be working in our day. God says that "your ways are not my ways"[387] and when we understand His "ways" from how He has responded in the past it gives us a better chance to understand what He may be doing in the present or in the future. The only thing that gives us those insights is that we have developed a bib-lical worldview. Without this grid through which we can evaluate what is going on around us, we are at the mercy of others who do not share our values and truth to interpret for us the meaning and sig-nificance of what we encounter.

2. We live in a culture whose worldview is in total opposition to a biblical worldview. This is illustrated easily by quoting the late Carl Sagan who hosted the television show, "Cosmos." He opened every show in a quasi-religious fashion with the words, "The Cosmos is all that is or ever was or ever will be." This is a statement that comes directly out of the worldview called *naturalism*. In commenting on this, Colson and Pearcey write, "Here. Sagan is capitalizing on liturgical forms. Ever since the early church, Christians have sung

the Gloria Patri: 'Glory be to the Father, and to the Son, and to the Holy Ghost. As it was in the beginning, is now, and ever shall be, world without end." Sagan is clearly offering a substitute liturgy, a cadence to the cosmos. The sheer fact that he capitalizes the word *Cosmos* just as religious believers capitalize the word *God*, is a dead giveaway that he is gripped by religious fervor."[388] Nancy Pearcey in her book, *Total Truth* describes picking up a science book for her little boy. It featured the Berenstain Bears and the book was titled, *The Bears Nature Guide.* She said she was amazed when she came to a two-page spread that spelled out in capital letters: "Nature….is all that IS, or WAS, or EVER WILL BE!"[389] This is simply a repackaging of Sagan's naturalistic religion for young children.

To show how far we are away from a biblical worldview, even in the church, let me cite a few statistics. George Barna has found in his recent polls that only 9 percent of students in evangelical schools believe in anything called "absolute truth."[390] In another survey he did, George Barna put together a list of biblical teachings that presumably Christians of every denomination or theological tradition could affirm: There is absolute moral truth based on the Bible; biblical teaching is accurate; Jesus was without sin; Satan literally exists; God is omnipotent and omniscient; salvation is by grace alone; Christians have a personal responsibility to evangelize. The statistics were revealing. Of Southern Baptist pastors 71 percent hold to this worldview; Of Methodists only 27 percent do; of other Baptist 57 percent do; of nondenominational Protestants 51 percent do and of charismatic or Pentecostal churches 44 percent do. Of those denominations that belong to the National Council of Churches only 28 percent could be described as holding a biblical worldview.[391] In an article in *The Economist* magazine an article appeared that demonstrated the unequal balance in political views held by university professors who supposedly believe in and foster diversity. The writer said, "Employees at both universities (University of California and Harvard) gave 19 times as much to John Kerry as to George Bush. Meanwhile a new national survey of more than 1,000 academics by Daniel Klien, of Santa Clara University, shows that Democrats outnumber Republicans by at least seven to one in the humanities and social sciences. And things are likely to get less balanced, because younger professors are more liberal. For instance, at Berkley and Stanford, where Democrats overall outnumber Republicans by a mere nine to one, the ratio rises above 30 to one among assistant and associate professors."[392] I could cite many other references to the disproportionate balance that occurs just in the modern universities, not including the news media, publishing houses, etc.

If we are ever going to help our young people stand up in the midst of such an educational worldview that embraces primarily naturalism or humanism as their operating philosophy or worldview, we must help them to understand the battle they are facing. Our entire culture is teleologically in opposition to the worldview we embrace as Christians and we need to understand that.

An example of the kind of grid we can help people develop is seen in the following example:

	Reality	Man	Truth	Values
Naturalism	The material universe is all that there is	Man is a product of evolution. He is entirely material and is basically good.	Only verifiable, scientific truth is real. It is detected by the senses	There are no objective values or morals. They are subject to evolution and change.
Theism (Christianity, Judaism, Islam)	A personal, infinite God exists. He created the world which is both material and spiritual.	Man is a unique creation of God. We are personal, eternal, spiritual and biological. We arte initially evil.	There three kinds of truth: 1)	Moral values are objective and given to us by an absolute, moral God.

3. We need to understand how to evaluate differing worldviews so we can effectively communicate and defend our faith. We are continually bombarded by information from many different sources, most of them are unbiblical. How do we evaluate them to determine what really lies behind what they are trying to say? If we do not help ourselves and our people to evaluate and assess these many world views, then we will welcome these ideas and solutions uncritically causing us to accept ways of dealing with issues of life that are wrong or at

best won't work. We need to know how to evaluate
ideas and truth we are exposed to.

The best tool I have found is outlined in Pearcey's
book, *Total Truth: Liberating Christianity from
Its Cultural Captivity*. In her Introduction as she
is setting forth how the book is laid out she says
that the first section is designed to "provide practical, hands-on worldview training. It will walk
you through concrete steps for crafting a biblically based worldview in any field using the struc-
tural elements of Creation, Fall, and Redemption.
It will also give you an opportunity to practice
apologetics by analyzing non-Christian worldviews.
After all, every philosophy or ideology has to
answer the same fundamental questions:

1. CREATION: How did it all begin? Where did we
   come from?
2. FALL: What went wrong? What is the source of
   evil and suffering?
3. REDEMPTION: What can we do about it? How can
   the world be set right again?

By applying this simple grid, we can identify
nonbiblical worldviews, and then analyze where
they go wrong."[393]

What she is saying is that when we are exposed
to a speaker, a book, a newscaster or analyst, a
professor in college, someone from another culture we can eventually determine their worldview
by asking ourselves: 1) Based on what they have
said, where would they say the universe or the
human race came from? Has it always been here?
Did it evolve or is it continually evolving? Is it
being continually reincarnated or is it cyclical?
As they answer that question, we discover their
definition of "god" for whatever has life in itself
as an uncreated entity has become by definition
"god." 2) What would they say is basically wrong
the human problem? Is it lack of education? It

is the wrong social structure? Is it the lack of self-restraining laws? Is it something innate in their genetic makeup? Is it a lack of money? Is it some inherent evil inside of each person that causes them to be self-centered? This is important because their solution to the social problems we are faced with will be determined by what they think it will take to correct their behavior. 3) What do they say it take to help human beings act properly? Is it giving them the freedom to do whatever they wish? Is it a good education? Is it correcting the social environment in which they live? Is it getting appearance enhancing surgery? Is it helping them to live in a better neighborhood? Is it electing the right political party into office? Is it found in giving them the right medication or drugs? Is it found in giving them freedom of sexual expression? How they answer this question will help you understand what they see to be the solution to the ills of our social culture or individual problems.

Unless we understand how to evaluate and analyze the different worldviews we encounter and understand how a biblical worldview answers these questions, we will never be able to communicate in a meaningful way with the people in the world that we live in.

<u>4. It determines the way we handle life.</u> In Psalm 73, Asaph is wrestling with the problem of envying those who are "wicked" because it does not seem to him that they are being treated properly. He lists the things that appear to be going right for them even though they openly flaunt God and His laws. It was bothering him deeply until he said this, "When I tried to understand all this, it was oppressive to me till I entered the sanctuary of God; then I understood their final destiny."[394] He was looking at this issue from a human perspective but when he went into the sanctuary of God, he was reminded that justice and fairness are not always

obtained in this life and that there is coming a time of judgment when what is unfair now will be set right. When he submitted this issue to a biblical worldview, the thoughts he was wrestling with resolved themselves and he could go on the say, "My flesh and my heart may fail, but God is the strength of my heart and my portion forever…it is good to be near God. I have made the Sovereign Lord my refuge; I will tell all of your deeds."[395]

When Paul wrote to the Corinthians a second time, he was forced to defend himself and to explain what he had done and why he was doing it that way. He said, "We are hard pressed on every side, but not crushed; perplexed, but not in despair; persecuted, but not abandoned; struck down but now destroyed."[396] How could he keep going through all of this difficulty? It was because of his biblical worldview. He would write just a few sentences later, "For our light and momentary troubles are achieving for us an external glory that far outweighs them all. So we fix our eyes not on what is seen, but on what is unseen. For what is seen is temporary, but what is unseen is eternal."[397] It was his worldview that told him that the reward that awaited him upon the final completion of his life would far outweigh any hardship or trouble that he might have to go through during this life. It was their worldview in both of these cases that enabled them to handle life.

The same is true for any follower of Jesus. We need to be continually reminding ourselves of what our worldview says about what the eventual outcome will be of the circumstances we are currently facing. It is our worldview that helps us be obedient to the will of God even though we might not be able to see how that obedience can possibly resolve the situation we presently face. It is our worldview that enables us to "give thanks in all circumstances" because we know that God works together for the good of those who love Him.[398]

HOW WE HELP PEOPLE DEVELOP A
BIBLICAL WORLDVIEW

1. We need to teach them to think biblically.
There are two parts to this step: 1) We need to
teach them to *think*. When my son came home from
his first year of college, he said to me, "Dad,
it is so frustrating. My friends don't know how
to think for themselves." He had encountered the
reality that most of us simply parrot back things
that we have been taught without deeply thinking
them through for ourselves. I heard a management
consultant say that he could find people to hire
who could do everything but two things: think and
do things in the order of their importance. A. W.
Tozer said, "I believe that pure thinking will do
more to educate a man than any other activity he
can engage in."[399] We need to help people learn how
to think, to be able to take an idea, mull it around
in their minds until there are auxiliary thoughts
that emerge, implications drawn, principles discovered and new, fresh conclusions arrived at. But
for this to happen, we need to help people put away
the entertainment of this generation that so fills
the airways and bookstores with things that would
distract and keep people from wrestling long and
hard with ideas and reason. We need to help them
learn how to think logically, how to reason from
assumptions and facts to consistent conclusions.
2) We need to teach them to think *biblically.*
To think biblically we need to help them learn how
to read the Bible for themselves. We need to teach
them how to study the Bible and draw forth truths
from its pages and principles from the truths that
emerge. We need to help them learn how to summarize what they have read and then build systems and
conclusions about what they have read and studied
that will change the way they think and live. The
Bible is the grid through which we see reality and
unless we encourage people to develop the skills

and heart necessary to immerse themselves in it, they will never learn to think biblically and build a biblical worldview.

2. We need to help them develop the *Creation — Fall — Redemption* paradigm. As mentioned above, this is the tool believers need to be able to evaluate ideas, philosophies, and other worldviews. To do this we need to help people understand the wonder of creation, the far-reaching devastation brought about by the Fall, and the logic and wonder of the redemption that God has provided for the human race. Then, armed with that understanding they can be exposed to other world views and isms and be able to accurately assess them and compare them to their Christian faith.

3. Offer college level courses that are designed to teach people how to develop a biblical worldview. These classes could be built around comparative religions, book studies together that use some of the better literature that is available or Bible study materials designed to focus on specific issues that need to become a part of one's worldview. We need to especially target our young people. Charles Colson, writing in Christianity Today wrote, "We must examine what our churches are teaching our kids about truth — assuming they're teaching *anything.* Youth leaders are good at activities like laser tag and Ultimate Frisbee. That's fine: Draw kids in. But they must couple this with a bracing dose of worldview instruction. In the Wilberforce Forum, we're been trying out some sample curriculums — and discovering young people hunger for it. We'd better ground our students in worldview thinking before they leave for college, where professors challenge everything they believe….Lay people can do this. A friend, Nancy Fitzgerald, has been teaching basic apologetics for teens in her home for years. Between 150 and 200 kids come for a lecture, then break into groups to discuss the material. They often continue the

discussion later via e-mail. The results among the kids — an ability to boldly witness to the truth — have been spectacular."[400]

4. Make good books available for your people to read. I have been greatly encouraged by the increasing amount of material that has come into print in the last 30 years that helps people work through many of these issues from a strong, biblical, logical viewpoint. To encourage this, put together small groups of people that are willing to work through such material together. There are excellent videos that are becoming available that can be shared and talked about that help people to think. The late Dr. Francis Schaeffer's video series, "How Then Shall We Live?" with its accompanying discussion guide is an excellent tool. The books mentioned in the bibliography are also good sources of study books. Many of them have discussion guides printed in the back of the books and some of them have separate guides that are available. I heard a speaker say, "Anyone who can read, and doesn't is no better off than a person who can't read." Help your people read good material.

5. Help people learn to submit their minds to the Lordship of Christ. By this is meant that we need to adopt the truth that the Bible sets forth as the truest truth we will ever discover and be willing to adopt that as our own. Regardless of how logical and simple the Christian faith may seem to a believer, it appears as foolishness to those who don't believe. Thus there will be a natural tendency on the part of a person to want to appear wise and learned before people who scoff at absolute truth. They will tend to waffle when made to appear out of touch or irrational to their contemporaries. In order to avoid this tendency, every believer needs to submit their mind and thinking processes to the Lordship of Christ. Jesus is the wisest person who has ever lived. The things that he taught about subjects and about life are truly

the most accurate and profound things that could be uttered about that particular topic. But unless we are willing to submit our minds to His Lordship, we will tend to try and amalgamate what He said with the latest thinking of this age and come up with a worldview that is acceptable to those in the world where we live but totally out of keeping with God's perspective. We do need to heed Paul's admonition to "Let this mind be in you which was also in Christ Jesus…"[401]

CONCLUSION

If we are going to be mature in Christ, we need to learn how to look at life from a biblical perspective. In order to do that we need to "renew our minds" away from conformity to the world's way of thinking and allow our thinking to interpret life through the grid of the Bible. To do so will enable us to establish a biblical worldview and to be more effective in our impact in the culture of which we find ourselves a part.

Chapter 23

They Know 54 Verses of Scripture

Anumber of years ago, the church I was pastoring had decided to add an educational wing onto the one existing building as the church had grown and was unable to accommodate the additional people that were attending. I could look out my study window and watch them at work. I was fascinated by the fact that they started by excavating about 15 feet down, filling it back up with gravel and sand and compacting it with lime into a very firm soil. When I inquired why they needed to dig it all up and then fill it all back in again, they said that since we were going to build a two-story building, it needed to be built on a solid foundation or else it would not withstand some of the possible things that might happen to it. I discovered the necessity of a good foundation if you are going to build any kind of stable building.

The same thing is true of building a mature disciple. The kind of foundation that is laid in one's life will determine to a large degree the kind of disciple they will eventually become. We know that Jesus Christ is the ultimate foundation upon which a mature believer's life is built[402] but once that cornerstone has been laid the rest of the foundation is the word of God. This is what Paul referred to in Ephesians 2:20 when he wrote about the fact that they "are no longer foreigners and aliens, but fellow citizens with God's people and members of God's household, built on the foundation of the apostles and prophets, with Christ himself as the chief cornerstone."[403] That foundation is the foundation of the words they both spoke and wrote that we find in the scriptures.

The way to lay that foundation is to take the word of God and hide it in the memory banks of our minds so that it can do the work there that only it can do.

WHAT IS MEANT BY THIS:

The memorized word of God forms the foundation for all that we have written in the previous chapters in this book. It is for that reason that I set this forth as the sixth thing a mature believer needs to know if they are to learn to be complete in Christ. The list of verses needs a little explanation. What I have done is to take each of the 18 characteristics that have been described in this book and have included three verses for each characteristic that has been enumerated. The reason for that is so the mature person knows that the foundation for this whole description is found in the word of God and is not just the thoughts of some author. Since the Bible must give us the foundation and motivation for who we are and all that we do, we need to be convinced that these characteristics come out of the word of God itself. This list is not intended to be the "end all" of scripture verses that ought to be memorized or even the sum of what any leaders should use in their ministry. They simply represent the best listing that I have been able to develop over the years of my personal ministry.

Category	Verse Set 1	Verse Set 2	Verse Set 3
Attitudes			
A desire to know God	Phil 3:10	Jer 9:23-24	Hos 6:3
A desire to glorify God	John 15:8	1 Cor 6:19-20	1 Cor 10:13
A desire to be Christlike	Luke 6:40	Gal 2:20	Gal 4:19
A desire to love people	John 13:34-35	1 John 3:16	John 15:13
A desire to serve people	Matt 20:26-28	Phil 2:7	Matt 23:11
A desire to be involved in the Great Commission	Matt 28:19-20	Acts 1:8	Col 1:28-29
Skills			
They know how to hear & follow God's voice	John 10:27	1 Sam 3:10	Isa 6:8
They know how to build relationships with others	Eph 4:29	Phil 2:3-4	Col 3:12
They know how to build a strong Christian Home	Gen 2:24	Eph 5:21, 25	Eph 6:4
They know how to use God-given abilities to build the body of Christ	1 Cor 15:10	Eph 2:10	1 Pet 4:10
They know how to articulate & defend their faith	Matt 10:20	2 Tim 2:24-25	1 Pet 3:15
They know how to disciple others	Matt 4:19	Luke 6:40	2 Tim 2:2

Knowledge			
They know who they are "in Christ"	John 15:5	2 Cor 5:17	Col 2:10
They know basic Christian doctrine	Rom 6:17	1 Tim 4:16	Tit 1:9
They know their unique temperament & abilities	Rom 12:3	1 Cor 4:1	Prov 11:2
They know a general Bible overview	Luke 24:27	2 Tim 3:16-17	Neh 8:8
They have established a biblical worldview	Isa 1:18	1 Cor 14:20	Phil 2:5
They know 54 verses of scripture from memory	Josh 1:8	Psa 1:1-2	Psa 119:9, 11

You will notice that there is a category for each chapter included in this book. You will also notice that each topic has three different sets in it. It is suggested that you help them learn their way through "Set 1" and when that is completed, have them then begin on "Set 2" and when that is completed move on to "Set 3." This repeated process will help to firm up in the believer's mind the eighteen different characteristics and they will remember them along with memorizing the verses that affirm the characteristic.

WHY THIS IS IMPORTANT:

There are a number of reasons why this is an important area of knowledge:

1. Memorized scripture is the tool the Holy Spirit uses to transform our thinking. When Jesus spoke to his disciples as they gathered together for one last supper, He told them, "….the Holy Spirit… will teach you all things and will remind you of everything I have said to you."[404] The scrip-

tures we have are the fulfillment of this promise that Jesus made. Therefore, the more of the scriptures that we can ingest and cause to be a permanent part of our memory banks, the greater will be our thinking transformation. Paul told the Romans when he wrote that he wanted them to "be transformed by the renewing of your minds."[405] The writer of Hebrews expresses how this process works. He wrote, "For the word of God is living and active. Sharper than any double-edged sword, it penetrates even to dividing soul and spirit, joints and marrow; it judges the thoughts and attitudes of the heart."[406] What he means is that the word of God is actually something that has a life of its own. When we take that word and memorize it so that resides in our minds, apart from our conscious thought processes, it is working to "discern" the thoughts and attitudes we have within. As it does its work, the Holy Spirit uses that work to either deal with wrong thoughts and attitudes in an unconscious way or bring them to our consciousness to enable us to see that here are issues that need dealing with if we are to become mature. In either way, our thinking process is changed because of the internal working of the word of God.

2. The memorized word enables us to become "thoroughly equipped for every good work." When Paul wrote to Timothy he commented on how Timothy had known the scriptures from infancy and that they had made him wise for salvation. Then he added this comment: "All Scripture (old and new) is God breathed and is useful for teaching, rebuke, correcting and training in righteousness, so that the man of God may be thoroughly equipped for every good work."[407] God has prepared good works in advance that He has created us in Christ Jesus to do.[408] It is a part of the ministry of the word of God to enable us to understand both what the works are that He desires us to do and how we should do them. Carrying the word of God around in our minds

because we have memorized it enables us to observe everything we encounter and become aware as to whether it is something He wants us to do something about or not. There are so many possible ways we can invest our time as we encounter people on a daily basis, that we need divine help determining which ones we should do something about. The word of God will help us understand which things are priority and which things we need to leave alone.

3. The memorized word enables us to "set our minds on things above." Paul admonishes the Colossians to "Set your minds on things above, not on earthly things."[409] I have found that one very practical way of doing this is by memorizing scripture and then using that as the content for my times of meditation and reflection. It is almost like a cow chewing on a large bite of food who then drops it into one of her stomachs. Later she regurgitates it and resumes ruminating on it a second and third time. The memorized word enables a person to be able to instantly recall a verse of scripture (things that are above) and then to use it as something to set their mind on. This becomes a wonderful aid during times of intense temptation when the mid is prone to wander off and fixate on things that are counter-productive to ones spiritual and mental well-being. When David wrote about the word of God (the Law, statutes, precepts, etc.), he said that it revives the soul, it makes the simple wise, it brings joy to the heart, it gives light to the eyes, and that the word of God is of greater value than wealth. He said that when we keep what they say they bring about a great reward.[410]

When God charged Joshua with the responsibility for leading Israel into the land that He was going to help them repossess, He told him "… not let this Book of the Law depart from your mouth; meditate on it day and night, so that you may be careful to do everything written in it. Then you will be prosperous and successful."[411] When whoever assem-

335

bled the book of Psalms in its present form did so, the first psalm that introduced the book told them that their "delight" should be in the law of the Lord and that they were to meditate on it day and night. If they would do that they would be "like a tree planted by streams of water, which yields its fruit in season and whose leaf does not wither. Whatever he does prospers."[412]

Memorizing scripture is of great value to a believer and a mature believer will be one who has memorized significant verses and portions of scripture.

HOW THIS IS DONE:

Scripture memory comes more easily to some than it does for others. Some are able to look over a verse or a passage a few times and come away having it totally memorized. Others have a much more difficult time and for them it takes much review and work to store the verses in their minds so they can be retrieved and used with skill. Research has discovered that for something to be memorized well, it takes about six weeks of reviewing it at least once a day for it to be thoroughly engrained in our minds. I have discovered that this is so. A person can easily memorize certain things to regurgitate on a test or for some kind of public performance but unless they are continually reviewed afterwards it will be lost to permanent use. With this in mind, let me make a few suggestions:

1. Purchase some blank calling cards and write the verses on them. These can be purchased by the box or now they can be purchased in sheets to be printed by a printer. It is wise when doing this to put the actual verse on one side and the verse reference on the other. Memorizing the references is important as well. Then when you are in conversation with another person you will be able to

open your Bible to the exact reference and point it out to them. These cards are small enough that they can be carried easily and then pulled out and reviewed at times through the day when there are a few minutes or even seconds. I also use 3 x 5 cards if I am memorizing a larger passage.

2. Start with "Set 1": Attitudes. See if it is possible to memorize one verse a week along with the verse reference and the topic title. It is more important to know the verses well and be able to use them than it is to generate a large number of verses. If one a week is too fast, then take two weeks per verse. The issue is to get them memorized and retrievable. You will find as you go along that it will become easier to memorize verses. If you have not done this for a while it is a habit that needs reestablishing and that will take time. You may also find that if you go too fast you reach a place where the verses, their references and the topics get all jumbled up. If this happens, take some time off and regain some sense of the flow of what you are doing. When you have completed "Set 1" then move on to "Set 2" and then to "Set 3." Remember, the goal of this discipline is the transformation of tour mind and thinking — and that will take time.

3. Find a partner. Having a "partner" that you can meet with regularly will help to establish an accountability that will prove beneficial. This needs to be someone that you trust and can be open with and in whose presence you do not feel intimidated. You should meet regularly at a place that the two of you agree on. It can be done for breakfast or lunch, at work during breaks, in a car pool going to and from work, in a mother's group where you are watching your children play, etc. In other words, the schedule and design is as varied as the people who are establishing it. Depending upon your marital relationship it may or may not be a good idea to choose your mate as your review

partner. Sometimes this puts an undue strain on the relationship where you establish the mentality of "checking up" and it turns negative. But having a faithful friend and partner goes a long way toward helping you be accountable for your memory work.

Don't be afraid to ask someone that you are with for a longer period of time to help you review even though you don't know them well or even if they are not believers. I have found that in the right circumstances people who were strangers will be willing to review your verses for you. I have done it by simply saying, "I wonder if you could help me for a few minutes. I am currently trying to memorize some verses from the Bible and if you would be willing to listen to me as I try and recite them I would appreciate it." I have had some pleasant conversations with people who were not believers because I took the initiative and asked them to listen to my verses. You will be surprised at what God can do — and remember, His word is living and active and it will do a work whether the other person is receptive or not. His word always accomplishes the purpose He intends it to accomplish[413] whether we are aware of that purpose or not.

4. <u>Use pre-printed materials as well.</u> The Navigators have a scripture verse memory system they call the TMS (Topical Memory System) which they make available through NavPress. Other organizations as well have other collections of verses that they make available for sale for you to use. These can be quite effective. The reason I suggest these 54 verses is because they fit within the framework of my definition of a disciple but they are not the only system that is available.

5. <u>Make note of any special verses that speak to you as you read your Bible.</u> Often God uses specific verses to speak to us about a situation we are facing or a decision we must make as we simply read the Bible on a regular basis. It is wise to make note of those verses. If they deal with a cur-

rent circumstance you are dealing with, it may be very helpful to interrupt your systematized memorization and work on that special verse or verses. This is God's way of speaking to us in a very precise way about that circumstance and to take the time to memorize the verse will help us make wiser decisions than we could have otherwise. Every time we open up the Bible to read it for ourselves, we need to ask God to open our eyes to what He wants to say to us as we read. When He does speak in that way it is wise to memorize the verse so we can come back to it repeatedly.

CONCLUSION

God's word is a very different book from any other we will pick up. Because it is "living and active" the Holy Spirit will use it as we are exposed to it to speak in detailed ways to us about specific situations we are facing. It will make us wise beyond our educational training and will become a light unto our feat and a lamp unto our path. So a mature believer is someone who sees the wisdom of this discipline and hides the word of God in their heart. Our mind is thereby being renewed and our thinking stops being conformed to the way our world thinks.

Chapter 24

How to Help People
Gain Knowledge

I f you are a Star Trek follower, you will remember
the times that Dr. Spock engaged in what they
called a "mind-meld." He would put his fingers on
the head of another person and then through a
process known only to the writers, would somehow
transfer information from his mind to someone else
or vice versa. In other science fiction stories,
they have created methods for attaching a willing
or unwilling person to a machine, turning it on,
and automatically downloading information into
their brain in much the same way you download a
file over the internet.

Wouldn't that be wonderful if it were possible?
Think of all the educational processes that could
be avoided and the expenses involved in getting
an education. But we cannot do that for the same
you cannot send someone else to the dentist for
you. Pure information that has not been processed
through experience and thoughtful reflection will
not do the recipient much good. So we must turn to
other alternative ways of helping people gain the
knowledge they need to become mature disciples.

Before proceeding with the methodology, however, we need to recognize two tensions connected

with the accumulation of knowledge. The first tension is the tendency of knowledge to cause a person to become conceited. When Paul wrote to the Corinthians about the issue of whether or not to eat food that had been offered in sacrificing to idols, he recognized this tendency. He wrote, "Now about food sacrificed to idols: We know that we all possess knowledge. Knowledge puffs up but love builds up."[414] He is saying that the real issue here is not the knowledge that idols do not have any real existence but whether or not we love those who have just come out of idolatry enough to forego certain freedoms we have in Christ for the benefit of those who are not quite as far along in their growth process as we are. Paul does acknowledge that knowledge for knowledge's sake can tend to make a person proud of their knowledge. So in helping people acquire the knowledge they need to function as mature disciples we need to be careful that they do not see the acquisition of that knowledge as an achievement that brings about pride. Larry Richards wrote, "Much of education is concerned with helping people know what their teachers know. Christian education is concerned with helping become what their teachers are. The unique task of building up men and women toward Christ's likeness is the task of making disciples."[415]

The second tension is that knowledge can under certain circumstances be dangerous. Information can be used for purposes other than that intended by the teacher. Frank Laubach, a man who launched the worldwide "Each One Teach One" method of stamping out illiteracy once wrote, "All learning is dangerous if the heart is savage. The skies of the world today are full of the latest scientific inventions for wholesale destruction. Much knowledge is more dangerous than a little knowledge for the same reason that a bomber is more dangerous than a bow and arrow." Some of the most difficult people I have encountered throughout the course of my ministry have been those people who started out embracing biblical Christianity. For a variety of reasons, they turned away from their faith and became aggressive attackers of that which they at one time whole-heartedly embraced. They have an insider's knowledge about our doctrine and life together and when they turn away from Jesus, that knowledge can be used to undermine the work of the kingdom.

We do not stop being diligent in imparting informational knowledge to those that we disciple but we do so with the realization that along with that knowledge we must communicate the right spirit and hunger. Having said this, let's look at five specific methodological processes we can use in addition to what has been spelled out specifically at the conclusion of each of the previous chapters.

1. Teach people how to love God with their minds. When Jesus was asked "…which is the greatest commandment in the Law?" he responded by saying, "Love the Lord your God with all your heart and with all your soul and with all your mind."[416] In saying this, he was implying that the human mind plays a very vital role in our relationship with God. God has given us a mind that is capable of thinking His thoughts to a partial degree. But in order to do that, we must learn how to develop our minds and train them in self-control and thinking. We have to help people see the absolute necessity of engaging their minds deeply in their walk with God if they are ever to become the mature disciples that Jesus called us to be. Paul wrote to the Romans that they were to "renew their minds."[417] He wrote to the Philippians and said they were to "have this mind in you that was also in Christ Jesus…"[418]

When he wrote to the Corinthians he said, "The weapons we fight with are not the weapons of the world. On the contrary, they have divine power to demolish strongholds. We demolish arguments and every pretension that sets itself up against the knowledge of God, and we take captive every thought to make it obedient to Christ."[419] We love God with all of our minds by realizing the crucial role it plays in our walk with God and by learning to discipline and train it, filling it with the kinds of thoughts, ideas and reasonings that will both be pleasing to Him and will help us become mature in our walk before Him.

One of the problems with much of modern day spirituality is that it is shallow and therefore intellectually barren. We are like the conversation Howard Hendricks had one day with a pathologist friend of his from Philadelphia. Dr. Hendricks asked him, "Have you seen many brains?" "Hundreds of them," the pathologist responded. "Have you ever seen one worn out?" asked Hendricks. The pathologist friend answered, "I've never seen one even slightly used." As far as our brains are concerned, there's plenty of room for improvement."[420]

2. Teach people how to read well. According to "The Economist" of Nov 2007, twenty percent of the world population was illiterate in 1998 by the United Nations definition. This is the inability to read and write a simple sentence in any language. And according to "Brian's Lines" of Sept/Oct 1996 only 5 percent of the people living in the United States will either read or buy a book this year (1996). A large part of the reason for these statistics is that we are not training people to be effective readers. All of this is true in spite of living in an increasingly informational society. It is estimated that one edition of the New York Times contains more information than a person living in the seventeenth century would encounter in a lifetime.[421]

So we need to be helping Christians learn how to read more effectively. When Paul wrote to Timothy, he asked him to bring along his scrolls and parchments the next time he came to visit him.[422] He knew the benefit of reading and did so to continue to learn and grow intellectually.

I can speak to this from personal experience. I had not learned how to read well from childhood for a number of reasons which resulted in the fact that even though I wanted to learn and grow, I was reluctant to work at it because reading was such a counter-productive process. Finally, when I was around forty years of age, I went to a local college and signed up for a class in developing better reading skills. As a result of three evening sessions and the required practice in between, I went from a reading speed of 275 words per minute to better than 1,700 words per minute and my comprehension more than quadrupled. You can imagine the change that happened in my life as a result of this. The material that was used came from a book entitled, "Rapid Reading With a Purpose" by Ben Johnson.(See Bibliography) It helped me so drastically that I purchased a companion book entitled "Rapid Reading Naturally" which teaches you how to lead such a class and have used it a number of times throughout the remainder of my ministry. I never cease to be amazed at the transformation that occurs in a person's life when they are finally able to overcome poor reading habits.

We need to help people develop the attitude that Groucho Marx had when he said, "I find television very educational. Every time someone switches it on I go into another room and read a good book."

3. Build a strong church library. Frank Laubach was a missionary in the Philippines for a number of years. One of the great hindrances he found to the gospel was people's inability to read. As a result he created his "Each One Teach One" system and as a result spent the better part of the rest of his life traveling around the world helping other nations and people groups learn how to read. When

he was in one of the African countries teaching them how to read and then teach others how, a young man who was a Communist came up to him after one session and congratulated him and thanked him for what he was doing. Laubach was surprised at the man's comments and asked him why he was so excited about that. The young man responded by saying, "You teach them how to read and we will provide them with the literature."

It does not make any sense to help people learn how to read effectively without providing them with profitable materials to read. To that end we need to be building strong church libraries. No one individual can afford to purchase all the good books by themselves. It is too expensive and does not represent good stewardship of the Lord's resources. These libraries need to contain at least three different kinds of materials. First there need to be good books. There are many excellent books available on the market to help develop the knowledge base we have been talking about. Many of these books are written in language that is easily understood by the average person and can be read well with good comprehension. There are other more technical and theological books that while they are more difficult to read and comprehend they are worth the effort involved in working through them.

Secondly, they need to contain quality CD's and audio tapes. As Americans we spend an inordinate amount of time in traffic and this time can be redeemed by listening to men and women who speak in areas of expertise that we need to develop in order to live consistently in our culture. Messages can be downloaded from the internet onto iPods or other similar listening devices that can be worn while exercising, shopping and waiting for appointments, etc.

Thirdly there needs to be a good supply of current, relevant DVD's and videos that can be used either in the confines of one's own home or as the basis for classes or small group discussions. One only needs to go online to discover the vast array of this kind of material that is available to us in this generation.

4. We need to offer college and seminary level classes in the local church. In the Parade magazine of April 19, 1998 there was an article that said that twenty-seven percent of American adults still believe that the sun revolves around the earth. That is almost unbelievable — except it is true. People are untaught because we have not helped them to learn how to think for themselves in many areas of life. Having been involved in church ministry for many years I have observed that what goes on in the average "Sunday School" class is far from educational. There is something about the traditionally practiced class room structure that prohibits people from having to do much thinking or deep mental processing. Couple that with the realization that very often the material being studied is far from life-oriented and culture-engaging and the result you get is that God's people are not well prepared to take their place in the world of ideas and thought.

Pollster George Gallup is concerned about the maturity of American Christians. Although some 53 percent of the general public says religion is "very important," he found only 13 percent live the faith they profess. Gallup said, "There is not a spiritual vacuum in our country, but spiritual chaos." According to his research, "Americans need instruction badly in Bible study, prayer techniques, and how to share the gospel. People are trying to be Christian without the Bible." Gallup is a Christian who thinks Americans need more spiritual maturity because they have become consumer-oriented and are practicing what he calls "a la carte religion." He noted, "People want the fruits of faith but not the obligations." Spiritually speaking, we need to grow up![423]

In his book, "They Like Jesus But Not the Church" Dan Kimball records a number of interviews he has conducted with young adults ages 18 to 35 about their perspectives on modern Christianity. One young woman named Alicia said, "Why aren't church leaders paying attention to what we are doing in university? All the emphasis in churches is on the pastor's one-way sermon. But in university, we don't like listening to the lectures in the big 100-level classes. They are the least favorite. The large classes are the ones which are the hardest to pay attention in and are the hardest to learn from. We learn best in upper-level classes, which are the smaller ones, and in the labs where discussion takes place and our voices can contribute to the learning experience. The church has it backward focusing their teaching all in a lecture. I would like church to be small enough to have dialogue and not just sit in a lecture."[424] Another young woman, Penny, said, "I'd like the church to be more like when you go to a philosophy meeting where people can dialogue and intelligently grapple with Scripture texts together. Not just sit there for an hour listening to one person telling like-minded people what they want to hear without questioning or talking about it."[425] Kimball has found that when churches offer credible, college level classes this younger generation is genuinely interested and wants to wrestle with the real intellectual issues of our day.

These classes probably need to be taught at times other than Sunday morning and need to require the same kind of reading assignments and involvement as college classes do. Granted, there may not be the high attendance figures that many churches like to parade but there will be a cadre of people who are desirous of working through some of the real issues in a way that will equip them for interaction with our culture.

5. Offer targeted Bible studies that deal with specific issues. Much of the material available from publishing houses is "life-oriented" which means it deals with issues of personal growth in emotional and relational areas. This is an important of a person's spiritual growth but if that is all that is presented then there are some major areas of life that are neglected. In-depth biblical studies need to be developed in the areas of authentic science, political, literature, the arts, ecology, modern education and other similar areas. Unless we work with our people to help them think biblically in these crucial areas, we will be absent in the meaningful discussions in these areas. We need to help our people think through what the Bible does and does not say in these crucial areas so that when they are confronted with conversations about these topics they can respond with a well thought through response from a biblical perspective.

We need to help people wrestle with truth in all areas of life. G. K. Chesterton, one of the great Christian authors of the twentieth century, was once asked what single book would he choose if he was stranded on an island. He answered, Thomas's Guide to Practical Ship Building. Commitment to God does at times require us to do the impractical, but there are also plenty of occasions where God expects us to use practical wisdom.

CONCLUSION

A young man came to Socrates to say, "I want knowledge." "How badly do you want it?" replied Socrates. The young man replied, "I must have it."

Socrates took him to the beach and they waded out up to their necks. Then he pushed the young man under the water in a ferocious struggle. When the young man finally emerged Socrates asked him, "What did you want the most?"

The young man said, "All I wanted was air." Socrates then said, "When you want knowledge like you wanted air when you were under the water, then you will get it."

Somehow we must develop this desire in the lives of our disciples. When we do that we will guarantee that the Christian faith will move meaningfully forward into the next generation.

Section 4

How to Use
This Book

Chapter 25

How to Use This Book

Introduction

This book is designed to be a working manual. This final chapter will give the reader some initial guidelines in how this book can be used. It will address the application on three levels:

1) Personally. This section is for the person who has been a Christian for a while and who desires to develop a working plan for their own personal growth. It gives both a definition as to what you are trying to develop in your own life and a tentative plan for attaining that. It assumes there has been previous growth in your life but that there is a desire to grow into greater maturity and Christlikeness. Although this can be worked out without anyone else being involved, it is a good idea to establish an accountability partner to whom you have given permission to ask hard, personal questions and who will meet with you periodically and "check up" on your progress.

2) Personal discipling. This section is for the individual who desires to meet with another individual to mentor and disciple them in their walk with God. You may already be meeting with another and have exhausted the "design" or material you

353

have been using and you are looking for where to go next with the individual. It will give you suggestions as to how to proceed with that relationship and move them toward this definition of a mature disciple.

3) Total Church or Group. This section assumes that you are a part of a local church or small group that wants to establish a definition of what a mature disciple looks like and then wants to focus your entire ministry energy and efforts on helping the people in your group become mature disciples. It assumes that this will become the focus for your corporate times together, your educational program at all age levels and the content around which you will pray and plan for your future. It will give you a clear definition of the desired end result which will then establish the standard against which you can measure your effectiveness and progress.

It goes without saying that these entire processes need to be undergirded with prayer. The church is a supernatural fellowship in whose midst the living God dwells. Maturity can never be attained by simply putting a program into action. All one needs to do is to study the prayers of Paul to discover how he prayed for his disciples and the variety of things he prayed for. His prayers certainly don't reflect the content of the average church or group prayer time. The reason that Paul was so effective comes out of his insights into the true needs of people and how he saw he needed to pray for them. Although I don't mention prayer in connection with each level of application, I assume it to be an integral part of the entire process.

PERSONAL

The normal tendency when we begin a project like this is to try and work on everything all

354

at once which becomes counter-productive and so overwhelming that we eventually quit. It is like belonging to a health club in January. Everyone comes in having made New Year's resolutions and with good intentions. The place is crowded. But usually by February 1 it is back to normal.

In order to prevent that, I am going to suggest that you set out for yourself a six-year plan, working on each of the eighteen areas for four months each in a sequence of your choosing. This will enable you to make some progress in specific areas which will begin to establish deeper life-style patterns. To try and change more than three areas a year usually means that the change never gets a chance to be deeply established enough to last the rest of your life. You might object that it is too long but if you start with the first things first, the changes will begin to take place and it will become a source of pleasure to God and encouragement to yourself.

Step 1: Using Appendix A you begin by evaluating your own personal life based on the eighteen characteristics described there. You may want to give the evaluation sheet also to someone who knows you fairly well and ask them evaluate your maturity and areas of need as well. This gives you at least two perspectives as you begin to lay out your longer range plan.

Step 2: Find an accountability partner. This will be the person you will meet with over the next six years who has your permission to ask you how you are progressing. You take the responsibility for locating and enlisting the person and for setting up the times when you will get together for your check-up. Explain to them what you are attempting to do and if necessary, give them a copy of this book to help them understand what you are trying to accomplish and why. In their reading of the book, they too might desire to start such a plan and perhaps turn your meetings into a time of mutual encouragement and evaluation.

Step 3: Set out an initial six-year plan for growth using the sheet in Appendix B. You will notice that it is broken into six years with three columns for each year. This will give you four months of concentrated time to work on one of the characteristics. If you find that an area takes longer or shorter time than you planned, simply revise your plan. Growth toward greater maturity is the goal, not completing your plan on "schedule." God has the rest of your life to develop maturity in you so don't get discouraged if it takes a little longer than you planned. After all, "A man's mind plans his way, but the LORD directs his steps."[426]

Step 4: Select the area you have determined is your number one priority or place of growth than needs to happen. Describe for yourself why you see it to be an area of need and what you hope to see happen in this area as you begin to work it through. You can use the description in the book as a starting place. This will give you a more specific target to work towards and a means of evaluating your progress.

Step 5: Determine specifically what you believe God wants you to do to change this area of your walk with Him. You can use the suggestions at the end of each chapter in the book or those at the end of each section. If you still have trouble, talk with a spiritually mature person you respect and ask them for any suggestions they might have. Make these steps things that are measurable and can be placed on a time chart and a "To Do" list.

Step 6: Lay out a sequential schedule for the four months that enables you to do what you have determined needs to be done. Put this into your personal computer, day planner or whatever else you use to schedule your time. This will become the "plan" that you will follow as you move toward this area of maturity. If, as you are doing this, God brings some variation that you did not antici- pate beforehand, feel free to substitute that but keep coming back to make certain you are moving toward your purpose for doing this.

Step 7: As you reach the end of the four months, evaluate your progress to make certain you are reaching what you sensed God wanted you to develop. As you do this, re-evaluate your six year plan to make certain that what you thought was the second area of growth to address is still where you want to go. If you have not accomplished what you sensed God speaking to you about, pray that through. Does He want you to spend more time in this area? Does He want you to move on and come back to this at another time? Is He satisfied with the progress you have made? Remember, this is a pattern that you can use for the rest of your spiritual life and so you will probably address this issue on a dif- ferent level again later in your life.

Step 8: Celebrate! Take some time to enjoy your walk with the Lord and look back with joy at what God has accomplished over the last four months. You have faced and worked on an area of growth that God has called to your attention and you have moved forward to that end. God is pleased with that progress and is already celebrating what He sees happening. Take some time to join Him in that celebration. This is not pride because ultimately the Spirit is the one who brings about the growth, but you have defined and addressed a specific area of growth that He was desirous of working with you in, and there has been progress toward that end.

PERSONAL DISCIPLING

When writing about personal discipling I am spe- cifically writing about a one on one relationship with another believer who you are walking along- side of to enable them to grow in their life to a place of spiritual maturity. This can be defined as "discipling, mentoring, or apprenticing." It is the activity of trying to put 2 Timothy 2:2 into practice. There Paul told Timothy, "...the things you have heard me say in the presence of many witnesses entrust to reliable men who will then be qualified to teach others." Paul was concerned that Timothy had been with him and watched him engage in active ministry. Now he was exhorting Timothy to find a few "reliable men" to whom he could do the same thing that he had done with him. If he would do that then those reliable men would turn around and find some "others" that they could do the same thing that Timothy had done with them.

In the world in which we live with its mobility, it is often difficult to plan on being in one place, related to another person in any in-depth way for much more than three or four years. Understanding that, I am going to suggest that the time line for working another through this model be shortened to three years. It has been my experience that to try and do anything one on one longer than that becomes very difficult. This means that you will only spend two months in each of the eighteen areas but this will introduce the disciple to the totality of the definition and then, when you break so that each of you can disciple another, they will have a definite model and strategy they can use to work with another. It also helps them to see the model so if they wanted to work it through personally they could do so, using the methodology described above.

Step 1: Explain the model you propose to use to the one you are discipling so they can gain a grasp of what you are suggesting and why you are proposing that you use it. Perhaps you might want to give them a copy of the book and have them read it through to gain a better grasp of what you are suggesting.

<u>Step 2:</u> Get their agreement about going ahead with this model. It is important that they are in agreement with what you are suggesting as their acceptance of it motivates them toward its completion and helps them see where you are going with the relationship. This will put you on the same page and it is reassuring to the one you are discipling to know that you know where you are going and what you are planning.

<u>Step 3:</u> Evaluate the person using Appendix A. It would be helpful, depending on how well you know the person, to have you fill out an evaluation sheet on them as well. If they are a relatively new acquaintance, you might want to get their spouse or some other close friend to fill one out as well. Another perspective is always helpful. In the evaluation determine a sequence that you will follow as you begin to help the person work through the model. This sequence will establish the tentative course that you will follow through the next three years.

<u>Step 4:</u> Using Appendix B set out a tentative three year or six year discipleship plan for them based on the evaluation. This is done in two month segments so the number of times you deal with a specific topic will depend upon how often you meet.

<u>Step 5:</u> Gather the materials, lessons, interviews, etc. that you will need to help the person work through the initial characteristic you will be working on. Sometimes when doing this it is good to consider having the person interview or meet with someone other than yourself that you know is mature in this particular area. It gives the person you are working with another person they can turn to and takes the full responsibility for helping in this specific area off your shoulders entirely. Another voice affirming what you are attempting to develop in their life is always a positive thing and should be used whenever possible. After all,

discipleship is the task of the body, not just of her individual members.

Step 6: Work them through the materials you have determined to use and then recommend other things they can do on their own to grow further in this area. Two months is not sufficient time for a new area of growth to become firmly implanted but God can use it to open the door for them and get them started in a disciplined way to work their way toward maturity.

Step 7: Review the remaining seventeen areas and reaffirm that the next area is still the direction to move. Then repeat steps 5 and 6 in this area as well.

Step 8: Celebrate the progress. You will want to plan something of a celebrative nature to affirm them and the progress they are making. It is setting a lifestyle of facing growth issues and planning to do something about them. Celebrating helps them feel positive about the process and gives them hope as they grow.

CORPORATELY IN THE CHURCH

As we move to the church or the small group of which you are a part, I again recommend using a three year planning calendar with two months being devoted to each trait. With the mobility of people we are fortunate to have some of the people for the full three-year cycle. Plus this makes each segment two months. We have found that most younger people simply do not attend church or seminars for eight straight weeks but if it is something special and the content is something they really feel they need they will make an extra effort to do so. For these reasons I recommend a three-year, two month format.

Step 1: This disciple definition needs to be worked through the leadership structure of the church or small group so that they can state with conviction that this is the description is the will of God for their growth strategy. This will probably necessitate having them work through this book together over a period of time so they fully understand the concepts and definition. This will help them come to some sense of understanding as to what is involved.

If there is professional staff, they need to be on board as well so whatever your leadership structure is, there must be the painstaking work of making certain everyone is on board.

Step 2: Have the leadership personnel determine in whatever decision making process your church or group uses that you are going to commit yourselves to this classification of attributes for a disciple. This makes certain that everyone is on the same page. It means that you will begin to build the entire church programming around this description. This includes the sermons from the pulpit, the content of Christian education classes, the material you either purchase or write for your small or home groups as well as any special seminars or workshops you will plan that focus at various times.

Adopting a specific definition of a disciple simplifies the decision-making process and procedures of the church. Once a definition has been adopted it becomes much easier to say "Yes" or "No" to programs and special emphases that come your way through publishing houses or denominations. If you are offered something that doesn't help you produce disciples as you have defined them, you can easily and quickly say "No" and no one can challenge the rationale behind the decision. It is not that some of the material is not well done, it is simply that it does not get you where you want to go.

Step 3: Use Appendix A to evaluate where you see the total church to be in terms of mature disciples. You will want to include not only your leadership people, both lay and professional, but you also want to include persons within the congregation that you know from experience are spiritually sensitive to what God is doing and who understand what the spiritual needs are within the body. The broader you can make the survey group, the more accurate will be the analysis you will have.

Step 4: Have your leadership review the survey to determine what they see to be the greatest area of needs within the congregation. Have them work through some kind of prioritization process to determine the sequence that needs to be established.

Step 5: Using Appendix b lay out a tentative schedule for the next three or six years that will then set your course for the next years. This can always be altered if something surprising arises during that time but it will give you a general plan for producing disciples.

Step 6: Begin to enlist teachers, mentors, workshop leaders, seminars, video courses, etc. that will enable you to present material that will move you toward your target plan. There will need to be good explanation and communication of what is being offered, how to enroll, etc in plenty of time for the people to seriously consider what they want to do so they can plan their lives accordingly.

Step 7: Implement the cycle of classes. Initially this means that you will be offering new classes, seminars, training sessions, etc. every two months. Eventually it would be a good idea to offer something new the first of every month so that newcomers to the church can have an immediate way of getting tied in to the fellowship life of the church and be assimilated with much greater ease. You will be able to do this because you will have enlisted teachers who can then repeat the same class or seminar whenever the need determines that it be rescheduled.

Step 8: Review and reschedule. Evaluation and review is to be an ongoing process. As you are involved in the specific classes or topics, the leadership can see more easily where the congregation is and what needs to be done differently to succeed at the task. Do not be afraid to rethink what needs to be offered next on an ongoing basis. God's ways are not our ways and there are times He brings things to our attention that we were unaware of that need to be dealt with before anything else. Continue to be sensitive to His voice.

CONCLUSION

Jesus called his disciples to go out after His ascension and the coming of the Holy Spirit to repeat the same process with other people that He had done to them. They did not need to have a description set forth on paper because they knew what He had done with them to bring them to where they were. They knew how to replicate the process and as a consequence they would get the same result. "Follow me and I will make you fishers of men."[427] They followed and in the following were transformed into fishers of men. In the years since they first started, the church has gone through so much change that what now passes for Christianity has very little resemblance to what He did and taught. It is time for us to address this and return to the task of "making disciples" as He did.

This book is not the last word directed toward that end — but it is a word that God has given me. I encourage you to go back through the book, reflect on the characteristics, evaluate the processes and if you don't agree with me, at least put together a description that is workable for you and those you walk with. Don't wait until after you take your shot before drawing your target. If that is the way your ministry goes, you will never see the things that your heart longs to see.

May God give you His grace and wisdom as you determine to become involved in the exciting process of "making disciples."

Appendix

Appendix A

Sample Evaluator
(Change for groups or churches)

Attribute	Low 1	2	3	4	5	6	7	8	9	High 10
ATTITUDES										
I have a desire to know God										
I have a desire to glorify God										
I have a desire to be like Jesus										
I have a desire to love people										
I have a desire to serve people										
I have a desire to be involved in the Great Commission										
SKILLS										
I know how to hear and follow God's voice										
I know how to build relation-ships with other people										
I know how to build a strong Christian family unit										
I know how to use my spiritual gifts to build my local church										
I know how to articulate and defend my faith										
KNOWLEDGE										
I know who I am "in Christ"										
I know my basic Christian doctrines										

I know my unique temperament, spiritual gifts and strengths									
I have a good general knowledge of the Bible									
I have established a basic Christian worldview									
I have memorized the 54 recommended scripture verses									

Appendix B

Sample Six Year Plan
(Change for groups or churches)

Attribute	Year 1	Year 2	Year 3	Year 4	Year 5	Year 6
ATTITUDES						
I have a desire to know God						
I have a desire to glorify God						
I have a desire to be like Jesus						
I have a desire to love people						
I have a desire to serve people						
I have a desire to be involved in the Great Commission						
SKILLS						
I know how to hear and follow God's voice						
I know how to build relationships with other people						
I know how to build a strong Christian family unit						
I know how to use my spiritual gifts to build the local church						
I know how to articulate and defend my faith						
I know how to help others become mature disciples						
KNOWLEDGE						
I know who I am in Christ						
I know my basic Christian doctrines						
I know my unique temperament, spiritual gifts and strengths						

I have a good general knowledge of the Bible					
I have established a basic Christian worldview					
I have memorized the 54 recommended scripture verses					

[1] Matthew 28:19
[2] Colossians 1:28-29
[3] 1 Thessalonians 2:19-20
[4] Frankl, Victor — "Man's Search for Meaning" — pg 123
[5] Tozer, A. W. — "The Pursuit of God" — pg. 16. Christian Publications, Inc.
[6] Philippians 3:10
[7] Jeremiah 9:23-24
[8] Hosea 6:3 (RSV)
[9] Exodus 33:18
[10] Psalm 46:10
[11] Philippians 3:10
[12] Ephesians 1:17
[13] 2 Peter 1:3
[14] Romans 11:33-36
[15] John 17:3
[16] Tozer, A. W. — "The Knowledge of the Holy" — pg 123 — Christian Publications
[17] Genesis 4:1 (KJV)
[18] John 8:55
[19] Exodus 33:18
[20] Morgan, G. Campbell — "The Best of G. Campbell Morgan." — The Westminster Booklets.
[21] Psalm 23:4
[22] Genesis 32:22-32
[23] John 17:3
[24] 1 Samuel 3:7
[25] Exodus 33:18
[26] Ephesians 1:17
[27] Colossians 1:10
[28] Exodus 6:2-3

[29] Psa 42:1-2
[30] Lewis, C. S. — "Mere Christianity" — pg 120.
[31] Psa 63:1
[32] Matt 5:6
[33] Psa 63:6
[34] Packer, J. I. — "Knowing God" — pg 20. — InterVarsity Press.
[35] Matthew 9:8; Mark 2:12; Luke 5:25-26
[36] Matthew 15:31
[37] Luke 7:16
[38] Daniel 2:26-28
[39] Genesis 41:16
[40] 1 Peter 4:16
[41] Revelation 4:11
[42] 1 Chronicles 16:28-29
[43] Leviticus 10:3
[44] Isaiah 42:8
[45] Isaiah 48:11
[46] Proverbs 16:18
[47] Edwards, Jonathan — "The Works of Jonathan Edwards — Volume II" — pg. 399.
[48] Romans 1:21-23
[49] Matthew 5:16 (RSV)
[50] Daniel 2:27-28
[51] Daniel 2:47
[52] Psalm 50:23 (RSV)
[53] Psalm 86:11-12
[54] Romans 15:7-9
[55] John 14:13-14
[56] 1 Peter 4:10-11
[57] 1 Corinthians 6:19-20
[58] John 17:4
[59] Romans 8:28
[60] Romans 8:29
[61] Genesis 1:26-27
[62] Colossians 1:15
[63] John 1:12
[64] Romans 8:29
[65] Colossians 1:15
[66] 1 John 3:1-2
[67] Philippians 3:8-16
[68] Philippians 2:13
[69] Luke 6:40
[70] Philippians 2:5

71 1 Peter 2:20-25
72 Hebrews 12:2-3
73 1 Corinthians 11:1 (RSV)
74 Galatians 2:20
75 1 Corinthians 4:16; 11:1; 1 Thessalonians 1:6
76 Yancey, Philip — "The Jesus I Never Knew" — pg. 23 — Zondervan Publishing House
77 Eldredge, John — "Wild at heart" — pg 7 — Thomas Nelson Publishers
78 Hebrews 12:2-3
79 Tozer, A. W. — "The Knowledge of the Holy" — pg 9 — Christian Publications, Inc.
80 Psalm 1:2
81 Joshua 1:8
82 1 Corinthians 3:18
83 Yancey, Philip — "The Jesus I Never Knew" — pg 130 — Zondervan Publishing House
84 Proverbs 13:15
85 John 10:10
86 Willard, Dallas — "The Spirit of the Disciplines" — pg 156 - HarperSanFrancisco
87 Ibid — pg 3-4
88 2 Corinthians 3:18
89 1 John 3:2
90 1 John 4:8
91 John 14:20-24
92 1 John 3:17
93 Vine, W. E. — "Vine's Expository Dictionary of Old and New Testament Words"
94 Philippians 2:3-8
95 1 Corinthians 13:4-6
96 John 15:13
97 Rusten, E. Michael and Sharon — "The One Year Book of Christian History" — Tyndale — pgs. 90-91
98 John 3:16
99 Romans 5:8
100 1 Corinthians 13:1-3
101 Lewis, C. S. — "— Mere Christianity" — chap. 9, para. T — pg 116.
102 John 13:34
103 Matthew 19:19; See also Romans 13:9; Galatians 5:14; James 2:8
104 Matthew 22:39; Mark 12:31
105 1 Corinthians 14:1

[106] 1 John 4:21
[107] John 14:21
[108] 1 John 3:11
[109] 1 John 3:14
[110] 1 John 4:7-8
[111] 1 John 4:11
[112] 1 John 4:20
[113] 1 John 5:1
[114] John 13:34-35
[115] Galatians 5:22
[116] Romans 5:5
[117] Foster, Richard — Leadership — Vol 3 # 1
[118] Hebrews 10:24-25
[119] Matthew 23:11
[120] Luke 22:27
[121] Romans 1:1, 9; Philippians 1:1; Titus 1:1.
[122] Barclay, William — "The Letter to the Romans" — pg 11-12 — Westminster John Knox Press
[123] Hession, Roy — "The Calvary Road" — pg 58-59 — Christian Literature Crusade
[124] Num 12:7-8; 14:24; Job 2:3; Psa 89:20; 105; 42; Isa 20:3; 22:20; Hag 2:23, etc.
[125] Jer 25:9; 27:6; 43:10
[126] Exod 9:13; 23:25; Josh 24:14-15, 31; Judg 2:7; 1 Sam 7:3; 12:20, etc.
[127] Rom 1:1; 2 Cor 4:5; Gal 1:10; Phil 1:1; Titus 1:1
[128] Matt 8:9
[129] Genesis 24:2
[130] Genesis 39:2-6
[131] Matt 18:23-35; 24:45-51; 25:14-46
[132] Luke 16:10-12
[133] Matthew 25:14-30; Luke 19:11-27
[134] Luke 19:26
[135] Matthew 23:11-12
[136] Jeremiah 33:3
[137] Psalm 50:15
[138] Sanders, J. Oswald — "Spiritual Leadership" — pg 135
[139] Genesis 18:3
[140] 1 Samuel 17:32
[141] Numbers 12:7-8
[142] Joshua 5:14
[143] 1 Samuel 3:10

[144] Romans 1:1; 2 Peter 1:1; James 1:1; Jude 1:1; Revelation 1:1
[145] Matthew 4:19
[146] Exodus 33:11.
[147] 1 Kings 12:7
[148] "Guardians of the Great Commission."— Christianity Today - Vol. 33, no. 17.
[149] Hession, Roy — The Calvary Road — pg 56 — Christian Literature Crusade
[150] Hession - Ibid — pg 60-61
[151] Willard, Dallas — "The Spirit of the Disciplines" — pg 182 - HarperSanFrancisco
[152] Hession — Ibid — pg 57
[153] Paterson, Sir Alec — Leadership Magazine — Vol. 1, No. 2
[154] Peterson, Eugene — "A Long Obedience in the Same Direction" — pg. 13 — InterVasity Press
[155] Moore, Waylon — "Multiplying Disciples" — pg 16-17 - NavPress
[156] 2 Timothy 2:2
[157] 2 Timothy 3:10
[158] Ezekiel 33:7-9
[159] 2 Timothy 2:2
[160] Coleman, Robert — The Master Plan of Evangelism" — pg 38-39 — Fleming H.Revell
[161] Luke 10:2
[162] Luke 24:49; John 20:22; Acts 1:8
[163] 2 Corinthians 3:17-18
[164] John 14:25-26
[165] John 16:13-15
[166] Romans 8:26-27; Luke 11:13
[167] Henrischen, Walter — "Disciples are Made, Not Born." — pg 54 — Victor Books
[168] Chambers, Oswald — Spiritual Leadership — pg 140
[169] Coleman, Robert — The Master Plan of Evangelism" — pg 39 — Fleming H.Revell
[170] Ephesians 4:15
[171] 2 Timothy 3:10-11
[172] 1 Corinthians 4:6 (See also 1 Cor 11:1; Eph 5:1; Phil 3:7; 1 Thess 1:6; 2:14; 2 Thess 3:7, 9)
[173] Hebrews 4:12
[174] 2 Timothy 3:16-17
[175] John 15:1-5
[176] 2 Corinthians 5:17

[177] Ezra 7:6
[178] 1 Corinthians 3:10
[179] 1 Kings 7:13-14
[180] John 10:5
[181] John 10:27
[182] Ephesians 5:17
[183] 1 Samuel 3:9
[184] Havner, Vance — "The Vance Havner Quote Book" — pg 98
[185] Genesis 22:9-12
[186] Matthew 3:16-17
[187] Acts 9:4
[188] Daniel 10:1-21
[189] Joshua 5:13-15
[190] Acts 9:7
[191] Judges 7:15
[192] Exodus 3:3
[193] Isaiah 6:1-13
[194] Willard, Dallas — "Hearing God" — pg 59 — InterVarsity Press
[195] Matthew 22:37; Mark 12:30; Luke 10:27
[196] Romans 12:2
[197] James 1:5
[198] Lovelace, Richard — Dynamics of Spiritual Renewal — pg 265
[199] Willard, Dallas — Ibid — pg 99
[200] Colossians 3:15
[201] 1 Corinthians 1:26-29
[202] Strong, Augustus H. "Systematic Theology" — pg 304 — Judson Press
[203] Genesis 1:26
[204] 2 Timothy 4:9
[205] 2 Timothy 4:16
[206] McBurney, Louis — Marble Retreat, Marble Colorado — Leadership Magazine — Vol 14, # 2
[207] Trent, John — "A Father's Heart" — "Christian Parenting Today" — November/December 1999
[208] Ephesians 1:23
[209] Ephesians 2:22
[210] Ephesians 1:17-19
[211] Ephesians 3:19
[212] Grubb, Norman — "Continuous Revival" — pg 15-16 — Christian Literature Crusade

213 Poole, Gary — "The Complete Book of Questions" — Zondervan
214 Drucker, Peter - Leadership Magazine — Vol. 16 # 4.
215 Briscoe, Stuart — Leadership — Vol. 11 # 1
216 Amos 3:3 (The Message)
217 Ephesians 5:21
218 Philippians 2:3-4
219 Galatians 3:26-29
220 Romans 12:2
221 Isaiah 55:8-9
222 Genesis 2:24
223 Judges 2:7
224 Judges 2:10
225 1 Peter 1:5
226 Ephesians 5:21-33; Colossians 18-19
227 Guest, Edgar — "Your Name"
228 Deuteronomy 6:4-9
229 Proverbs 1:8-9
230 Deuteronomy 6:7
231 1 Corinthians 15:31
232 Luke 9:23
233 Romans 12:4-6 (RSV)
234 Romans 12:6
235 1 Corinthians 12:4
236 1 Corinthians 12:29-31
237 Romans 12:6
238 Ephesians 1:23
239 1 Corinthians 1:7
240 Ephesians 1:23
241 Ephesians 3:20-21
242 Matthew 19:21
243 Colossians 3:1-2
244 Matthew 4:19; Mark 1:17
245 Matthew 22:37; Mark 12:30; Luke 10:27
246 Ephesians 1:23
247 Romans 10:14-17
248 Matthew 10:7;
249 1 Peter 3:15-16
250 2 Timothy 2:24-26
251 Isaiah 55:10-11
252 Lewis, C. S. — "Letters of C. S. Lewis" — pg 209
253 Matthew 10:7; Mark 3:14
254 Acts 10:42
255 Acts 1:8

[256] Acts 3:15 (See also Acts 5:32)

[257] Acts 22:15

[258] 2 Corinthians 3:15

[259] 2 Corinthians 4:3-4

[260] Romans 10:14

[261] Ministry Currents, Jan.-March, 1992, p. 5

[262] 2 Timothy 3:7

[263] Mark 6:7

[264] Lewis, C. S. — God in the Dock — pg. 183.

[265] Acts 18:9-10

[266] Luke 12:11-12

[267] Luke 21:14-15

[268] See chapter 7, "A Desire to Be Involved in the Great Commission."

[269] Moore, Waylon — New Testament Follow-up" — pg 27

[270] 1 Thessalonians 2:6-8

[271] Galatians 4:19

[272] 1 Corinthians 4:15

[273] 2 Corinthians 4:12

[274] Coleman, Robert — The Master Plan of Evangelism — pg. 108-109

[275] Wilson, Carl — With Christ in the School of Building Disciples — Chapter 1 — pgs 17-43

[276] Pearcey, Nancy — Total Truth —"Part 3: How We Lost Our Minds" — pg 249-348

[277] Henrischen, Walter — "Disciples Are Made, Not Born" — Victor — pg. 153

[278] Chambers, J. Oswald — "Spiritual Leadership" — pg 140

[279] Isaiah 43:4-7

[280] Wilson, Carl — Ibid — pg 218

[281] Coleman, Robert - "The Master Plan of Evangelism" - pg 106

[282] Kuhne, Gary — The Dynamics of Personal Follow-up" — Zondervan — pg. 145

[283] Wilson, Carl — With Christ in the School of Disciple Building — Zondervan — pgs 79-170

[284] To order these materials go to navpress.com and enter "Lessons on Assurance" in their search engine or write to NavPress, Colorado Springs, Colo.

[285] Moore, Waylon — New Testament Follow-up — pg 27-28

[286] Matthew 24:21-23

[287] Matthew 4:19

[288] 1 Corinthians 4:16

[289] 1 Corinthians 11:1
[290] Philippians 4:9
[291] 1 Corinthians 8:1
[292] Stanford, Miles — The Green Letters — Zondervan — pg. 167
[293] Rom 6:3, 6, 16; 7:1; 1 Cor 3:16, etc.
[294] Romans 5:20
[295] Romans 6:2-3
[296] John 6:56
[297] John 14:19-20
[298] John 14:23
[299] Colossians 1:27
[300] Galatians 2:20 (See also Romans 8:9-11)
[301] 1 Corinthians 6:19
[302] 2 Corinthians 5:17
[303] Ephesians 2:1-2
[304] Ephesians 1:4-5
[305] Romans 8:15-16
[306] Galatians 4:4-7
[307] Romans 8:17
[308] Romans 5:12-19
[309] Hebrews 7:1-19
[310] Nee, Watchman — The Normal Christian Life" — Christian Literature Crusade, Inc. — pg 40 -
[311] 2 Corinthians 5:17
[312] "Emancipation Proclamation," *Microsoft® Encarta® 98 Encyclopedia.* © 1993-1997 Microsoft Corporation. All rights reserved.
[313] Colossians 2:10
[314] 2 Peter 1:3
[315] Revelation 12:10
[316] 2 Corinthians 10:3-5
[317] Vine, W. E. — Expository Dictionary of New Testament Words."
[318] 1 Timothy 1:10
[319] 1 Timothy 4:1-8
[320] 1 Timothy 4:16
[321] 2 Timothy 3:16-17
[322] 1 Timothy 5:17; Titus 1:9
[323] 1 Timothy 6:1
[324] Titus 2:10
[325] 2 Timothy 3:16-17
[326] 2 Peter 1:20-21
[327] 2 Peter 3:14-16

[328] Ephesians 2:20

[329] Ephesians 4:14

[330] Lewis, C. S. - Mere Christianity - pg 136

[331] Hebrews 5:11-14

[332] Hebrews 2:1

[333] Matthew 15:9

[334] Colossians 2:20-23

[335] 1 Timothy 4:1-2

[336] 2 Timothy 4:3-4

[337] Romans 15:4

[338] Titus 1:9

[339] Titus 1:9

[340] 2 Timothy 4:2

[341] 1 Timothy 6:1

[342] Titus 2:10

[343] 1 Samuel 17:26

[344] Psalm 139:13-16

[345] Jeremiah 1:4-5

[346] Isaiah 49:1

[347] John 17:4

[348] Clinton, J. Robert — The Making of a Leader — Chapter 2

[349] Romans 12:1

[350] Romans 12:3

[351] 2 Corinthians 10:12

[352] See chapter 13, "They Know How to Use Their Spiritual Gifts to Build the Local Body of Christ"

[353] Clinton, J. Robert — "The Making of a Leader" — pg 43

[354] Merril, David W. & Reid, Roger H — Personal Styles and Effective Performance — Chilton Book Company - pg. 1-2

[355] Buckingham, Marcus & Coffman, Curt — First Break All the Rules — Simon & Schuster — pg 57

[356] Proverbs 27:2

[357] Joshua 1:8

[358] Baptist Standard, Dec. 4, 1996, p. 1

[359] Associated Press, Sept 14, 1992

[360] 2 Timothy 3:16-17

[361] Psalm 19:1

[362] Psalm 19:7-11

[363] Exodus 6:3

[364] Isaiah 55:8-9

[365] Tozer, A. W. — Of God and Men — pg 25

[366] 1 Peter 3:15-16
[367] Joshua 1:8
[368] Psalm 119:11
[369] Psalm 1:1-2
[370] Garfield, Charles — Peak Performers — pg 160
[371] Hebrews 4:12
[372] Ezra 7:10
[373] Nehemiah 8:5-8
[374] Ezekiel 34:2-3
[375] John 21:15-17
[376] Acts 6:4
[377] 2 Timothy 4:2
[378] Romans 12:2
[379] Sire, James — The Universe Next Door: A Basic Worldview Catalog — InterVarsity Press — pg 15-16
[380] Colson, Charles & Pearcey, Nancy — How Now Shall We Live? — Tyndale — pg 14
[381] Pearcey, Nancy — Total Truth: Liberating Christianity from Its Cultural Captivity — Crossway Books — pg 23
[382] Genesis 3:4-5; John 8:44
[383] 1 Corinthians 1:18-25
[384] Romans 12:2
[385] Hebrews 11:3
[386] Ephesians 6:12
[387] Isaiah 55:8
[388] Colson, Charles & Pearcey, Nancy — How Now Shall We Live? — Tyndale House Publishers, Inc. — pg. 53
[386] Pearcey, Nancy — Total Truth: Liberating Christianity from Its Cultural Captivity — Crossway Books — pg 157
[387] Colson, Charles — Christianity Today, December 2004 — "Worldview Boot Camp" — pg 80
[388] Veith, Gene Edward — WORLD Magazine — February 7, 2004 — pg 25
[389] Lexington — The Economist — December 4th, 2004 — pg 36.
[390] Pearcey — Ibid — pg 25
[391] Psalm 73:16-17
[392] Psalm 73:26-28
[393] 2 Corinthians 4:8-9
[394] 2 Corinthians 4:17-18
[395] Romans 8:28

[396] Tozer. A. W. — Man" The Dwelling Place of God — Christian Publications, Inc. — pg 145

[397] Colson, Charles — Worldview Boot Camp — Christianity Today — December, 2004 — pg 80.

[398] Philippians 2:5

[399] 1 Corinthians 3:10-12

[400] Ephesians 2:19-20

[401] John 14:

[402] Romans 12:3

[403] Hebrews 4:12

[404] 2 Timothy 3:16-17

[405] Ephesians 3:10

[406] Colossians 3:2

[407] Psalm 19:7-11

[408] Joshua 1:8

[409] Psalm 1:2-3

[410] Isaiah 55:11

[411] 1 Corinthians 8:1

[412] Richards, Larry — A Theology of Christian Education

[413] Matthew 22:37; Mark 12:30; Luke 10:27

[414] Romans 12:2

[415] Philippians 2:5

[416] 2 Corinthians 10:4-5

[417] Hendricks, Howard - Teaching to Change Lives - p. 61

[418] Knight-Ridder Tribune News - 1989

[419] 2 Timothy 4:13

[420] Baptist Standard, May 12, 1993, p. 24; Facts & Trends, May 1988, p. 3

[421] Kimball, Dan — They Like Jesus But Not the Church" — Zondervan — pg 218

[422] Kimball — Ibid — pg 219

[423] Proverbs 16:9

[424] Matthew 4:19

CPSIA information can be obtained at www.ICGtesting.com
Printed in the USA
LVOW110920131011

250307LV00002B/168/P